WHEN EVERYTHING ELSE FAILS, SAY **NO** TO POVERTY

MEMOIRS
Cirencester

Published by Memoirs

MEMOIRS
PUBLISHING

25 Market Place, Cirencester, Gloucestershire, GL7 2NX
info@memoirsbooks.co.uk www.memoirspublishing.com

All Rights Reserved. Copyright © 2012 B. B. Goldsmith

No part of this publication maybe reproduced, stored in or introduced into a retrieval system, or transmitted, in any form or by any means (electronic, mechanical, photocopying, recoding or otherwise) without the prior written permission of both the copyright owner and the publisher of the book

The right of B. B. Goldsmith to be identified as the author of this work has been asserted in accordance with the Copyright, Designs and Patents Act 1988 sections 77 and 78.

This is a true rags to riches story, though some parts are fiction. Names of some characters have been changed and are used fictitiously, and any resemblance to actual persons dead or living in some events is entirely coincidental.

ISBN:978-1-909304-35-2

TABLE OF CONTENTS

Dedication
A Letter to Amai Na Baba (Mum and Dad)
Acknowledgements
Note from the Author
Foreword
Words of Encouragement and
the Eleven Forgotten Laws of the Universe

CHAPTER 1	The Zibigihauzi Family
CHAPTER 2	Tanaka Zibigihauzi and her Family Growing up The River Adventures The Scariest Moment of my Life
CHAPTER 3	The Apple of my eye: Kenzo Jamukoko My First Love Letter to Kenzo My First Love Letter from Kenzo
CHAPTER 4	The Cultural or Traditional Marriage Bridal Mentoring: Cultural Bridal Preparation (Kurayiwa in Shona) Female Genital mutilation: "Africa's shame and a heap of ignorance!" "Bridal Labour" (Huroora)
CHAPTER 5	Tanaka and her Husband Kenzo Jamukoko (who slept with prostitutes enough to fill a double decker bus plus standing passengers)
CHAPTER 6	The Confrontation
CHAPTER 7	Roy Pender-Hurst: The Multi-Millionaire with African Values
CHAPTER 8	What Goes Around Comes Around
CHAPTER 9	The Affair

CHAPTER 10	The Social life of Black and White Men in the early 80's.
CHAPTER 11	The Beautiful Zimbabwe and Her Secrets: Heterosexuality and Homosexuality Why do Men and Women Cheat?
CHAPTER 12	Sex and Money
CHAPTER 13	The Stalker and the Murderer
CHAPTER 14	Tanaka's Smuggling Adventures
CHAPTER 15	A Fool in London
CHAPTER 16	Looking for Gold in the Streets of London
CHAPTER 17	Gold Panning along the River Thames
CHAPTER 18	Where there is Shit there is Brass!
CHAPTER 19	The Expert Bum Cleaner (aka Carer)
CHAPTER 20	Femme Fatale with the American Millionaire
CHAPTER 21	In Search of Love Again
CHAPTER 22	Life in the Women's Refuge: Homelessness
CHAPTER 23	Going Back to my Roots
CHAPTER 24	What I did when Everything Else had Failed
CHAPTER 25	Applying the Law of Attraction
CHAPTER 26	Out of Sodom and Gomorrah
CHAPTER 27	Food for Thought: The Secrets of a Better Relationship or Marriage
CHAPTER 28	True Love: What it is and What it Takes plus The Definition of True Love
	Concluding Notes
	About the Author

DEDICATION

This book is dedicated to my beautiful daughters Lolo (Yorlandah) and Shana (Shona) who I adore and love very much. These two girls are my life savers and my reason for living; they are my everything and they mean the world to me. These girls have seen me through many difficulties and have stood by me through thick and thin.

- To my #1 people: Girls, I would never trade you for a million shackles. *I love you very much girls and I will always love you; thank you for being there for me all the time.*
- *I love you very, very, very much; words cannot express how much I LOVE YOU.*
- *I sob, sob, sob with happiness, as I never wanted to die and leave you behind with debts to pay, but with untold wealth in property to enjoy your lives with your children and children's children.*

As the Bible commanded: "A good man leaves an inheritance for his children's children, but a sinner's wealth is stored up for the righteous."(Proverbs 13:22.)

.

A LETTER TO AMAI NA BABA
(MUM AND DAD)

IN LOVING MEMORY OF MY LATE PARENTS

To my late mum, the wisest and most loving woman ever, and dad the most wonderful, caring and hardworking man ever.

Mum and dad, you were the most wonderful people I have known; my mentors, you taught me the basic entrepreneurial skills from an African market that has turned out to be amazing and fantastic. I love and miss you every day. I wish you had lived a little bit longer to see my achievements. You always taught me to work hard, to be charitable, to have **faith, inspiration, motivation and determination.** You are the greatest entrepreneurial teachers I ever had, and this has enabled me to move from an African Market Vendor to owning businesses in a developed country. You taught me to take calculated risks and never to do anything blindly.

You always taught me to believe in myself, to have respect for others and to call upon God Almighty in times of need, and to thank God for the gift of life, knowledge and everything He has done for me. You taught me to learn by observing, to love everyone as a brother and sister, mother and father, to have morals, to say sorry when I have wronged someone, to appreciate and to thank those who helped me, to stand up for my rights and to remain grounded. You taught me the benefits of working very hard to achieve my success and giving and sharing.

I did not have everything in life, but I was very happy as a child because you cared for me. Though I did not eat any fancy food, I never went to bed hungry, which meant a lot to me. I enjoyed the usual sadza and vegetables and meat stew once in a while and rice and organic chicken cooked with tomatoes, onion and madras curry on Christmas day. We never ate out or went on holidays, it wasn't right, but it was okay for us as a family.

I miss and love you very much. Mum, I miss that song you always sang for me, when I visited you, and that lovely motherly cuddle you always gave me. You changed the scene around when I was older and you called me your parent as you thought God had replaced your parents, with me. I tried very hard to provide for you, build a house with a toilet for you and I sent you money for shopping every month without fail; I sent you to specialist doctors, but in the end your time was up and you were called.

If only God had enabled you both to live a little bit longer, I would have made your wishes come true; to fly up in the sky above the clouds in an aeroplane and sail across the mighty oceans. I may have wronged you as child but you always had room for forgiveness.

I was blessed to be your offspring, and still am. I would never ever wish for another mother or father, you were simply the best.

I love and miss you very much.

Till we meet again, your loving child.

B. B. Goldsmith. xxx

ACKNOWLEDGEMENTS

I would like to thank my family and friends who have been there for me for all my life and new friends for the time I have known you, some through prayer meetings and some through business coaching sessions. I would also like to thank all the doctors and nurses who looked after me and who will continue to look after me during my lifetime. Writing this book has brought back memories of my life. On reflection, I had the opportunity to learn from my past experience and this has helped me to change for the better. This book is based on my inspirational life story, so just relax and enjoy as I know that by reading this book your life will change too. Honestly, my life is a very interesting story and it had to be told. Therefore, I share it with passion and with my million-plus fans around the world: enjoy and learn as you read! Let me tell you something: WHEN ONE HAS SURVIVED SO MANY TEMPTATIONS AND MANAGED TO PASS THROUGH MANY OBSTACLES IN LIFE, THEY WILL NEVER HIDE THE TRUTH FROM ANYONE AS IT BECOMES A LIVING TESTIMONY. I WILL NEVER BE ASHAMED OF TELLING THE TRUTH ABOUT MY PAST, AS THE TRUTH SHALL SET ME FREE.

Finally, I would like to thank the people who allowed me to use their names, the seminars that I attended that changed my life, and my mentors. The author's agency, especially Charles Muller for editing and polishing the work and the publishers.

A big thank you to my girls Lolo and Shana for making my dreams come true.

My #1 girls, I love you all and always will.

My thanks to you *especially, El Shadai*, for making everything possible for me.

When Everything Else Had Failed, You turned things around for me and You helped me to reject POVERTY!

I beg for your forgiveness God Almighty, for I know that I am a sinner. I know that without you nothing is possible. I repent and am born again; please accept me as one of your children, as I shall worship you forever and ever. Amen.

DISCLAIMER

This book is based on my inspirational life experience, for my life is a genuine story. Names of persons have been changed to protect the innocent. It will inspire a lot of people who think they have been unlucky in life, unlucky in love whether married or divorced, single mothers and fathers, the homeless and those in debt, those who suffered domestic violence, disability discrimination, humiliation and those who think Everything Else Has Failed, and those who think they can't do anything and are at the end of their tethers.

For those of you who are looking to start something big and think you cannot do it alone, my advice for you is *go for it*, follow your dreams and seek advice from the experts and those who have done it before. Money is out there and very easy to make only if you know how! If you get the right mentor, you can make it big, and make big money within no time at all! Good luck to you all in your endeavours. I know you can do it and I want you all to achieve your dreams with all my heart! I say this hand on my heart, and I give you God Almighty's blessings to acquire your wealth because I know that anyone can do it. I did it, so can you!

Having said this, bear in mind that the publishers of this book and I will take no responsibility for any loss or damages that might occur with respect to anyone who follows what I did and fails.

B. B. Goldsmith

NOTE FROM THE AUTHOR

I learnt the hard way and found out that in life when one is husbandless, moneyless and broke, homeless or poverty stricken, friends are few or nowhere to be found - they "don't wanna know you or hear from you"; but when you are rich and famous and when you have acquired some wealth, everyone wants to know you, make friends with you and some ask for money from you; even when it comes to people you have never met in your life, you will receive letters and e-mails from them that pour in like a river in flood, not in a bad way, but that's the truth. Letters will travel many, many, miles to find you. You know what I mean: some people just want to see you, touch you, feel you or just touch your clothing. This phenomenon is very true. For example, if one of the world's richest people should set up a stand charging people to come and see them, talk to them, have pictures taken with them, shake hands with them, I bet they would raise billions in a day, and the poor will even resort to borrowing to go and see these rich people. Consider, for example, that the majority of people will queue up at Madame Tussauds to have photographs taken with waxwork effigies of the wealthy and famous; it goes without saying that most people will be even more in favour of being photographed with the originals - the real persons. It is surely a niche market, to parade the rich and famous for a fee, such as the world's richest men and women.

The gospel truth is, however, that you can make yourself one of these rich and famous guys if you believe in yourself and have the faith to break the fear and chain of poverty!

B. B. Goldsmith

FOREWORD

When Everything Else Fails, Say No to Poverty, do something to get yourself out of the situation as no-one else will Do It For You!!!!!

If I hadn't suffered the way I did, and if it wasn't for my courage to be able to shake poverty off, this book would not have been written.

I went from being *husbandless as a widow at the age of thirty-five*, being broke, suffered domestic violence in the UK, lived on Home Office vouchers as an *illegal immigrant*, became homeless and refused to embrace the situations as they were thrown at me by nature. In the bondage of being broke, single and alone, tethered as a single mother, I had to unshackle myself and break away from this depressing situation. I bounced back to become a natural hard working person... an Entrepreneur, Business owner and an Investor. It wasn't an easy journey, but because I had imagined (visualised) my life out of poverty, I had imagined my life in prosperity and I believed that I could do it and just wanted to carry on. Believe me, guys, it wasn't easy, but it was funny as every day was different. I applied all the Eleven Forgotten Laws of the Universe - and here I am.

For those who want to take the greatest challenges of their lives, I advise you to OPEN THE EYES OF YOUR MIND and START SEEING POTENTIALS. **Desire it, imagine it** and **create** the life you want to live; boost your energy, boost your vision, boost your mind, boost your needs. Gold Dust and Silver are veritably lying around, everywhere on this planet, even in Zimbabwe where there are many Poor Trilionnaires!

When Everything Else Fails, would you just sit there and PRAY... or ACT?!

This is the story about the adventures of an African damsel that grew up in paucity, married in haste, and started smuggling to earn a living till the time she flew to England to seek the Gold she heard that paved the streets of London in a veritable gold-paved paradise.

This is a fascinating and inspiring book, for young adults as well as mature men and women. The story reveals a true life adventure of a Zimbabwean girl and her culture - of a girl brought up under the then Rhodesian colonial rule in Zimbabwe, and of her life in London without any family members around her. She married a serial cheat who bedded enough women to fill a double decker bus plus standing passengers. When she got bored with making love in the good old missionary position and suggested something saucy to her old-fashioned husband, he labelled her a **Nymphomaniac** - upon which she left him for greener pastures. Hurt by his spiteful words, she then plotted a grim revenge and developed the desire to do great things for herself. The book reveals all of the string of events that have never been told before. It's all about Pain, Suffering, Endurance, having Faith and the ability to take Action, and to Persevere through hardships. All this determined the results when she Became Rich, which made some men wonder as they didn't know what they had got till it was gone!

This is a true Rags-to-Riches story; now that you have a copy of the book in hand, relax and enjoy the experience as you turn the pages through this AMAZING JOURNEY!

WORDS OF ENCOURAGEMENT &
THE ELEVEN FORGOTTEN LAWS OF THE UNIVERSE

When everything else fails, who should you turn to...? Take Action and Have Faith and Perseverance, because praying without Action will not help; take Action and you will reap your rewards!

Act and take full responsibility of your life, don't just sit there and moan that life is just so unfair, because negative attitudes will only demoralise you and prevent you from doing the right things. Take Action to remove yourself from whatever bad situation you are in, because in everything that happens to us, most of it is a result of our own actions! For example, if you don't pay your rent you will be evicted and find yourself homeless! Hence, it is called a priority debt! Keep the roof over your head!

I command you to be the boss of your own life today; start acting now and find out how to do it from those successful people who have done it - believe me, it helps! As the Bible says, "He who walks with the wise grows wise, but a companion of fools suffers harm" (Proverbs 13: 20).

Stop watching these stupid blaming each other shows on television as you will only learn to be bitter, and take action now! Honestly, why would someone who wants to grow rich, wealthy and knowledgeable, waste time watching a Jerry Springer show, and other inane chat shows? All they will do is fuel the anger in you and build a sense of hatred towards your family - apart from turning you into couch potato. I would rather work hard to find myself on chat shows like that of Oprah Winfrey, a show that talks about progress and genuine achievements in life.

Apply all the ELEVEN FORGOTTEN LAWS OF THE UNIVERSE in your life, thus:

- The Law of Thinking
- The Law of Supply
- The Law of Attraction
- The Law of Receiving
- The Law of Increase
- The Law of Compensation
- The Law of Non-Resistance
- The Law of Forgiveness
- The Law of Sacrifice
- The Law of Obedience
- The Law of Success

When you apply the Eleven Forgotten Laws of the universe and do it correctly, you will definitely see results that will shock and surprise you when you reflect on the way your own life was before applied these laws.

Stop being a couch potato and start taking responsibility for your life. Say **no** to poverty, say **no** to watching rubbish on television, and start reading proper books. Learn and ACT, I repeat, as it sucks to see people who were created in God's image change to look like baby elephants due to lack of exercise and eating the wrong food, fostered by watching rubbish on television.

Blame no-one for your life's failures - not your parents, not your siblings, not your wife, not your husband, not your child, not your neighbour, not the government, and finally, not God, because when He created us we all came into this world with nothing. Blame no-one but yourself. ACT, and start by applying the Law of Thinking: have FAITH and PERSEVERE, and you will see a change for the better begin to take place; RECEIVE, harvest and enjoy the REWARDS of your hard work and you will be very successful - but only if you take *Action* to change your life!

PRELUDE

When Tanaka was growing up as a young girl, she never heard about millionaires, billionaires or very rich people, especially from her social network of black people in the old Rhodesian days and early Zimbabwean days; not until the time when Zimbabwe was hit by massive inflation and there were loads of poor billionaires and trillionaires. She grew up thinking that only white people were destined and chosen to be rich, and blacks to suffer. Whilst observing her parents working very hard, she thought black people would never be rich and the spirit of slavery would continue; they had no choice but to work very hard till death came to their rescue to release them from their burden.

Tanaka observed her dad working very hard, sweating buckets whilst chopping firewood for them to make a fire and cook dinner for the whole family. She felt sorry for her dad since he would have spent the day working very hard as a builder's assistant for a company called Costain. Tanaka's dad would fall asleep whilst they were still eating due to excessive tiredness. At the same time Tanaka would be heating water in a large twenty-gallon tin for him to have a bath so that he could wash the sweat from his body and retire to bed, to have a rest a be refreshed for another day's hard work.

It was never easy for Tanaka and her family since they had fields to go and work in for the maize that would be ground after harvest to make stiff porridge known as sadza, the Zimbabwean stable food. Tanaka had a very difficult childhood compared to that of her kids but she was nevertheless very happy and contented.

Tanaka's dad Kufa changed his job to work for a company called GMB - the Grain Marketing Board. He used to start work at half past seven in the morning and finished around six in the evening. Sometimes he would work overtime, till nine at night. Tanaka remembers crying one day when she saw her dad Kufa carrying the ninety kilogram bags of maize on his head all day long. Yet Kufa was happy since he considered the job to be better paying than his previous job.

"I don't want to grow up," Tanaka told her mum.

If Tanaka had heard about Peter Pan, I'm sure she would have related to a PETRA PAN, the girl who wished she would never grow up.

"Why don't you want to grow up?" asked *amai* (mother). "If I have to work hard, like *baba* (dad) then it means I will die young," she replied. Tanaka's mum tried to reassure her little girl and said, "No my girl, it will not be like that for you; as long as you go to school and pass your tests, after high school you could work for a *Murungu*" - meaning a white man - "as a copy typist and earn good money or even marry a *Murungu* if you are smart!" Tanaka was then reassured and felt happy, because most people were made to believe that only white people had money and by associating with whites one would become wise and rich; whereas being black meant hard work and poverty.

Nevertheless, Tanaka grew up very quickly and used the skills she had learned from her parents to make money. She married at the age of seventeen and separated when she was thirty-two, by which time she was a mother of four. Since her late husband Kenzo had cheated on her several times, she did not look back or give a DAMN but left him and moved on. I must admit the girl married in haste and repented at leisure.

Her husband Kenzo had called her a Nymphomaniac when she told him she was not enjoying making love in the same old and boring missionary position. She wanted to try something new, hence the indignity of being called a Nymphomaniac. After being called a Nymphomaniac, she plotted a shocking revenge by becoming a real "BITCH"!

She went to Harare and started her own business using the skills she had learned from her parents and some which she had taught herself. The following year she managed to buy herself a ticket and flew to London, where she had heard the streets were PAVED WITH GOLD. In her mind it was a real Gold Paved Paradise.

Whilst in London she worked very hard in and around Surrey, sending money home on a weekly basis to feed her children and mum as well as building a better house for her dear mum. Tanaka worked very hard and earned between six hundred and seven hundred pounds per week whilst working seventy to eighty hours per week - until she realised she would never get rich by working for someone else.

She later trained as a nurse, hoping her salary would double from what she earned in the late 90's as a healthcare assistant. However, nursing jobs became scarce due to the NHS' and other private companies' recruitments of foreign nurses from countries such as the Philippines and Africa. This is when Tanaka's Nursing and Recruitment Company was born, followed by hair salons and investments in property. When Tanaka started her own business, things became a bit different for her. *Phew!* No one can ever become rich whilst working for someone else, she sighed, sipping a cup of green tea.

Tanaka hated the idea of queuing for benefits and borrowing from friends and being seen as the one suffering from poverty diarrhoea and so took the initiative to launch her own businesses and writing career in order to generate passive income.

The company started to earn a good income, sometimes in excess of one thousand pounds per day. She did not have any capital when she started her company but invested much of her time working around the clock and recruiting nurses and carers; then she launched #a sex school and eventually #a celebrity lottery! Tanaka had hit on a NICHE market, aka SEX SCHOOL - who had ever before thought of a school that teaches people what to do in bed, or how to make a request in a celebrity lottery?! Like MONEY, SEX remains a taboo subject that teachers and parents do not feel comfortable to teach children about.

Hey, it is everyone's #1 dream to receive MILLIONS from Bill Gates, Donald Trump and Sir Richard Branson, to name only a few of the rich and famous in the world, but never dreamt about how to make millions for themselves. Several people cherish the wish that they could get a MILLION pounds or dollars from these global icons.

Tanaka did not have any bank loans or credits cards as the bank declined to lend her money, saying it was too risky for a new business. All it took her was applying the forgotten ELEVEN LAWS OF THE UNIVERSE, starting with the law of THINKING - by de-cluttering any junk from her mind-set which might stop her from moving forward; and she brainstormed on NICHE markets. Secondly she added **#1 Faith, #2 Perseverance, #3 Inspiration, #4 Determination, #5 Motivation, # 6 Wisdom, # 7 Knowledge, # 8 Vigorous Action and #9 Belief in the Laws of the Universe**. It was her desire to make it and to become **RICH**, especially **When Everything Else Had Failed for her…** and she took **Action** to follow her dreams as she took the biggest **RISK** of all, starting a business without **CAPITAL.**

What inspired her more was her courage to hate the words, I HAVE FAILED and I CAN'T AFFORD IT; also, her mother, a successful woman in her own way though not in terms of wealth, taught her the value of the words: *never give up!*

One day as she listened to the radio (BBC Radio 2), she heard a comment by the then British Prime Minister, David Cameron, saying people should not listen to wealth creators as they are snobbish. Tanaka thought, what stupid advice, advising people not to become financially independent! What was the alternative - to become reliant on benefits? Politicians just made her skin cringe and crawl! They enjoy seeing their people struggling while they might be earning a six-figure income or more.

As I mentioned before, most things that happen to us in our lives are a result of our own actions; if you listen to bad advice you become daft and demoralised; if you steal from your employer you will get sacked; if you don't pay your rent, you will get kicked out; if you don't pay your bills, you will get a bad credit history and no-one will ever lend you services or money; if you sleep all day, you will become lazy and forget to find ways to earn a living; if you eat too much you will become overweight; if you borrow too much and fail to pay back the money you owe, you will get into serious debt; if you badmouth or backstab your friends or family, you will lose them; if you have multiple SEX partners and have unprotected SEX, you will get AIDS and other STI's; if you cheat on your partner you will get divorced or dumped; if you do not RESPECT others, no one will RESPECT you; if you pursue your DREAMS and take ACTION, you will accomplish them.

My mum criticised me a lot when I was growing up and her constructive criticism made me who I am today.

We definitely get what we deserve in life according to our own capabilities. Some people win millions, but within no time the millions will be gone and they become broke. This is due to their lack of capabilities in handling loads of cash. Some people are much calmer when dealing with loads of money yet some go bonkers and completely insane.

"In life, if you mingle with fools you will become a fool; if you mingle with the wise you will become wise; if you mingle with the rich you will become rich; if you mingle with the famous you will become famous" - that is what my mum always told me. It's time to take responsibility for our own ACTIONS and STOP BLAMING others for our life failures.

This is the author's message for you.

CHAPTER ONE

THE ZIBIGIHAUZI FAMILY 1958-1981

RUNNING AROUND, mucking about, joking and laughing were normal for the Zibigihauzi family. No bad language such as swearing was ever used in the Zibigihauzi household. Passing wind loudly was never a joke but an embarrassment. Good manners were taught, and to be creative and ambitious was encouraged.

The Zibigihauzi were a very loving and close-knit family. They were well known by their neighbours due to Tanaka's parents' hard working, kindness and being members of the Salvation Army. Tanaka's parents were entrepreneurs, but she did not know the meaning of the word. She thought because her parents were illiterate and poor, selling stuff at the market to make a living, they were trapped in their lifestyle. Nevertheless her dad built a big house which had two large rooms, constructed with brick and cement under iron sheets whilst their neighbours lived in pole and dagga huts, or the famous African round hut - hence the name *MuZimba* which they tried to translate into English *Zibigihauzi* (the big house).

Tanaka was born on the 28th of August, 1963, in a small pole and dagga hut in Mutare, Zimbabwe. She was the third of five children. She was her mum's third child and her dad's first child. Tanaka's mum Kirera had two children from her previous marriage. Tanaka and her siblings grew up not knowing that they had different fathers till she was seventeen, when her mum inadvertently let it out whilst having an argument with her dad. These are some of the very common family secrets in Zimbabwe. It was a traditional thing that mum's children automatically become dad's children; and it was a norm for the man to take on his wife's children and bring them up as his own without letting the children know. This is usually supported by the famous Zimbabwean saying that "if you pull a branch of a tree, you pull it with its leaves". Thus, if a man falls for a woman with her own children, he should take the children on as though they were his own.

Tanaka felt sorry for her two elder siblings as they never got to know who their biological father was since it was never spoken of. It was also considered rude and a breach of morals to try and question your mum about the identity of your father. The family lived in a two-roomed house which Kufa had built using the skills he had learned whilst working for Costain building company, which he joined in Mutare. Since

CHAPTER ONE

Costain was a building construction company, the Zibigihauzi family moved from place to place till they landed in a small town, called Karoi, surrounded by farms. Karoi was a small town that was represented by a small sign of a witch riding on a broom. People believed there were a lot of witches living in that small town, hence the name Karoi.

Their house had a nice flat roof which was made of iron sheets. The roof sloped at the back which was handy for collecting water into drums when it rained. The water thus collected in drums was used either for baths or for washing clothes and dishes. There was also an old drum that was cut in in half along the middle, lengthwise, that was used as a bath tub. The family used to have a bath outside in a closet made of grass or reeds, called the change house. Outside there was a drainage trench that was made to drain the water and urine. The floor was made of concrete slabs. There was a tap a few metres away from Tanaka's house where they used to get drinking water, and water for cooking, as it was treated and came from the local dam. This was around 1968 when Tanaka was five years old.

Karoi also used to have some public toilets for sections of the community. There was a particular public toilet that was nearer to Tanaka's house in a location called *kwa Julius*. This public lavatory was just something no one would ever want to be near. A natural bad smell used to emanate from it. If one walked past the toilet around midday, loud buzzing noises were heard coming from huge green flies that congregated by the toilet. These large green flies, known as green bombers, celebrated, feasted and multiplied. The flies would buzz and make exultant tunes to show that they were feasting on human shit and of course celebrating. Tanaka resented these public toilets, so much that she just wanted to die. Two men she knew as toilet cleaners for these public toilets became lunatics and eventually died. It was just too much to bear for a man to stand the sight of such huge amounts of human shit on a daily basis. Maggots were a common sight in and outside the toilet, most probably what the *varoyi* (witches) fed on, because there were just millions of them.

However, Tanaka developed a habit of going to use the toilet very early in the morning when the toilet would still be clean. If Tanaka's digestive system was slow to produce the expected body waste, she would invite her best friend Anna to come along; then, together, the girls would carry a hoe on their trip to the bush to empty their bowels. They used to carry a hoe so they could dig holes to shit in and cover the shit with earth, just like cats. There were myths behind this, since they were brought up to believe that if someone shitted (poo'ed) anywhere other than in the toilet and left it exposed, wicked people would spread crushed red chillies onto the shit and the victim would have a very red and sore asshole. It was a legend developed by the elders to discourage people from shitting everywhere.

CHAPTER ONE

Later on the family moved into a community housing where a toilet was shared amongst eight families - still not ideal, but much better by far than the fly-infested toilet.

Nevertheless, as time moved on, Tanaka's parents managed to acquire a council house with its own toilet (*the type of African toilet without a toilet seat with a hole in the floor over which one had to squat - tough!*) and a tap inside the house; there was no sink under the tap, for the washing up was to be done outside. This was complete luxury for the whole family. Even though the toilet was situated outside the house, it was a considerable improvement because it was their very own toilet which was for the family's use only. It also came with a long chain that we used to pull and flush after use. There was no toilet seat but a large hole was dug in the floor and had a silver cover; people had to squat over the hole to defecate. Tanaka was very happy as she had moved away from the life of using a public toilet, to having a toilet that was for the use of her family alone, and there was also a shower. The council house benefited and saved Tanaka's head from carrying gallons of water. (Containers of water were usually carried by being balanced upon the head and held steady with one or both hands.) It was a relief for Tanaka, since her hair was beginning to look straight and flat.

The council house that the family acquired was a three-roomed house. There was one bedroom for Tanaka's mum and dad, a living room and a small kitchen. The kitchen had a small wooden shelf that was fixed on the wall which Kufa had made, and Kirera used to display her nice plates on it. The family always had to make a fire outside to cook dinner as it saved firewood as compared to the wood or coal cooker that was in the kitchen. Many people had previously died from the use of that kind of cooker due to carbon monoxide poisoning. Also, the kitchen was used as the girls' bedroom at night where Tanaka and her sisters slept on the floor on a mat made out of reeds.

The girls used to wake up early in the morning and fold their blankets and put them away in their parents' bedroom. The family could never afford any nightdresses; neither did they know about them. The girls used to fold their clothes at night and used them as pillows. They used a bucket at night in lieu of a chamber pot, which they emptied and washed in the mornings since it was too dark to go and use the public toilet at night. Thank God no-one seemed to have had an episode of diarrhoea during those days.

The living room was empty with no furniture in it; and it was much bigger than the kitchen. It had one small window that measured one metre by one metre in size. This is where the girls' brother Petros slept, on the floor on a mat made out of reeds. Whilst growing up, we never slept on beds, but on hard solid floors.

Kirera and *Kufa* always taught their children that if any of them got into a mess, then it was their responsibility to get themselves out of that situation; don't get me wrong - these parents disciplined their children accordingly. For example, they always said God only helps those who help themselves; thus, if are you are about to be attacked by a lion, don't just stand there praying constantly waiting for miracles to happen: pray, yes, but do something! Either find something to fight the lion with or find ways of escaping whilst praying. Unfortunately the majority of people pray and just wait for miracles to happen instantly; if they fail to see the miracles, they give up and start blaming God.

People who make it in life don't give up easily; they don't pray and wait - they pray and take action, even take a risk and believe, and then they see the results. Surely, persistence has priority over resistance. Persevere and fight your way out of poverty!

CHAPTER TWO

TANAKA ZIBIGIHOUZI AND HER FAMILY: CONTINUATION

ON A LOVELY SUNNY Monday morning, two men appeared from nowhere. At first we did not notice them as we were busy playing *nhodo* (a game of pebbles) with my friend Anna on this lovely and beautiful day. The sun was radiating its heat rays which we enjoyed and which made us feel relaxed to the extent that we forgot to stay alert. Just like lizards enjoying the sun on rocks, we remained relaxed - until these men got nearer to us. Gosh, the sudden realisation of their presence might have caused our tachycardiac readings to peak, for our heartbeat rate surely accelerated to over 100 heartbeats per minute due to fright. These men were looking for *amai* (mum). I did not ask them who they were as that would have been considered rude. I held my heart in my hand to support it, so to speak, as I felt it beating even faster by the second.

CHAPTER TWO

Breathing heavily, like an Olympic Athlete, I went straightaway to fetch *amai* from our neighbour's house where she was chairing the local ladies' meeting about work that needed to be done at our church and the matter of handing over some money to one of the ladies from their savings club. Due to the effect of tachycardia, I forgot to say hello to the mothers as a way of showing respect.

"Did you greet the mothers?" asked amai angrily. "What did I teach you?" she echoed.

Gasping for breath, I apologised quickly and greeted amai's friends. They all replied at the same time (*tripo hedu*): "We are all well thanks!" My Aunt Mable said, "Here is a cup of water - drink and catch your breath; it is too hot out there." I thanked her without delay, bending my legs to show respect. Every woman brought some money on a monthly basis which was given to one woman to start a business or save for something. They did this every month between the six of them, rounding up everyone, each one paying exactly the same amount each time. *Amai* seemed to know who these guys were as she came out with a big smile on her face. Since it was her turn to receive the money the previous month, she must have bought something, I assumed.

"We have brought your delivery," said the men.

"Bring it over please, then I will show you where it is supposed to go," said *amai*. She quickly showed the men the way to the bedroom. I could tell from the smile on *amai's* face that she was very proud of her achievement; but what in this Whole Wide World had she bought, I wondered?

My friend and I and all the children from our community became anxious to find out, so we all went to the main road to watch the big lorry with big words: "GOTOBED & SONS LTD for all your furniture requirements." GOTOBED! We giggled as the name sounded so funny! I tried to put letters together to make a few words from the name and came up with Got-O-Bed or Got-A-Bed. It didn't make sense so I tried again. "Maybe it means a GOAT has BED!" shouted Anna.

"Oh, don't be silly, how can a GOAT have a bed?" I asked as I was getting annoyed, assuming that my friend had called my mum a goat. Then the penny dropped. "It means 'GO-To-Bed' - I got it, I got it!" I screamed with excitement, jumping up and down. My mum must have bought a bed so that she can now Go To Bed and sleep comfortably! Better than the hard floor, I thought. I could feel the excitement running down my spine and through all my nerves. Even if it was not *my* bed, the mere thought that my parents could afford to buy a bed when all the locals failed to do so thrilled me.

We saw the men carrying something that looked like a table with iron legs and chains in the middle. It can't be a table, I thought, and wondered what it was, still not convinced; then I plucked up the courage to ask these two men what it was they were carrying.

"It's a bed," said the man.

"Yes!" I screamed again. "*Mum has bought a bed; mum has*

bought a bed!" I sang with my friends. I got told off for asking though, since it is not a characteristic of our culture to be nosey and to talk to strange men. My friends and I nevertheless cheered loudly, as this was not very common; buying even the cheapest piece of furniture was considered a luxury. We kept on cheering and making lots of noise, because we were very excited that mum had bought a bed - a very big achievement. We grew up, you see, thinking that beds were only for white people and the rich.

The cheering made all our neighbours wonder what was happening. They all came out to stand by their doorways to watch. You know, in developing countries any stupid thing can draw a large crowd due to lack of entertainment; even public fighting will draw loads of people. This was indeed a great achievement for an African family - to be able to afford a bed!

When the men finished offloading the bed and were on their way back to town, all the kids ran after the truck, some trying to jump on it, some just wanting to touch it, while some were actually racing with the truck; it was all done in good faith, having fun the African way. *Baba* felt very proud of *amai* as he quoted a verse from the Bible (Proverbs 14:1): "The wise woman builds her house, but with her own hands the foolish one tears hers down." "I am glad that I married a wise and God-fearing woman who uses her hands," said *baba*, showing his appreciation of *amai's* works.

CHAPTER TWO

For the very first time mum and dad had bought a bed, which brought all our neighbours round to see it. This was after ten years of marriage, and please, do not even try to guess for how long these folk were sleeping on the hard floor! This made our family stand out from the crowd, and neighbours began to view us differently. The bed was made of iron and springs. It made squeaky noises that we could hear with every roll or turn that mum or dad made when they sat or lay on it. It had a mattress that had some large buttons on it. It felt really soft and much better than sleeping on the hard floor. When mum was out at the market, I would get my friend Anna to come round. We would jump and bounce on this spring bed: *chiki chiki chiki chiki* went the bed! We totally enjoyed it as we had our own trampoline. We had to make sure we didn't get caught jumping on the bed, of course, or we would be punished.

My family was such a loving and close-knit one. We always washed our hands in a large bowl and ate with our hands, together, outside, by the fire. The good thing was since we did not know about spoons, forks or knives, we used our hands and always had to wash our hands thoroughly before eating and after eating.

The next thing *amai* bought was a table with six chairs. Imagine that, we started eating together at a table! It was a luxurious life, a veritable heaven on earth - *kudya namambo*, like eating with the Royal family.

CHAPTER TWO

My mum and dad would take it in turns to tell us stories after supper, called *Zvingano*. We really enjoyed listening to their bedtime stories. Eventually my two elder sisters got married and moved in with their husbands. It was now my turn to cook for the whole family and do all the household chores. I grew up very quickly and worked hard both at school and at home, practising all the womanly chores. My aspiration was to make it big one day and turn the life of my whole family around.

When I was seven years old, I started school. My desire was to be able to speak and write in English. At the age of ten I could write and speak fluent English and I started to translate for my parents when we went shopping for food, clothes or furniture; but I wanted to do better than that. I used to go to sleep late at night, as I had to practice my maths and reading. I used to have a small lamp made from a small empty jam jar. In the lid of the jar was a small hole made by punching a sharp nail with a hammer. A thread from the jute bags was threaded and pulled through the hole and one hundred millilitres of paraffin was poured into the jar. The small paraffin lamp produced so much smoke in the house that it caused the nostrils to turn pitch black; but I had no other choice because spirit was considered lethal as well as exorbitant. I just wanted to pass and gain my primary school-leaving certificate to enable me to go to high school. I did not know about candles at that time - perhaps they were too expensive. By these means I passed my grade seven, even showing shades of distinction which made my parents the most chuffed of all about them.

My eldest sister Eunice also found a job and started working for the Hersellman family as a nanny. My sister would bring home second-hand clothes and food which she was given by Mrs Hersellman and some which were bought from the white neighbours at work.

It was really luxurious for us, as I had my first pair of knickers! Even if they were second hand, the fact that I had a pair of knickers thrilled me because I knew that amongst my friends none of them had knickers. All we girls were always taught to sit with our legs crossed and wore dresses long enough to prevent anyone seeing our genitals or thighs; this would also stop sand or any dirt contaminating our vaginas. *Hey, growing up in Africa is very sad but it is also very funny - growing up without any material things, yet enjoying every moment of it!* It all helped me to condition my mind that material wealth is worth nothing; nevertheless, financial freedom cannot be devalued: today, being able to have cash coming in, being able to sleep at night and making more money whilst sleeping gives me a peace of mind that I had not known in those early years. It is something I never realised till I received the financial education in later life as an adult.

My younger sister was called Roselyn. We became the

happiest of girls in our street, because we had knickers - even though these knickers were as huge as boxer shorts, which some old white woman had been tired of wearing! We were happy that we had something which our friends didn't have. I must admit these knickers were even bigger than Bridget Jones's; they had to be fitted with a draw string that would be tightened up, or with elastic, in order to fit. The local people used to call these knickers parachutes because they were so big! I recall pulling the elastic and making knots to make it fit our waists. We always washed our big knickers before having a shower, a procedure that enabled our knickers to dry in the sun whilst we took a shower.

My desire to make it in life grew stronger day by day, as I vowed never to bring up my children under similar circumstances. I thought, if my parents were impressed by my big sister working as a nanny, how happy would they be when I become a nurse, teacher, doctor, or even a copy typist, or the wife of a *murungu* - a white man; but deep down I wanted to be more than that, a person without a 9 to 5 job but who would be self-sufficient, someone who worked only when she wanted to, not because the boss wanted her to be in at a certain time. Running a business, I mean, and being an entrepreneur.

Amai was not educated at all, yet she was a very intelligent and wise woman - the woman who is described in Proverbs. She used to ask me to help her memorise all the names in the Bible from Genesis to Revelation. She memorised the majority of the songs in the Salvation Army song book. If she was leading the church service, she would memorise the verses and chapters as well as the page numbers she was going to be talking about. She would pretend she was reading, then ask someone from the audience to take over. Her favourite song was always HOW GREAT THOU ART.

Amai would pretend she was reading the first verse which she had memorised:

> O Lord my God, when I in awesome wonder,
> Consider all the worlds thy hands have made,
> I see the stars, I hear the rolling thunder,
> Thy power throughout the Universe displayed.
> *Then sings my soul, my saviour God to thee:*
> *How great thou art! How great thou art!*
> *Then sings my soul, my saviour God to thee:*
> *How great thou art! How great thou art!*

Amai would sing in a trembling voice, showing emotions of how great she felt God was, with tears running down her cheeks; it just felt so heavenly!

I thought that was wisdom, as none of *amai's* friends knew till the time of her death that she was not able to read or write.

Amai was born in a royal family which made her a princess. Her father was known as Chief *Maunganidze* (meaning a person who gathers) from Birchenough Bridge. However, they were not as rich or popular as the British Royals. Kirera taught her children to work very hard to achieve whatever they wanted in life. She always said, *"Mwana wamambo muranda kumwe"* - meaning, a King's child is a servant elsewhere, therefore one has to do what everyone else is doing to better oneself and to fit in the society one finds oneself in.

My *baba* (dad), Kufa, originated from Chipinga. Unfortunately, I never got to know or meet any of his family members, since they were displaced during the war of liberation in the 70's. *Baba* tried to find his family after the war in the 80's but could not find anyone. The village was deserted. Maybe they all died during the war and *baba* lamented their loss. *Amai* comforted him and said, "Now you've got us and the kids, you are not alone." In Zimbabwean culture, having a loving family means more than wealth or fame. I could see that *baba* was heartbroken due to the loss of his family, but no-one could help as many people had moved into Mozambique and South Africa and the only means of communication was by writing letters. Where could a letter be sent with an address? How could one communicate with people with telephones or mobile phones? I could feel the frustration but could not do anything about it, due to my age and lack of knowledge. At this point I vowed that I would always keep in contact with my family

CHAPTER TWO

and loved ones as they meant the world to me. For some of us who have broken families and know where the other family members are, I advise you to apply the Law of Forgiveness and find one another or else you will regret it for the rest of your life.

Baba worked very hard for his family as it was a norm that the man has to be the breadwinner. As time went by *baba* changed his job and started working for the GMB (Grain Marketing Board). He used to carry ninety kilogram bags of maize, wheat, sorghum, soya beans, sunflower seed, and rice on his head all day long. The sight of seeing her dad working very hard made Tanaka resent growing up. She told her mum that she did not want to grow up anymore. Kirera told her daughter that if she married an educated man, then she would live happily as she and her husband would be able to afford everything. Nevertheless she was already intimidated by adult life responsibilities.

One day dad (*Kufa*) had a nasty accident at work, when one of the machines that carried the bags of maize caught his little finger. According to dad, his little finger was crushed and he said he had never felt pain like that in his life. He was rushed to hospital but nothing could be done to save his finger, which was amputated; believe it or not, no compensation was paid to *Kufa* for the loss of his little finger - such was life during colonial rule. *Kufa* stayed in hospital for a long time and no money was forthcoming from his company for the family to live on.

"My little finger has been taken as *a sak-ruh-fahys*, a sacrifice for the company," cried baba. "It's gone, all gone, lost for ever; how shall I work and feed my family?" he cried in pain and frustration.

"It shall be fine, God shall provide and his will shall be done," said *amai* trying to console *baba*. "We will survive, just be brave for us and concentrate on getting better; we will find ways to feed ourselves," *amai* added with tears running down her cheeks, holding and rubbing *baba*'s left hand. "We shall pray for wisdom to get ideas from God Almighty, and work hard to look after the children. I know and believe that God will guide me; all I need is to do something, take action and stop sleeping." All this she said, sobbing her heart out.

Amai and I started to think of ways of making money, as **everything else had failed** and we were determined to reject poverty. We all depended on *baba* financially; we prayed and abstained from food (fasting), but God seemed to have gone on a vacation, we thought. It took us some time to come up with an idea.

As young as I was, aged ten, I managed to hatch an idea of picking corn from our small field, cooking it and selling the corn to travellers and commuters on buses. Little did I know, that was the first sign of my destiny as a real life entrepreneur. I hatched this plan to stop *amai* (mum) from begging for money or food from some better off neighbours who would in return have to marry one of the girls when they were older. This was known as *kuzvarira* in olden Zimbabwean culture. **I resented the idea of marrying an older man or allowing any of my sisters to be given away as a child bride to an older man in exchange for food or money, which, as I said, was known as *kuzvarira*. It also appeared to me that God only helps those who help themselves; no matter how much you pray, without action it will be difficult to receive those miracles as in the old biblical days. One has to do something, I learnt. If one does something, God will help one and one will see the miracles of today.**

My family worked very hard and managed to raise some money to buy peanuts (*nzungu*) and ground nuts (*nyimo*) from the local farmers, boiled them in salted water and sold them together with the corn. We managed to earn money enough to pay rent and buy food whilst *baba* was still in hospital. Later on when *baba* was discharged from hospital he returned to work and was very impressed by the family's achievement during his long stay in hospital.

My family continued with the buying and selling business, this time adding bottles of Coca-Cola, hot cross buns, sweets, matches, creamed doughnuts and cupcakes called candy cakes. We sold some of the goodies to patients who were hospitalised at the local hospital.

One day, as I was in charge of the vending bike, a young man dressed in white came towards me from the hospital. He grabbed a bottle of Coca-Cola and a candy cake. "$1,20 please," I said as I raised my hand to receive the payment.

"I am not paying for anything; you guys shouldn't be selling stuff at this hospital," he blurted out with his red eyes wide open.

I didn't know what to say as I was just a young girl; his voice and height scared me and made my heart pound very fast and those huge eyes were just enough to make me pee myself with fright. My worst fear was being grabbed by the arm and ending up being raped by this evil man - for rumours had circulated about his behaviour towards young girls. I kept quiet and prayed quietly to God to spare me from the evil that was in front of me. Honestly, he marched away without paying but I gave thanks to God, because he had not laid a finger or nail on me. I just watched him, helpless, as he disappeared into the hospital to partake of the free goodies. Some people just bring bad luck into their lives, I thought, because I was made to believe that when someone says bad things about you, it attracts bad luck to you.

When *amai* (mother) came in the evening to take me home, I started crying at the first sight of her. I was scared and did not know what or how to tell her about the incident, as I thought all that had happened was my fault. I was scared that *amai* was going to blame me for the shortage of a Coca-Cola bottle and a cake. I assumed that *amai* might blame it on me, saying that I drank the Coca-Cola and ate the cake

CHAPTER TWO

and was now lying to cover it up. Instead, she was very sympathetic and wanted to know what had happened. I explained everything to *amai*, who asked me to come along and point out the man who had done this.

As we entered the hospital I saw the man, still dressed in his white uniform. I pointed at the man saying to *amai*, "That's him there, dressed in white!" *Amai* promptly approached the man and asked him to pay for the drink and cake he had taken from the vending bike.

"You guys don't pay any rent for selling stuff outside the hospital!" he yelled. He was much younger than my mum, probably half my mother's age.

"Who the hell do you think you are, asking me for rent?" she shouted. "All the senior doctors and the hospital matron allow me to sell and they pay for all their goodies!"

"I will not pay for anything, because I work and pay taxes; what about you people, just making money and paying no tax?" he barked again.

This made *amai* really angry and she snapped back: "It is your choice to work as a 'LEARNER DOCTOR' and it was my choice to be in business." She continued to fire back angrily: "When I fall ill, I will make sure that I do not get treated by you, a 'LEARNER DOCTOR', a mere medical student and a thief!"

I dared to look at this man's name badge; it read *Tonde Mukwamuri*, Nurse. I wondered why my mother thought he might have been a trainee doctor whom she called 'LEARNER DOCTOR'. I found this humorous as I told *amai* that he was not what she thought he was. "Thanks *mutanami*," she said as she walked briskly to the matron's office to report Tonde. He was called in straight away, asked to apologise to *amai* and pay for the Coca-Cola and cake. From that day I realised that working-class people were never happy about paying income tax, but it did not mean much to me at the time.

Since Karoi was surrounded by farms, the farmers started to produce more and more grain which was later exported to neighbouring countries such as Zambia, Malawi and Tanzania. The family business later developed into a mini-restaurant, where we cooked *sadza* (grounded maize, stiff porridge, served like mashed potatoes) and *nyama* (beef stew); the stiff porridge made from ground maize and beef stew was sold to the truck drivers and workers at GMB, and we made money; funny enough, *baba* never had a bank account, so we made money and blew it as my parents both concurred that too much money would make people insane. Every Zimbabwean knows that it was believed that too much money was not good and too much education could make people insane.

Baba and *amai* started talking about profit and loss which was a new thing for me. Baba explained this to me in a simple way to understand: "You see, Tanaka, you take twenty-four dollars to buy a case of Coca-Cola bottles; then, after selling them you get thirty-six dollars. You will then say thirty-six take away twenty-four and the answer is your profit. If you paid two dollars on the bus to go and buy the case of Coca-Cola, you will need to take it out which means your profit will be ten dollars. If you sell anything for less the amount you paid when you make your order, that will be a loss."

"Thank you *baba*," I said as I stood up to bow and bend my legs (*kutyora muzura*), as a way of appreciation...

My parents managed to make good profits from their business, to the extent that they managed to buy proper though cheap furniture for the whole house. When I was around fifteen, *baba* became prey to the local prostitutes. He started having one-night stands and affairs and eventually *baba* and *amai* divorced in 1981. It was heart-breaking and I felt like my parents had died whilst they were still alive. It was the hardest time for us as a family. Divorce does not only affect the two married people, it affects everyone in the immediate family including the pets.

It was a common thing for Zimbabwean men to have an affair as they thought it gave them status. Also, the majority of single women saw prostitution as a lucrative business.

Local single women sold sex for a living and bought small council houses and herds of cattle for their parents in the rural areas. It was often wished by some young men that if they had vaginas they would strike it big by trading sex.

Homosexuality was not spoken about very much,

especially publicly, and it remains illegal in Zimbabwe. It is also considered a taboo practice. However, some men still found and find ways of making money in the same ways as the single women (prostitutes) do through streetwalking; however, it is swept under the carpet and never spoken about in public as it was seen as taboo. Male prostitution is a huge business for those who want to get rich quickly in Zimbabwe.

The majority of these male prostitutes are either married or single men who use emotional and financial blackmail as a means to receiving financial gain from their rich foreign lovers, especially by threatening to report them to the local authorities such as the famous CIO. Honestly, no man would want to be locked up in an African prison such as Zimbabwe's Chikurubhi where there are bed bugs and lice, and where he will also be faced with the prospect of hard labour. In some other African and Asian countries these *bendos* or "queers" could be kept in prison till they die or actually get killed. These men would give whatever they had in a bid to stay alive and to return to their countries in one piece. As I said, it is illegal to be GAY in Zimbabwe and some other countries, in as much as it is frowned upon in Christianity; even God himself condemned Sodomy.

GROWING UP: TANAKA ZIBIGIHAUZI

My beginnings were tough going but I had to face the challenges in-order to grow up; even though *amai*'s constant criticism knocked my confidence at times, it helped me to become a strong woman. I am not ashamed and will never be ashamed of where I emerged from, as this determines who I AM today. I AM a Zimbabwean and an African and will always be proud to be who I AM; thus the powerful words, I AM; Me, Myself and I. Despite the fact that I did not have any material things as a kid, I must acknowledge that I had a very blissful and adventurous childhood. Running around like monkeys with my siblings and mates without knickers on, climbing trees, jumping up and down from trees and low buildings, playing hide and seek, going to Sunday School, being members of the Brownie and the Girl Guides, and prying on the whites at the Country Club - you know, those then 'no go' areas for blacks - were just a few of our fun-filled activities.

We never went to bed hungry; we always ate nutritious meals though not so posh; it was mostly a vegetarian diet, *sadza* and *covo* (green kale leaf or *sukuma* in Swahili). Baba was a very industrious man. Once in a while he would go fishing and caught plenty of bream (*Tilapia fish*) that filled big containers and we ended up smoking and drying some for later and also sold some to friends and neighbours just to earn a bit of cash. He also used to go hunting at times, but mainly for guinea fowls and rabbits as it was illegal to hunt down any large wild animals for meat. We also had a massive vegetable garden which we had to work hard on; thus digging the ground, making beds, planting the vegetables, watering them, weeding and pruning. *Amai* was very strict in her teachings; if any of us refused to work in the garden then there would be no food for us for that day. As such, she taught us to work hard to be able to put food on the table rather than rely on hand-outs such as state benefits; she was trying to destroy the dependence culture of our lives.

"I shall not breed any lazy offspring!" she shouted every morning as she encouraged us to get up early each morning and do our daily chores. "The house needs to be swept and cleaned on a daily basis; sleeping has no bonus, it will only bring sorrow and poverty to your lives," she warned. "Learn to rise before the sun rises and you will collect all the blessing of the day before your fellow neighbours," she encouraged us.

By the time our neighbours woke up, we would already have made a fire outside our house, swept the house yard, had a wash to make sure our faces were presentable and ready to face the day. Most of our neighbours would come to our house to ask for red hot coals to make a fire; by this time our twenty-litres of hot boiling water for domestic use would be making a loud bubbling noise just like a waterfall. A pot of maize porridge with peanut butter would be sending an appetising aroma about the place, all ready to be dished out.

By waking up an hour or more earlier than our neighbours, we were always admired by most of the people around and envied by some.

Ours was a very traditional family with traditional family

values. I do not recall eating at a friend's house at any point; we always had enough to eat; even if there was nothing to eat, we had to go hungry till *baba* and *amai* found something for us to eat. We would get punished very severely and harshly should *amai* or *baba* find out that we ate at the neighbours known as *Kukwata*. *Kukwata* was a taboo as parents feared we could be poisoned by some wicked people through food.

I would say we were better off regarding food than apparel, for we did not have much to wear. I remember walking barefooted to school up to the age of fourteen and the only time my parents bought a pair of black shoes for me was when I had joined the school choir. Every member of the choir had to have a pair of shoes as we had to attend a district school's show to compete against some regional schools; as such it was a must that every child who participated had a uniform, complete with white socks and black shoes.

One day in August, a day of dazzling sunshine, the grass was very short having been burnt by the locals. The smell of the burnt grass and mud after the rain was evocative, drawing my imagination into an unknown world. The entire township just felt and smelt heavenly, as I did not know any other unnatural scents. Soap, which was known as *Lifebuoy* and *Choice*, were the only unnatural scents I had been accustomed to. On the other hand the smell was also nauseating, unholy, disgusting and sickening and I just wanted to regurgitate! What on earth was this ungodly smell and where was it coming from? After stumbling on a heap of raw-shit, I realised that my friends and I should not use the public lavatory, so we opted for the bush instead. However, I did not know that once human shit got rained upon it started to decay, causing a strong and unwanted odour. The stench made me realise that we were polluting the environment.

I could not use the bush for my bowel movement since the grass was too short to provide cover for me and my friends. I was left with no option but to visit the public lavatory after all. Wearing these slippers by *Bata* called Pata-pata, I pata-pated into the public lavatory to do the big one. I stepped into the first cubicle and my step picked up a large lump of dough, human poo, on my Pata-pata! My Pata-pata started to stick to the floor as I carried on walking, trying to find a hole that was not so full; I stumbled on a slippery floor, slipping as I had treaded on shit already; in fact, I slipped and fell onto my back and landed on my bum with my arms and head landing on shit and more shit! It must be said, African public lavatories are disgusting as people poo on the floor! I panicked and cried and cried my lungs out. I crawled out completely covered in human excrement like a mad girl. *Amai* heard me crying and quickly came to my rescue.

The smell made me sick and I regurgitated, till my tummy was completely empty. "What on this planet has happened to you?" asked *amai*.

"I treaded on human shit, then slipped and fell, landing on more poo in the latrine... *ooooucccchhh!!*" I answered, crying my eyes out; in fact, I cried buckets and buckets of distress. *Amai* quickly helped me remove my clothes and poured some water for me to have a bath. Thank God for *amai*'s wise idea of having boiling water ready by the fireside all the time. This worked like our boiler. *Amai* used warm water and Surf washing powder to scrub my body as I wept. "I will never ever go into that toilet again!" I cried. Mama helped me pour more clean water over my body. I think I had five good baths and scrubbings from head to toe that day. I took the hump and begrudged visiting the public latrines. As I write, I recall how to this day I hate those public latrines in less developed countries - I really do! I threw my clothes away and my Pata-patas and never wanted to see them again as they were only going to remind me of my misadventure. By the way, this happened before we moved to our new house with its own toilet. I thought, is this what my people mean when they swear life is shit and can be really shitty!

That evening I could not eat anything at all as my throat felt blocked by a huge lump. As I listened to my parents talking, I heard *amai* telling *baba* about my inadvertent mishap. *Baba* replied, "These public latrines really need to be demolished as they are dangerous; they have clear cemented floors which are very slippery and they are untrustworthy, unsafe, dirty and water keeps leaking from the pipes; as for

Tanaka, I feel sorry for her mishap but happily I know this will bring good luck into her life."

"What do you mean *baba*?" asked *amai* anxiously. "Good luck when she has slipped into a heap of shit?!"

"Oh *amai* Tanaka, it is a saying from our elders that say shit in dreams and in accidents is associated with much, much wealth, so watch this space! It shows and proves her ability for endurance. Her life will never be the same again."

"Is that what you actually *think*?" said *amai* with that expression which said 'how dare you!' and 'what's wrong with this man?' *Amai* wanted to keep it simple as it has always been believed that the husband is the head of the house and as such should be considered to know everything, and whatever he says should not be criticised, especially during the presence of visitors and children - as kids will learn to criticise their parents.

"When I was growing up, my granddad used to ask me to drink a raw egg when I was going to sit for any exams or going for interviews," *baba* said. "He told me that if I endured the taste of the raw egg and allowed myself to believe that I have already passed my examination and I have got the job before the interview, everything would turn out to be true - and it worked for me on several occasions!" *Baba* smiled and added: "This shows that there is power in believing and in the words we speak."

From that moment I thought *baba* was out of his mind, yet as I grew older I found his philosophy was working for me.

CHAPTER TWO

I could not eat for a few days and only drank clear fluids till I felt really hungry. I started eating small amounts till I completely forgot about my nightmare. Yet for some strange reason I kept on dreaming about shit, maybe once or twice a month, swimming in it or maybe treading on it. Funny enough, sometimes I had dreams about very big green fields with corn or rice. I told my parents about it and *amai* was quick to say, "You are still thinking of what happened to you, *mutanami*" (my child); but *baba* always said, "It has to do with finances, my girl - money, big, big money, and the green scenery is life; that means you will live longer." For some unknown reason I started to feel more positive energy as a result of what *baba* had said.

I developed much confidence in myself and became wiser even in choosing boyfriends when I was big enough. I started vetting my potential boyfriends on how ambitious and creative they were as opposed to their level of education and looks. I had to vet their families as well to find out if there was effective bonding and that family values were respected in those families. I also looked for personal presentation, noting how my potential boyfriends carried themselves, dressed, whether they were tidy and had a good sense of humour. Any unkempt boys, smokers, drinkers and those who lacked self-confidence and bad boys were dismissed from my register. I was a smart dater as a young girl. Shoes and a belt on a pair of trousers said it all for me; not what we see these days, boxer shorts way up above the waist and the trousers cutting the buttocks in half - what a disgrace! Is it fashion, the times, the generation, western culture? What is it actually that makes people walk about half naked, wearing next to nothing? God help us!

My baptism of fire followed me all the days of growing up. One day I dressed up nicely and was about to go out with my best friend Anna and her two sisters. I wore a nice green and off-white dress, which was bought for me the previous Christmas, but I did not have any shoes to wear. I recall I was about fourteen years old - that time when the boobs were starting to grow and feeling very painful to the touch, and felt really heavy as they grew bigger by the week.

My friend Anna had a pair of wedge heels which she had received as a gift from her sister who worked for an American family; these shoes are now back as retro fashion. She did not wear them as she could not walk in them. She lent me the shoes for a day. We had scrubbed our bodies and applied body lotion and Vaseline; our legs were shining, looking very hairy and greasy in the sunny weather. Talk about waxing! We had never heard about it, and everything on us was purely natural - the body odour, the breath and everything; it was just us, purely us.

I wore the borrowed wedge heels to add a dash of glamour and a pinch of height and off we went. Everyone was gazing at me as I stood out of the crowd due to the American wedge heels. I could see everyone's set of eyeballs rolling towards me. I stood high like a celebrity walking on a red carpet in an African Township as I swung my hips like a model doing a catwalk and held my head high with much confidence and pride. Wow, the recipe came out well! I chuckled as I continued to walk confidently, all these eyeballs following me. I shall soon be famous, I thought to myself.

When we were about to reach the market we had to go down a set of stairs. I did not know what to do as I had never worn wedge heels before. Instead of going down, step by step, I jumped from the fourth step onto the ground, hoping to land gently! *Ouuuchhh!* I fell like a sack of maize and twisted my ankle. All those people who were eyeballing me felt sorry for me whilst some laughed out loud: *"Kubatira chirungu padenga!"* they yelled. (Meaning, "Trying to grasp the western culture from the top, you've been brought down!") Surely, pride comes before a fall, I thought as I was being rushed to hospital on *baba*'s bike - for there were no ambulances - and there I stayed in for a week. As a result of this I took refuge in my hood; even if one were to ask the hens that ran around the market, they would confirm they knew me. Yes, Tanaka became the talk of the township. I was known as the girl who wore parachute knickers, or the girl who fell from an American mango tree, meaning the girl who fell from the American high heels!

When I returned from hospital I got told off by mum and

dad as they shouted together like a pair penguins: "You could have broken your leg! Why were you wearing high heels, for goodness's sake! Are you after boys then?" I did not answer back to my parents as it was considered to be very rude. I let them speak and shout at me till they thought it was enough.

The truth is I was just a young girl who never ever pondered about boys, for the thought of boys was far, far from my mind. But I was contemplating a successful adulthood with loads and loads of money and fashion, American fashion in the then Rhodesia.

I was just an innocent young girl who wanted to have adventures and fun with my friends as we enjoyed being teens. As I had developed a hankering after British and American fashion, my friends and I started to go to the local country club where whites congregated over the weekends for swimming, tennis, hockey, volley ball, golf and other sports. It was clearly marked 'European Country Club' and underneath were the words: "Blacks, beware of the dog! Trespassers will be prosecuted!!" Honestly, the then white guys where very racial. See the quote below:

Company Rule

> Company rule on behalf of Britain was very harsh on the Africans as the companies

practiced an apartheid-like system during their rule. In spite of the numerous blunders of these companies in running colonies in Africa, the British government allowed most of them to rule for a very long time. Interested only in making profits, the companies were ill suited to administer territories or colonies, and they found that doing so was neither easy nor profitable. To increase their profit margins, they employed racist and draconian policies. Unfortunately, the adverse policies they enacted were continued when the British government took over administration of the colonies. These policies had far-reaching effects that lasted into the postcolonial period.

Settler Rule

Another system of British colonial administration was the settler rule system that occurred where Britain had large populations of European immigrants. These immigrants settled and established direct rule over the colonies in Africa especially in southern and eastern Africa. They planned to make Africa their permanent home. British settler colonies were founded primarily in South Africa, Southern and Northern Rhodesia (Zimbabwe and Zambia), and South-West Africa (Namibia). Settlers from Holland, Britain, Germany, and Portugal colonized these areas. In addition, settler rule was practiced in Kenya, a British colony in East Africa. These settlers, who came to Africa to exploit the natural resources, made sure that laws were enacted or forces created that enabled them to dominate the numerically larger African populations, economically, socially, and politically. **In colonies with settler rule, there was harsher treatment of native Africans than in the colonies with the indirect rule system or where there were no sizable white settler populations**. West Africa was spared settler rule because of the harsh hot climate and because of malaria. Malaria killed so many early European adventurers and colonial agents in West Africa that Europeans nicknamed it the "white person's grave."

Settlers regarded themselves to be naturally superior to the "natives," as the British called their African colonial subjects. They saw the Africans as people who must be subjected and who were good only for being domestics to the

white settlers. The methods of oppression and repression by the European settler populations were not known in pre-colonial Africa. At least the internal conquerors in Africa prior to the Europeans did not see themselves as genetically superior to the conquered. The white settlers appropriated to themselves to the exclusion of the Africans all the good and arable lands. These lands were designated "crown property." This practice was notorious in South Africa, Zimbabwe, Zambia, and Kenya. Some of the postcolonial and independent African countries did the same thing; government officials nationalized huge tracts of communal lands and distributed it among themselves, their families, and their cronies. This occurred in Nigeria, for example, when the government passed the Land Use Decree of 1977.[1]

We, as blacks, were not allowed to join in at the local Country Clubs, even if one could afford the membership fee; it was a complete white people only zone. Black people were seen as the white men's donkey or domestic, not a social being but a labourer.

---

1. Read more: TYPES OF BRITISH COLONIAL RULE IN AFRICA – Colonies, Government, Ethnic and African – J.Rank. Article: http://encyclopedia.jrank.org/articles/pages/5921/TYPES-OF-BRITISH-COLONIAL-RULE-IN-AFRICA.html#ixzz1xdNnVoca

CHAPTER TWO

We started sneaking into the country club by crawling under the razor fence or barbered wire. We all know the taste of the forbidden fruit, hence taking the risk. I led a group of teens, both boys and girls. We would sneak in and watch the whites playing all their games and young men and young women kissing in corners of buildings; for us this was like watching a movie or a play at a theatre. "What are they doing?" we asked each other as we had no idea what was going on and had never seen that sort of act before. "I think they are doing what animals do, cleaning each other's faces with tongues," we concluded, or perhaps they are giving each other kisses of life, which we had learnt about at school during first aid lessons. As we watched the boy proceeding to touch the girl's boobs we then realised that there was more to this than the kiss of life. We continued to hide and watch this free romantic scene. Within no time the girl was on the floor and the boy took his shirt off which he laid on the ground for the girl to lie on. The boy quickly climbed on top of the girl. They continued to have their mouths glued to each other but moving about, touching each other everywhere. We had never seen anything like it! We grew up without televisions but as time went on we watched free films from the government where they used the wall of a building as a screen; and nothing of what we saw the young white folk doing was ever screened there. This was called 'Bioscope'

CHAPTER TWO

which was delivered by a projector, mainly outside. Please see the quote below:

> Therefore films that were regularly shown to all audiences in Cape Town and Johannesburg were forbidden to African audiences in Rhodesia. Until the late 1950s virtually the only films screened for Africans in these colonies were heavily edited American westerns. African elites in the 1950s tried to "improve" the quality of films shown in Rhodesian bioscopes, with limited success. *Flickering Shadows*, Chapter 6.[2]

Thus, in Rhodesia (Zimbabwe after independence), people watched heavily edited movies. I still remember characters such as Charlie Chaplin and Oliver Hardy; it was pure comedy and there was nothing cynical about it. It was in later life as adults when we started watching the adult Hollywood movies that were realised such things are part of human lives.

Since what was happening to that boy and girl at the country club did not make sense to us, we ignored watching them and proceeded to watch my favourite sport which was swimming. I watched swimming most of the time and

---

2. Read more: TYPES OF BRITISH COLONIAL RULE IN AFRICA – Colonies, Government, Ethnic and African – J.Rank. Article: http://encyclopedia.jrank.org/articles/pages/5921/TYPES-OF-BRITISH-COLONIAL-RULE-IN-AFRICA.html#ixzz1xdNnVoca

hankered after being like the white people. I thought life must be good for them. I would close my eyes and see myself swimming and relaxing on sun beds in my bikini or floating on a float and going into this unknown world with Dolphins pulling my float to the other side of the world - a world yet to be discovered, a world where one does not need to worry about paying bills and what to eat, you just get up and sit by the table, eat as much as you like, then someone will do the washing up and cleaning after you: a real piece of heaven, I imagined. I found the imagination calming and relaxing. "One day I will be exactly like them, in my own private pool, at my very own large mansion or diving from a very large boat into the big blue sea," I told my friend Anna.

For a minute my un-ambitious friend thought I had lost it or was just about to lose it.

"Are you mad!" Anna exclaimed.

"No, I'm not," I replied.

"I've never heard of any black person who lives like them, it's only a dream and fantasy!" Anna hissed like a Gabon Viper and spat like a Black Mamba.

"So, you don't believe I can be like them?" I asked Anna, angrily this time.

"No, not in a million years! This kind of life is not for Africans," concluded my friend with a frown on her face, her chest slightly bent forward to emphasise her point - just like a Black Mamba that was ready to strike.

Shit, what a heap of intimidating ignorance, I thought.

I did not want to argue with Anna; she was my best friend, but her negative mind and lack of vision pierced my heart to the extent that I did not want to be friends with her again, since we were not on the same wavelength. However, I had to let her down gently. Sure, she was entitled to her option but had no right to try to discourage me by brainwashing me, making me think that black people would always live in the traditional round hut and shit in the bush... I respected her option but deep down inside me, I hated people without a vision and people who were not focused and those who lacked insight and ambition.

Let the fools mingle together, I shall not be seen hanging around with them; I shall seek the wise and mingle with them, I declared.

To this day, I love people who let their imaginations run away with them; people who ask why, constantly, people who try new but moral things, have adventures, create new things; and those who make things happen, like creating BRANDS, PRODUCTS and SERVICES that have never been heard of before, finding and satisfying new NICHE markets - you know what I mean. Walt Disney is my hero, the guy who created Mickey Mouse, the widely known and the most popular character mouse in the world. Even though his family tried to discourage him, he ignored them and as such he created his own world of fun: Disney Land in LA, California, Disney World in Orlando, Florida, and Disney Land, Paris in France.

One day as we observed the whites swimming, some white woman saw us and screamed: "*Kafir, Kaffir, help, help!!!!!*" - meaning "Blacks, blacks!" She screamed so loud you thought she had seen a pride of lions! I checked myself out and my mates. Do we have fangs? No. Do we have horns? No; do we have hooves? No; do we have tails? No; do we have any contagious diseases? No. Are we carrying machetes and spears? No!! Then why is the woman screaming like she has seen a pack of wolves or a pride of lions, or a leap of leopards, I wondered?

My mouth trembled with anger and terror as I wanted to say something but unfortunately the words stuck in my voice box and could not come out, suppressed by FEAR.

The guard came chasing after us with a vicious dog, which he set on us. Blimey, the dog himself was as racist as his owners and keeper! When it came across white people he would stop barking and wag his tail; but for black people this was different. The dog would bark and show his sharp teeth as if he was ready to fight a tiger. We ran for our lives as we begged our legs to carry us and not to give up on us, since our lives were in danger. Honestly, these guys used dogs for the wrong reasons; it was not surprising therefore that not many Africans were keen on dogs.

As the black guard chased after us, a group of white children almost our ages followed, calling the dog to come to them and they were throwing sausages at the dog which then stopped from chasing us as it concentrated on the sausages. When we saw that the dog had stopped we stopped as we were tired and gasping for air. The guard shouted at us: "Don't ever come back here ever again; do you hear me! This is strictly a whites-only area; I repeat, it is an area for *white people only!*"

We shouted back, "*Nyon'o nyon'o nyon'o*" - *in other words*, "*Na-na na-na na-na*, you think you are white like them!" We shouted again: "If they don't allow blacks then you shouldn't be there!!"

One of my friends, called Nyasha, stood on a large rock, cupped her mouth with her hands to make herself heard and shouted without any fear: "Are you a white man who escaped from a crematorium half-way through? Then you are almost like us, so stop discriminating, old man, and start living!" She jumped off the rock quickly and ran with us.

The guard was really annoyed and he shouted, "I am a black man you know, I am only doing my job!"

"Oh!" shouted Jabu. "You are a black man, but I thought you were a white man who was half- burnt alive or something; how come you are black and everyone is white!"

We laughed loudly and continued to run away.

"This country club is in our zone, our range, our territory; we patrol this area on foot, with our bare feet, and the CC is in the land of our ancestors, so why should we be barred from just observing? We cannot take anything with our eyes!" I snapped. "This is just racial segregation!" I puffed.

We shouted at him again, "But we did not take anything, we are just spectators - we want to learn how to swim, hence observing what these people without knees are doing!" Our elders used to call whites people without knees (*vanhu vasina mabvi*) because they could not kneel down like us; also, our knees are darker than our legs whereas with whites there is no difference colour-wise. The only way one could identify the knee is because it bends!

"Go and swim in the rivers, not here, it's never, never for Africans!" regurgitated the black guard again.

"This man must be fast asleep, hence being used like a slave!" I snapped. Surely, I thought, he did the job of four or five men by himself, yet was paid for one. He would cut the grass, do the garden, clean the swimming pool, clean the toilets, make teas and coffees and was also the security guard. Why? Because they did not want to introduce many blacks to work there! "Watch what you disgorge, old man!" I shouted at him. I had spent much of my time trying to swallow the dictionary, hence my coming up with some unusual words!

The white children came along and put the dog on a leash and pleaded with the guard to speak to us nicely. They also wondered why we were not allowed to intermingle with them and they wanted to make friends with us.

"Please stop chasing them and be nice to them," said one of the white boys who was a bit older. "Why are you being so mean to your own people?" the boy asked again. "Allow us to talk to them please, Mugwagwa," asked the boy.

"Of course you can talk to them but not a word to your parents as I might get sacked," said Mugwagwa.

"We promise we won't tell," said the older boy.

"Hey *shamwaris* (meaning friends), come here, to us," called out the bigger boy.

"Oh yes we can come to talk to you, but you need to take the dog back to the club first," I replied. Most whites in those colonial days used these innocent animals for the wrong reasons, to set them on Africans and enjoyed watching the dogs biting people; hence most Africans were scared of dogs. It was horrible and I don't even want to think about it, since I have many scars from dog bites on my legs.

The boy took the dog and handed it over to Mugwagwa. "Please take him back, we will be back as soon as possible; if anyone asks after us, you haven't seen us, right?"

"Yes, *pikini boss* (little boss)," replied Mugwagwa as he started walking back to the club.

We started chatting to these white kids. Their names were Ricky, Harry, Tim, Mark and the girls were Natalie, Jessica, Kate, Sophie. Ricky was the eldest of the group, aged about fifteen or sixteen. The group wanted to learn our language and culture. They had sweets and biscuits which they shared with us. We sat down in a large circle and started talking and introducing ourselves.

We went on to dancing as one of the boys had a tape recorder. We started dancing to Michael Jackson's 'Rock with You' and 'Don't stop till you get enough'. We enjoyed dancing and Nicky said, "This is what they do in America and Britain; I don't see why we can't do that here, and also, this music is by a black musician; yet my parents love it so much whilst deep down they hate African people."

We black kids did not say anything but just looked at each other with an expression that said, "Did you hear that!" while the white kids looked at one another with an expression that said, "What on earth is he telling these black kids this for?!"

When we finished dancing we sat down and Ricky, the most talkative one, asked, "Hey, Tanaka, what do you call a Willy in Shona?"

"A Willy is a Willy," I replied.

"Noooo come on, you should have a name for it," said Ricky again.

Actually I could not figure out what a Willy was - I thought it was short for William. I braved it and swallowed my pride. "Which Willy are you talking about, Ricky?" I queried smartly. The truth is I did want to appear a fool in front of my friends by saying I didn't know what a Willy was; instead, I chose to ask which one, as if I knew.

"You know what I mean," Ricky went on. "I am talking about the one your brother uses to pee."

CHAPTER TWO

It was getting worse. My brother doesn't pee at all, I thought. Let me just be smart here, otherwise I won't understand a thing!

"Oh Ricky, can you please use the dictionary English," I said.

"I see," said Ricky. "I mean the small stick between your brother's legs that he uses to urinate; what do you call it in your language?"

"Oh I see, you mean his boyhood toy!"

"Yes, you are right," said Ricky.

Phew, I sighed for a minute; never in my life had I thought or imagined that my brother had something different from us girls. I used to see it, but for some reason it did not mean anything to me. No one had ever called that boyish thingy by its name. What a shame, I thought, these white kids must be cursed because they use the forbidden language. Those are some of the things we black kids were not allowed to talk about.

"How about paying ten cents for every word I teach you?" I said.

"Okay, that's fine by me," concurred Ricky.

"Now pay first, before I teach you," I said. "I will teach you the words but to tell you the truth, my parents will disown me if they happen to find out," I told Ricky.

Ricky paid the ten cents and I told him that it is called *Mboro*.

CHAPTER TWO

"M'*boro?*" said Ricky, struggling to pronounce the word.

All the black kids burst into laughter. Ricky felt embarrassed and his face turned red straightaway. That was the first time we actually realised that a white person's face could turn red just like that. We panicked and felt very scared that we might be in serious trouble. Ricky noticed that we were scared and he burst into laughter as well as his group, just to make it easier for us. As we laughed together, Ricky leaned forward toward me to give me a hug and to say it was all okay.

"No, no, don't do that!" I protested loudly. "I am not allowed to do that; we don't do bodily contact with boys - please stay away from me."

"Okay Tanaka, I am sorry, I just wanted to make it up to you."

My mind had raced to the wrong conclusion. I thought he wanted to do that thingy we had observed before, with a boy and girl having their mouths and bodies glued together and touching each other everywhere. Silly and ignorant me, it was only a hug! See, we did not grow up doing things like giving each other hugs; but as time went by people, even our people, started doing that hugging thing; times had indeed changed.

He went on asking for more rude words and by the end of the day I had made about $10, since for every single word I charged ten cents! By the end of the day Ricky made an effort to string a sentence together in my language. He chose one of the youngest girls of the group and said the funniest joke that made everyone roll on the floor with laughter. Pointing at the youngest girl he said, *"Mbori yake, uyo agere pansi inenge nariti"* - meaning. "That one, who is sitting down, her penis is as sharp as a needle!" This appeared to be the funniest joke we had ever heard, as we wondered how on earth a girl could have a PENIS, and then one that was as sharp as a needle! We all rolled about laughing our lungs out. It was unbelievably funny.

"Hey Ricky, you made your sentence up correctly, but hey, girls do not have penises!" I corrected him. "I will not teach you any more rude words as you are now using them to verbally abuse my people. I shall teach you only the moral ones," I declared.

"Oh my God, is she a *girl?*" Ricky said, looking aghast. "I thought he was a boy!" He apologised to the girl and explained that he didn't mean to be rude. We all understood as our friend was enjoying the excitement of learning a new language.

As the sun was about to set we saw a group of white people heading towards us. I said to Ricky, "Look," pointing at the group of parents coming towards us.

"Oh My God, Unholy Shit! We're in trouble guys!" Ricky swore and screamed to his fellow friends. "Run for your lives, look at the pack of them!"

CHAPTER TWO

"*Rickyyyyyyyyyy*, come here now!!" called the larger white man who appeared to be the leader of the group.

"Okay dad, I'm on my way," replied Ricky meekly.

We watched our friends as they walked towards their parents.

"What have you been doing with those Kaffirs?" interrogated Ricky's dad. "Answer me - I am asking you a question! Why are you not answering? Have you gone deaf all of a sudden?"

"No dad, we were just mucking about, chatting, dancing and making friends with them," said Ricky.

"What have I taught you about intermingling with black kids?" he bellowed. "I taught you never, *ever* to make friends with these people who are uncivilised, who eat tripe and all, and who eat with their bloody hands!" he added.

"Stop it dad, please do not spurn their food - that is not very kind; we eat finger food with our hands and our ancestors ate with their hands before knives and forks were inverted; what's wrong with that? Just be nice to the poor kids," pleaded Ricky.

"I said, shut up! What's got into you? And you have no right to tell me what to do, young man!" yelled Ricky's dad who was very obnoxious and pig-headed.

"No dad, I am not going to shut up!" Ricky cried, standing his ground. "I am entitled to my say. You are just a nasty, horrible, horrible man, a bully and a racist!"

Ricky's dad grabbed him by the arm and bellowed, "How dare you speak to me like that, young man! That's enough! Now come with me and consider yourself grounded for the rest of your life!"

Even though Ricky resisted and retaliated, he could not win as his dad was a giant, but he refused to be mortified. We watched our friend being dragged towards the country club. All other white parents were having a go at their kids but not as bad a Ricky's dad.

We observed that our cultures were totally different, for we were not allowed to answer back to our parents; our friends were considered rude for not saying anything.

I felt sick with anger and wondered, how dare he call us black and uncivilised kids! We grew up being told that we were brown in colour and not black. My dad had always told me that being civilised meant having a good education, respecting your neighbours and everyone in society, not taking anything that doesn't belong to you, giving to César what belongs to César - meaning paying taxes and giving God what belongs to God (Tithing) and by not displaying too much affection in public; somehow these standards seemed quite unlike the behaviour we witnessed when we sneaked into the swimming pool area and watched these so-called 'civilised' people. We always saw some of them kissing and boob sucking and licking in-front of each other. Is this what civilisation is about? It must be said, we as Africans were asked to observe the heights of decorum, in our dress sense, when talking and behaviour in public…

On reflection, I must admit that as young children we never feared playing outside, never heard about children who disappeared and were found killed by so-called paedophiles. However, in these more civilised societies, we hear almost every week of a number of children who have been snatched and killed by paedophiles. Some of these things might be happening in some parts of the world including Africa, so where are the civilised people? Which country has civilised people? I doubt if any country deserves to be called civilized. In each and every country there are some civilised and uncivilised people, but to classify a whole nation as 'uncivilised' was just not right and was just unfair.

In the UK police spend most of their time chasing car offenders instead of chasing after paedophiles, or stopping and searching suspicious vans and cars. Police respond faster to car crimes than domestic violence. It is always about drink driving, MOT and Car Insurance! What about making the society a better place, tackling crime, keeping an eye on sex offenders and the so-called paedophiles, to make sure that people can live without fear in a civilised society?

Ricky received a very hard slap from his father who emphasised the point, "Never, ever talk to those black kids! We are not like them and they are not like us; and none of the black people will ever be like us, not in a million years."

Today, as I write, I am just saying how dare he undermine the reputation and dignity of blacks like that?

Look at America today: who is in the white house? A black man and his family, of course. Look at Bin Laden, the world's most wanted terrorist - whose government found and killed him? It was the black man's government of course. Look at Oprah Winfrey, Beyoncé, Jayz, Will Smith, Usher, Kanye West, Puff Daddy aka Sean Combes, Will I AM, the late Michael Jackson, Solomon Camberwell, Naomi Camberwell, Ashley Cole - even if they were not born in Africa, they are blacks and have some African connections and some are wealthier than a lot of whites. But, funny enough, this racial man had predicted that none of them could ever be like us, not even in a million years. How wrong he was!

The richest self-made woman on the Forbes 400 remains, of course, the talk show queen Oprah Winfrey. Her net worth is staggering, still pegged at $2.7 billion;[3] and she is a black woman, of course. Oprah, you make us proud to be blacks! All I want from you is a handshake and an opportunity to talk to you on your chat show. You are a wonderful black woman.

Ricky spat in his father's face, and said, "I am not going to be like you under any circumstances; when we are at home in the west we talk to them and you pretend to be very nice

---

3. On 13/06/2012 - see www.forbes.com

to them; yet out of here you are a complete racist! Watch me dad, I will continue to make friends with black people: they are human-beings, just like us, and I am going to marry a black girl. These people are nice and warm." He concluded with tears in his eyes: "They may be poor, but they are very caring and are very nice; please dad, understand."

His dad got very angry on hearing this and pulled Ricky as he grabbed him again by the arm. We got really annoyed watching this and we started throwing stones at Ricky's dad. Some stones where thrown by an African stone thrower known as *Rekeni*. Ricky's dad was apoplectic with rage. "Go away you BLOODY KAFIRS, I don't want to see you here ever again!" he roared again.

"This is just ludicrous, you know, being horrible to your own son for being kind to us!" I shouted, my lips trembling with fear. I was ready to run for my dear life if he came towards me.

Every parent dealt with their kid differently, but most of them were taken by surprise by what Ricky's dad did to his son as they all eye-balled him with their mouths wide open. Some white ladies were in total shock. We watched them disappear into this large building and we went home weeping as our kind friends were in trouble.

Ricky's dad was completely different from the other whites and missionaries we had met at home. He was just a horrible man, a complete racist. It's worth noting that not all whites were racist, for some were extremely nice and kind. Because of his actions I became curious and wanted to know what was so special that some white people did not want blacks to know. I started reading a lot and making more white friends.

THE RIVER ADVENTURES

We did not mention this to our parents at all. The following weekend we could not return to the country club as we feared we might get shot or have the dogs set on us. Thank God we were born before television was introduced into Zimbabwe; otherwise we might have turned out to be couch potatoes or perhaps become overweight by eating junk food in front of the box and having no exercise. We decided to go to the River for more adventures as suggested by the guard.

We were putting theory into practice, doing what we had observed the whites were doing. As we walked we observed some beautiful wild flowers. They were beautiful, very nicely scented, orange and red in colour with some yellow in them. We fell in love with these wild flowers and we started to water and weed the area where they were growing. We called the place our secret garden. Every single day we would go there to water the flowers.

Next to these flowers grew some greenish plants. We uprooted one of them and found out they had large bulbs as roots. We smelt them and thought they might be edible. We took some home and fed them to the rabbit. We observed the rabbit for two days; he was still alive so we concluded the plants were not poisonous.

We showed my mum one of the roots and she recognised it. "They are called *tsenza* and they are edible," said *amai*. "They are just like carrots but wild because they grow in the forest. This is what our ancestors and the Bushmen ate." My friends and I were very pleased with our discovery.

The following day it had rained and the smell of the damp soil was so tempting we just wanted to go out and play. We ended up going back to the bush where we picked the wild flowers and the wild roots. We changed the way we used to go home. We went via town instead as we wanted to kill time. Whilst in town we went past a service station and saw a middle-aged white woman who was sitting in the car whilst someone refilled her car with petrol. "Oh, what beautiful Flame Lilies!" she shouted, pointing at us. We thought she had called and we ran towards her. "Yes, madam, *siyathengisa*," said my friend Lulu. The white lady just smiled but shook her head to show that she did not understand the language.

"How much are the flowers?" asked the lady. I knew that I had picked twenty-four flowers so I wanted ten bucks.

"Five dollars for a dozen, madam," I replied, pushing my way through from the back. The lady pulled out a ten-dollar note and handed it to me. I handed the flowers to her and said, "Thank you madam, if you want some more, we can always bring them to you."

CHAPTER TWO

"You 'stealed' my customer!" shouted my friend Lulu in broken English - the kind of English which is spoken in Nigerian movies.

"No, Lulu, that's not fair," I protested, "I did not steal your customer and she is no-one's customer; how did you expect the lady to understand you when you were saying *uyathengisa* (I'm selling)? You expect everyone to understand our vernacular - you should have made an effort to string together a sentence in English, not *siyathengisa*."

"Okay guys, stop arguing please," the lady smiled. "I will need a weekly order - can you supply me weekly?" she asked.

"Yes, madam, that is not a problem because there is no school over the weekend," I replied. "I can do that for you."

"That's good, weekly will do for me as I visit my dad's grave every Saturday at the Methodist Church Cemetery," she said, and asked, "Do you remember the old man? Your people used to call him *Kamufuseni* or Mr Roadman. He worked for the council - he was my dad."

"Oh, I see," I smiled. "You mean that old man who used to wear khaki shirts and shorts and a cowboy hat? He used to supervise the road workers."

"Yes, yes, you are right, that was him, my dad!" she said. "He used to bring home Flame Lilies every time he came across them and I know he will love them."

The white lady was very impressed by my command of English.

CHAPTER TWO

"Oh, my name is Tanaka madam, and you are...?"

"Call me Mrs Janesa Brown," said the lady.

It was very common that most whites during those days did not like the idea of being called by their first names by black people; it always had to be MR or MRS So and So, or Sir and Madam.

"That's okay, Mrs Brown," I said, as I extended my unsteady hand to shake hers. "It's been nice to meet you - I will see you again next Saturday."

I could not believe I was shaking hands with this gorgeous white woman! She had lovely blues eyes, clean white teeth that showed when she gave her broad smile, and brownish hair which they call brunette. No wonder I felt nervous! This was my first actual handshake with a white person! She must be an angel, I thought to myself. I thought I had received a dash of good luck - you know, that feeling that shoots down one's spine when you have met a famous person, say, for example, Bill Gates, or Sir Richard Branson! Immediately my people perceived me differently.

"My pleasure, enjoy your week - bye," she said and drove away after paying for her petrol.

The petrol attendant watched from a distance with his jaws dropped, looking shocked as if he had seen a ghost. Mrs Brown had been very nice to us and it was also not a common sight to see a white person shaking hands with a black person. As the petrol attendant continued to gasp in amazement, I developed imaginary wings - you know, that feeling that says you have seen us, that we can do what was thought to be impossible.

Mrs Brown was very kind and ended up buying from everyone. She was completely different from Ricky's dad.

Some of my friends turned green with envy, as I could speak good English and was never scared of white people - because I grew up wanting to be like them from the early age of four. The impression the white people of those days made on us was that life was very easy. They had house maids, nannies, gardeners and cooks. They bought houses and large bungalows that were worth between £10,000.00 and £20,000.00, a veritable fortune way beyond the reach of blacks in those days. So, when they converted their foreign money to Zimbabwean money, ordinary people appeared very, very rich. Understandably, therefore, I wanted to be just like them - you know that kind of feeling that says if other frogs can swim, so can I, and if other people can jump, so can I!

I told *amai* about my new business venture and she was thrilled. My friends and I kept on going back to the secret garden to pick flowers every Saturday to sell to Mrs Brown. One Saturday I decided to go and wait by the gate at the entrance to the cemetery and wait for Mrs Brown. We saw another white lady walking towards us. She wanted to buy flowers, and behind her came yet another woman *and* another. I thought about doing away with the dozens and sell the flowers individually. We made good money and continued to do so. I bought myself my first pair of shoes and a pair for *amai* and all my siblings. I was very happy as I had stopped borrowing shoes. The following week I bought two pairs for my younger siblings Rose and Petros.

As time went by we were well into business. We went to the bush and uprooted the wild roots to take home. One of my friends called Evaristo ate one of the roots. It happened so quickly - his tongue swelled up to the extent that it could not fit in his mouth! We rushed home and Evaristo was rushed to hospital. He had eaten a different type of root that was similar in appearance to the edible one. His tongue continued to grow and grow, till we were not allowed to see him. He kept his face covered in a jumper and he never came out to play. This misadventure stopped us from going back to our secret garden for flowers as we thought that this might have been caused by the flowers.

We later ventured into swimming, diving and sunbathing. What we did not realise was that the rivers were polluted, had dirty water, with tree branches and stones as well as broken bottles and old tins.

One of our friends called Abudhu dived into the river and banged his head on a rock and started bleeding profusely. He could not swim. We helped Abudhu out of the water, but unfortunately he had lost much blood. By the time one of the boys had gone to call the adults, they found him dead on their arrival. We got told off and punished. Abudhu was buried the following day and we were heartbroken to lose a friend who was only sixteen years old.

After a few weeks we had forgotten about Abudhu. We went back to swim in the river, without our parents' knowledge. We promised one another that there should not be any diving, and we all concurred. The day was very hot. We enjoyed soaking and it felt so nice. As we enjoyed swimming, one of our friends was showing off as she said she had learnt a way of swimming underwater. As she went under we stood there and watched her swim to the shore completely submerged. We clapped our hands for her and cheered. On hearing this, she got carried away and started showing off. When she was underwater we saw a fierce human-like figure that emerged from the water. It was beautiful and amazing to watch. The figure went underwater and came back out again. At that moment we forgot about our friend as we kept on watching this human-like figure swimming. After half an hour we remembered our friend *Chiedza* who was still underwater. The human-like figure disappeared and we started calling our friend, who was nowhere to be seen. No one was brave enough to go into the water in search of her.

Once again we sent for the elders. Two brave men arrived who went in and they swam and swam about but Chiedza was nowhere to be found. The police were called and divers went in, but Chiedza's body was nowhere to be found. The elders gathered and consulted Spirit Mediums and *Nyangas* (Herbalists), Wizards and Witches who all confirmed that Chiedza was taken by mermaids and they believed strongly that one day she would return as a Spirit Medium. Our parents were advised by the mediums that they should not tell us off or punish us as Chiedza might not return. Chiedza's parents were advised to stay positive and behave as nothing had happened and to believe that Chiedza would come back one day.

We stopped going swimming as we were scared that Chiedza and Abudhu's spirits might be patrolling the river in search of friends. This disappearance of Chiedza was a big blow to us; we could understand death, but not total disappearance. We put a stop to swimming and started something quite different.

My adventures on the farms

After all the mishaps, we decided on something new. We decided on going onto farms, climbing over and under the barbed wire fences. It was daring and exciting. As the weather continued to be roasting hot with the wind blowing all the time, staying at home become somewhat boring, so this new venture was appealing.

We started going onto the farms, privately owned and government owned, for more adventures. One day as we were up a *Muzhanje* tree - three of us in the tree and four on the ground, to be exact - and we started to pick these small round fruits called *mazhanje*. The group on the ground would pick up the fruit we threw down and pack them into plastic carrier bags that we had brought with us.

As we were up the tree, the group on the ground saw someone we thought to be the owner of the farm on horseback galloping toward us. The crew on the ground alerted us about the horseman who kept coming towards us, and then ran for their lives. Two of my friends quickly climbed down the tree. "Can we outrun a donkey?" cried Lulu.

"Shut up and just run!" screamed Jabu.

"My legs are getting weak and I want to wee!" cried my sister Rose.

"Just run - hold my hand and just let the wee flow as you run!" I shouted, not yet down from the tree.

"The donkey seems to be galloping very fast," said Jabu, kneeling down. "I can't run! If he is going to kill us, so be it! It looks like one of those horses that do the OK Grand Challenge annually at Borrowdale Race Course in Harare - we can never outrun one of those!" Clearly he had given up at the outset, and added, "I will walk as my legs are already frozen with FEAR - I can't run, or outrun the donkey!"

"It's not a donkey, for the Universe's sake!" I yelled. "It is a horse! Don't you know the difference between the two?" I was still trying to show some vestiges of bravery as I prepared to scramble down the tree trunk. Jabu had allowed fear to take over and as a result it crippled him. Honestly, he did not even try to run but just sat there trembling and shaking like a reed in a flooded river.

Poor little Rose had wet herself and was just wondering what was going to happen to her sister Tanaka.

I had wanted to do everything very fast, and had jumped from the tree and had landed part-hanging from a branch that had caught in my big knickers and my crimplene dress. So there I was, hanging like a headless chicken on a butcher's hook. I wiggled and wiggled but could not free myself from the branch. When I saw the owner coming towards me, fear took its toll and I passed out.

In the state of passing out I felt like someone who had fallen into a pit full of hungry lions. The lions ripped my body open and tore me into shreds. One of the lions went for my face and as he was pulling and tearing my face, my eye popped out and went straight into the stomach of the lion. Inside the lion's stomach, I saw my whole life flashing in front of me. I saw a tall handsome black man stretching his hands toward me; he had two children in each hand and he was saying, *come with me*; there were loads of other women holding onto his legs. *I will give you all the things that you desire*, he said.

On the other side there was also a tall white man, who was very attractive. In his one hand he had bundles and bundles of money and in the other hand he was pointing at a beautiful bungalow with an outside swimming pool and large manor house with an indoor pool; he spoke the words, *come with me Tanaka, I will give you romance, love and the life you have always desired, silver and gold; together we shall trade with it.*

The white man in my imagination kept calling, *come with me Tanaka, all you need is to open the eyes of your inner soul, the eyes of your mind and see the opportunities of a lifetime; take action now and grab the opportunities as they come.* He went on: *Wake up and open your eyes…*

At that point I woke up from this weird dream or imagination. I saw the owner of the farm, Mr Porter, kneeling right next to me as I lay on the ground. "Thank God you are back," he said. He covered me with his large coat which he carried about just in case it rained. He advised me to lie down for a while as I was in a state of shock.

Mr Porter had just brought me back by means of mouth-to-mouth resuscitation. My black friends thought Mr Porter had kissed me. They started shouting abuse at Mr Porter saying, "Leave her alone or we will go and call the elders to bring machetes and axes as well as spears!" Some of the kids were even shouting in Shona: *"Iwe, musiye mhani, haunyare here, takuona uchimukitsa takuno kutaurira kuvakuru! Ibavapo"* (Hey, aren't you ashamed? Leave her alone, we saw you kissing her, we are going to report you to the elders!) My gang started throwing stones with a *Rekeni*, a V-shaped part of a tree that is attached to a rubber made from a tyre tube. The stones came, stone after stone, and Mr Porter feared for his life.

Mr Porter understood a little bit of Shona, so he apologised to me: "I am sorry, all I did was to unhook you from the branch and as you had passed out I helped you come back to life again by giving you mouth-to-mouth..." Since I had done first aid at school, I understood what he meant and thanked him. He said the next time I saw him, I should not be afraid or try to run away.

"This farm," he said, "part of it belongs to me but the other belongs to the government, so much of it is state land; so gather your fruits and go home when you are ready."

"Thank you very much sir, I really do appreciate your help," I said.

Mr Porter helped me up and tried to avoid being hit by the stones that were still coming and remounted his horse. A few stones landed on him nevertheless and he had to dash away quickly before losing an eye or a tooth.

"Goodbye, take care of yourself, kid!" and off he rode. My friends ran up to me and asked what had happened. I explained to then what had happened to me.

"Oh, we thought he was about to rape you!" said Lulu.

"No, he didn't," I replied.

My sister Rose walked towards me and burst into laughter.

"What are you laughing at?" I asked angrily.

"I am laughing at you because I thought I had lost you and now I don't know what to do!" cried Rose as she gave me a hug. "I am happy you are back, and I am laughing at you because you are my sister and there is nothing you can do about it; you don't know how I felt when I saw you hanging up like a headless chicken in that tree; that was the scariest moment of my life!" She added, "Please Tanaka, do not ever attempt to jump off a tree like that again."

"I won't, my dear, I promise," I replied. "Actually," I informed them proudly, "Mr Porter told me that we could come back anytime and not to be scared when we see him because he is now my friend." I did not tell my crew that he had said we shouldn't worry because this was all state land.

THE SCARIEST MOMENT OF MY LIFE

When we had collected our wild fruits we took the shortest way home. We walked past a lot of clustered trees. Small and large birds were tweeting and singing whilst enormous birds where flying and circling above one particular spot.

We headed towards the spot where the birds were flying over as we were told that normally there would be an animal not feeling well and the birds would be waiting patiently for the animal to die so they could feed on it. We thought there might be a waterbuck, antelope or wild pig, so we made our way towards the spot as we thought we might be able to find an animal to take home for meat.

CHAPTER TWO

As we walked closer the birds started making very loud noises, becoming a bit aggressive. We continued as this made us more suspicious. We walked and walked until we came to a huge pit. The smell coming from the pit was unbearable, quite sickening. We covered our noses and mouths and leaned over to find out what was in the pit. Large flies called green bombers were coming and going into the pit. "Oh my God!" shouted Lulu, who ran away and started retching. "I wonder why they are sleeping in such a smelly pit?" she added. The second one stumbled and looked, "Oh God Almighty, have mercy on us!" said *Jabu*, praying.

I wondered what was in there and gathered my courage, expecting to see the worst. I stumbled upon a heap of earth. The sun was very, very hot; a refreshing breeze was coming from the trees and from the dam, to cool down the heat of the September sun. I started sweating with fear as the smell from the pit became unbearable, drawing a step closer each time. Finally, I drew in a large breath and braved it.

"Oh God of Abraham, Jacob and Isaac!" I cried and prayed louder than everyone else. "Please God, why, why?!" The three of us who had seen what was in the large pit held each other tightly, and together we cried and cried and prayed.

"Tanaka, what have you seen in that pit?" asked Rose.

"Come on babe," I said, "you don't need to know. Let's get out of here quickly." We carried our fruit and we started running. I held my sister's hand and ran as fast as we could.

CHAPTER TWO

The moment we reached the dam wall, I soaked my feet in the water and washed my face. I sat down for a while since my heart was sinking with fear. My legs felt like jelly, as if I suddenly had no bones in them. My hands were shaking like reeds in a river on a very windy day. We continued with our journey home. After we had walked about two miles we saw an army helicopter flying over us; it continued its loud noise till we saw it landing somewhere around the radius of the pit.

When we arrived home we pretended everything was okay. I went to have a shower and my sister Rose had a shower after me. I helped *amai* prepare supper, which was the main meal of the day. We sat down and said grace, then started eating. I did not eat much as everything was sticking on my throat.

"Why are you not eating, Tanaka?" asked *amai*.

"I am not enjoying the meat," I said. "I wish there was some lacto" (Sour milk which tastes a bit like natural yoghurt).

"Here is some money, go and get yourself some," *amai* said.

I ran as fast as I could for I didn't want *amai* to have time alone with Rose. I was scared she might tell *amai* what had happened. By the time I returned Rose was fast asleep, exhausted from the hard exercise of the day.

I ate up my *sadza* and *mukaka* (Lacto) quickly. At home it was always a must to wash up before going to sleep as this stopped cockroaches from crawling over dishes, especially in our bedroom which was the kitchen. I quickly made my bed and wished *amai* goodnight and I went to bed to join my sister Rose.

As time went by I became very scared, to the extent that I started wetting my bed. *Amai* was very concerned. She worried over me and thought maybe I was raped or something nasty might have happened to me. Because of the mores of my culture, *amai* could not ask me any sensitive questions such as whether I had been raped or experimented in sex; instead, she assigned some two older women from the community to come and talk to me. Sex is a subject that is never open for discussion between parents and children in my culture. The two women spoke to me nicely and told me that *amai* was worried that I might be hiding something. The women asked me if I had been raped. They told me to be as honest as I could as they told me they were prepared to remove my knickers and check. I did not want the embarrassment of having my bits inspected so I told them the truth as it was.

"No, I have not done anything like that at all, and I am scared of losing my virginity to a boy who won't take responsibility of his child like my friend Anna. I will keep my virginity till the day of marriage," I reassured them. "My lips have never been near a boy's lips, my boobs have never been touched, licked or sucked by a boy, and this will remain as such till my day of marriage." I reassured the auntie that this was the gospel truth. I was pure, holy and untouched.

"Hang on a minute, if you have never done these things, how do you know that is what boys and girls do?" asked Aunt Phoebe pointedly.

"We have pried on white people on several occasions at the Country Club," I admitted. "That is where we observed these things, but we have never tried or experimented in what they were doing as we were scared we might get killed by our parents by way of being punished. Also, I remember when I started my periods you made me promise you that I would never allow a boy to touch me, since allowing boys to touch me will make me pregnant." This was my somewhat naïve reply, but it was sincere as I genuinely feared the punishment that losing my virginity might invoke.

"So what happened to you then?" Aunt Phoebe pressed me for an answer. "Why are you wetting the bed?"

"The thing is," I sighed, "last week when we went to pick wild fruit, I almost died." I explained to the aunties what had happened. "On the same day I thought I would never ever see anyone else again."

"Okay Tanaka," Aunt Phoebe replied, "thank you for letting us know; if there is anything you want to talk about you know where we are."

"Okay Auntie Phoebe and Auntie *Matirasa*, thank you for your concern."

"Okay kid, take care of yourself and please don't go swimming in the river and don't go for wild fruit; try to stay at home and try to preserve your virginity as it will shame us if you get married as an empty vessel." Satisfied that she had uncovered the truth, Aunt Phoebe said, "Bye Tanaka."

"Bye *vana aunty* (aunties)," I said.

When they had left the ordeal got worse. I could not go into a dark room. I would come out crying after having seen human-like images. I would come out of the room screaming my head off. I was petrified. I could not sleep at night as I saw these human-like images walking on their heads with their feet up. I cried and cried. They could walk through the wall. *Amai* and *baba* consulted the spirit mediums to see if our house was haunted. The spirit medium confirmed that the house was not haunted at all but said there were people who wanted Tanaka to tell what she saw. "So, what is it?" asked *amai?* "What is causing Tanaka to be scared of the dark and keeping her awake at night?" The spirit medium suggested that Tanaka sleep with a lamp on at night.

One night I was fast asleep when I felt a hand tapping on my shoulder lightly. I thought it was Rose. I turned around and whispered to my sister, "Not now Rose, please." The tapping happened again and this time I could feel that it was not Rose's hand as there were as many as ten hands tapping on my body. I drew a deep breath and opened my eyes and there stood an image of a human being who was walking on his head, pointing at a group of others walking on my roof and the wall on their heads with their feet up. Some had parts of their bodies missing, such as eyes, ears, lips, foreheads, arms, legs and even with stomachs ripped open. I screamed and *amai* came in immediately. She looked around but could not see anything; however, this time *amai* was convinced she had heard a group of people laughing at her but could not see them.

Amai went back into her bedroom and picked up a Bible and a bowl of water. She placed the water on top of the Bible and we began to pray very hard. We could hear the voices laughing as we prayed. *Amai* started spraying water in the house and praying. After that we managed to sleep for a while.

Eventually word travelled around our neighbourhood. Uncle Misheck came to see us and sat me down. He asked me over and over again what I was seeing. I explained exactly what I was seeing. He asked again, "Tanaka, have you ever seen a dead body?"

"Yes, uncle, I have seen bodies, not just one body."

"How many?" he asked anxiously.

"They were uncountable, more than twenty," I replied.

"Where on earth did you see the bodies, *kido* (kid)?" he asked.

"One day as we were looking for *mazhanje* (wild fruit) on the government farm we stumbled on a pit full of dead bodies. Decomposing bodies, some of them with parts missing, some with skulls open, as if they had been shot at close range," I recalled.

"Can you remember the place?" asked uncle.

"Yes, of course, I can," I replied.

"Can you come with me and show me this place?"

"I will need Lulu and Jabu to come as well," I said, "just in case I have forgotten the place."

We invited Lulu and Jabu to come along. We walked and walked. As we were about a mile away, we saw the green coloured helicopter taking off from the place we were heading to. We told uncle, "That's the place, where that helicopter is taking off." By the time we reached the place there were logs of wood burning like coal that was in a furnace.

"It's there, uncle," I said, pointing. "That's where I saw loads of bodies, in the pit. All three of us saw them, Uncle."

"There is no doubt that there are human bodies in there, due to the smell," concurred uncle. This was sometime around 1978 and 1979, if I am not mistaken, just before they called for a ceasefire in Rhodesia.

"Okay kids, let's get away from here as soon as possible," said uncle.

We left hurriedly as we thought the helicopter might return and that we might get gunned down. Uncle Misheck went to tell *amai* and *baba* what we had seen. It was a relief as the haunting kind of stopped a bit. We promised never ever to go to that farm for wild fruit ever again.

I managed to stay at home for a few more weeks. As staying at home was becoming a bit boring, I decided to go and join a local youth club. I had kept my twenty-five cents in my tin bank for some time. I went to pay my membership fee and felt very thrilled.

CHAPTER TWO

The membership entitled me to all the types of sport that were offered at the club as well as trip to other towns for competitions. One Saturday I woke well prepared and looking forward to going on the trip. This was going to be my very first time on a coach trip and you can just imagine the excitement of someone who had never been on a coach.

I had my packed lunch and a drink for later. I arrived at the youth centre very early. I waited by the coach nervously and for my name to be called; deep down I was very excited that at last I was now embarking on another adventure, hopefully a less dangerous one. All the people boarded the bus - and I was the only one left waiting outside.

"There is a young girl still waiting outside," said one of the caretakers to the bus driver.

"What is her name?" asked the driver

"Tanaka, Tanaka is my name sir," I replied.

"Tanaka - what is your second name please, Tanaka?"

"Zibigihauzi. Tanaka Zibigihauzi is my full name."

"I know you are a fully paid member, but you do not partake in any of the activities; therefore I don't think you should board the coach; it's best if you go home, then we can organise something next time," said the sports organiser.

"What?!!" I queried anxiously. "I paid a joining fee you know, therefore I am entitled to full membership and deserve the same treatment as other members," I declared. "If I am not allowed to go on the trip, then I want my twenty-five cents back now or I will go and tell my grandmother to curse you all!" I stood firm on my two legs, gesticulating with my two hands to emphasise the point.

"Well, if Tanaka is not allowed to go, I will remain behind," said one of the girls who was in the netball team.

"Good!!" I cried in approval.

"And me," said another girl.

At this point the sports organiser eyeballed Tanaka like a hungry lion with an expression that said, "If I was, I would..."

"Good job!" I shouted with much delight that showed I was winning.

The sport organiser looked daggers at me, giving me the evil eye that said, "You may have won for now but I will get you at some point."

I did not care at all and smiled sweetly to show that I was the winner and would always be.

"I can't go without the goal shooter and the goal defence," the sports organiser conceded. "You have made your point - girls, get on board now, including Tanaka."

Everyone cheered as I was finally allowed to board the coach. We travelled for the next hour singing and dancing as we were heading for *Mhangura Mine* for the intensive and vigorous competition.

When we arrived at *Mhangura Mine* the boys played first and they lost 3-0 against *Mutorashanga Mine*.

We walked briskly across the sports fields to the netball

side. I kept on walking closely to the people from Karoi as I feared getting lost. This was my first experience of being in such a big gathering.

Our girls wore red and the opposition team wore yellow. They started the game full of energy and enthusiasm; when a girl from our team caught the ball we would shout "RED FOR DANGER!!!!" If they happened to score we would run across the netball pitch singing and dancing; when we got to the centre we shouted "Hooray!", then sang "*KINDI KINDI BEWUUUUU!!!!*" after which we shouted, "*Вешишиш* aa hey !! *BEWUUUUUU!!!!*"

We would bend and flip our dresses or skirts towards our heads showing the bloomers and all the kinds of knickers girls were wearing and some with no knickers at all because they could not afford them. It was all in the name of fun, as we revealed all the different shapes and colours of asses and knickers!

After our shooter had scored one goal the girl on the centre started retching. She was driven out of the pitch to be checked by the first aider. Now here came the problem - they did not have any substitute. The same sports organizer and the driver who did not want me on board in the first place thought of me and came running towards me. "Tanaka, Tanaka, please, can you go and play the centre position for now till the girl recovers?" they asked shyly.

"No, I can't, I only came in to cheer," I said. "I can't play

CHAPTER TWO

netball and I have never practiced; and again, you guys never wanted me to come on the trip in the first place."

"It doesn't matter now, we apologise and that's forgotten - please can you go and stand in for now? Here is the uniform - go and change quickly and go to the pitch," said the sports master. "I am begging you," he added.

"Okay, I will play," I replied.

I rushed to the changing room even though my heart was pounding very, very fast. I pretended to be confident but my legs were shaking like a reed in a river. I thought, I can't run: I have always been given the sobriquet *dhadha* (meaning *duck*) due to my heavy legs. I had never played netball before, so what was going to happen? Oh God, please help me, I prayed quietly.

When I finished changing, I went onto the pitch and the game started, still with my heart pounding very fast. I didn't know what was referred to as 'being over bounce' or any rules for netball.

As the game progressed, one of the girls decided to pass the ball on to me... and I got myself well prepared to catch the ball. Since the girl who passed the ball to me was a bit taller, I had to jump high up in the air to catch it. The ball was heavy and I felt the full weight of it as it landed on my chest whilst I was still high up in the air. The force made me make a summersault, still with the ball in my hands as I rotated like a windmill - and the whistle went

CHAPTER TWO

Peeeeeeeeeeeeeeeeeeeeee! When I finally landed on the ground, I could feel my head spinning. I looked at the people and they were all going round and round in a continuous rotation. I could not understand what was going on as everything, even the ground I was standing on, was also rotating.

"Stand still, you Zombies!" I shouted. "Why are you all going round like people on a Merry Go Round? I said stand still!" I shouted again.

Man, I appeared a fool! I finally noticed that no-one was spinning and realised it was my head. I braved it and tried to pull back my confidence though with a nervous grin.

The girl who was standing next to me wanted to take the ball off me. "Pass the ball over, you just heard the whistle going." I looked at her and started laughing as she began to go round in a circle in my vision. Finally, the dizzy spell ended and everyone appeared normal once again. I must be damn crazy, right, I thought to myself. Netball not as easy as I thought - right, I concurred.

Tanaka was just being Tanaka you know, and she started her games. "What are you trying to do, ha? If you want a fight, see me after the game."

"Hey, it's not about fighting, it's about the rules of the game; don't forget, you went flying up there like an enormous bird without wings, with the ball in your hands; how could you fly without wings? This aint no gymnastic man, it's a netball pitch, we got rules here," emphasised my opponent.

"If you wanna play netball, then follow da rules!" she declared.

"Oh, bloody shut up!" I screamed. "Who the hell do you think you are?" I was now using the language I had learned from an American film.

"Oh my God, watch your patois girl!" shouted the referee.

The referee and one of the girls from my side came to explain what was going on. I then placed the ball on the ground instead of giving it to my opponent. Apologise? No I didn't. Why? Because I was such a fool, a pig-headed fool.

We played and played, but that was the first and last ball I had encountered during the match. Luckily, it was a knock-out game and my team won 7-2 and we stayed on… "Hallelujah!" I shouted as I thought I had done a great job for my team.

When we went back I boasted on the coach that they wanted to leave me behind, yet I was the girl called upon to play in the end. I told *amai* and *baba* about my experience and they laughed. "*You* playing netball!" *baba* exclaimed. "I would have loved to watch that because you look like you enjoy playing boyish games more than girlish ones."

"Honestly," I said, "you should have watched me! I made them win anyway. It was all down to me because I played really hard," I boasted. The sports organiser later made me join the junior team; at least I had something to occupy me rather than going to the river and onto the farms.

CHAPTER TWO

Time went by and I grew up to a bright young lady. I stopped hanging around with girls and boys and concentrated more on home making. As I grew older my boobs grew bigger and began to sag a bit. I needed a harness to help give my boobs a lift. My poor parents could not afford to buy me a bra, and my strict and old-fashioned Zimbabwean culture also barred young girls who had never known men, or never had children, to wear bras. They believed that all virgins should have natural boobs that had a natural boost and needed no under-wired bra, or a bra with some gel or cotton in them. These were considered a shame because in the olden days all virgins paraded with their boobs exposed to the public to show that they were holy, pure and untouched.

Times had changed, however, and I desperately needed a bra, even though *amai* kept telling me that a virgin should not wear a bra. I was a size 34 double FF who had played netball; honestly, I needed a harness to give my huge melons a lift! I realised that all the sports we were doing, such as running, netball, and riding bicycles, were something *amai* and my grandparents had never engaged in. They always wore bottom clothes that looked like mini-skirts at the front and a G-string at the back, called NHEMBE, and that was in the distant past. In the days of my youth no-one wore those, for times had changed.

I asked my sister Eunice for a bra, but she could not give me one, not even her old one. Since she was now working in a shop called Broomstick Boutique owned by a very rich family, the O'Connors, my sister had a selection of bras, second hand and new ones; but she could not even give one old one to me! One day I went to her house and saw these nice 'cross my heart' bras, and I stole one and left. When she came home from work she noticed that someone had been into her drawers and she found out that her bra was missing.

She came home to *amai* and *baba* fuming that I had pinched her bra. I explained to her that I was desperate for a bra as my boobs were very big and heavy. I tried to explain to my sister to make her see sense, by saying, "When I run, my boobs run too! When I jump they jump too; so I wanted to have something like a bra to stop them from running and jumping about!"

Instead of reasoning with me or allowing me to have an old bra, my sensible sister decided to cause a big scene. She went outside and started shouting at the top of her voice that she wanted her bra back as she had paid for it! She was escorted by her two step-daughters who were also shouting at me. The neighbours came out to watch this free drama. I had never felt so embarrassed in my life! All the boys who had an eye for me started saying bad things about me. It became very difficult for me to date a local lad. My dear sister just didn't appreciate that life changes. Poverty, hey, is not a good thing, and having poor parents really sucks, I thought! I definitely needed to do something for myself, I concluded.

I told myself I would work very hard and one day I would be able to buy myself a bra to harness my huge melons!

After all our adventures, we tried going back the Country Club to see if there were any changes. After all, we were a bit older now. To our surprise the notices about black people not being needed had been removed. This was during the 80's. Actually, the white guys were now looking for black kids to use as golf club carriers (caddies, what amounted to *child labour*) as they played golf, and they would pay them a few dollars at the end of the day. I would not do that. "I want to be the one that plays golf and tennis rather than the donkey!" I declared as I walked home and left some of my friends carrying the golf clubs.

CHAPTER THREE

THE APPLE OF MY EYE: KENZO JAMUKOKO
1980-1998

KENZO was born in a family of six. He had three younger brothers and two younger sisters. He was the first born of the family. Kenzo was born in a small mine near Chinhoyi called Alaska mine. Neither Kenzo's mum nor his dad where educated. However, they worked very hard in order to send Kenzo to a boarding school. His parents made many sacrifices to improve the prospects of their children and became vegetarians whilst Kenzo was still at St Phillip's secondary school in Sipolilo, now known as Guruve, so as to afford the fees.

Kenzo was very bright and managed to pass all his subjects at Cambridge Ordinary Level which is now GCSEs. On completion of his secondary school Kenzo decided to start working, aged nineteen. He found a job within a grain marketing company in Karoi. This job obliged him to move

CHAPTER THREE

away from his parents and start to live alone. Since he was educated he got the job as a clerk. He took over the responsibility of sending his younger brother Donald to a Salvation Army missionary school called Howard in Chiweshe rural area. He did this since he earned a few bucks more than his dad and wanted to help out.

It was not long before Kenzo discovered girls, and shortly afterwards he met his wife to be, Tanaka. "Hello, my name is Kenzo," he said at their first meeting, "could you tell me your name, please?"

"Oh hello, nice to meet you Kenzo; my name is Tanaka Zibigihauzi," I replied, feeling a bit shy though my heart was filled with excitement that Kenzo was chatting me up; but the feeling of being able to deal with the opposite sex totally destroyed my confidence.

"I have seen you several times, but I lacked the courage to come and tell you that I-I-I-I l - o - ve you and have felt like this since I first set my eyes on you," stammered Kenzo "Surely, I fell for you from the first day I saw you and have never slept properly since!" he went on. "W - ou - ld y - ou be… my gir - l fri - e - nd please?" he asked awkwardly.

"Oh Kenzo!" I gasped. "Give me some time to think about it, dear," I said shyly. As I spoke I felt butterflies in my tummy and felt embarrassed as I thought I was about to pass wind in front of my admirer and my wannabe husband.

"How long do you want - a day or two?" asked Kenzo.

CHAPTER THREE

Concentrating on trying to control the impending wind, I replied in an embarrassing squeaky voice, "Two weeks will be fine. Meet me at 6 p.m. by the corner of Boundary Road and Karoi dam." I knew I was blushing. All I wanted was to disappear before the unwanted embarrassment of passing wind in front of my potential boyfriend.

"Okay dear," Kenzo agreed. "I will be looking forward to seeing you; but please don't keep me waiting too long."

"No, I won't," I replied with a smile that expressed it all - an expression that said "I got you babe and all I want is to run away as fast as I can." This was in keeping with our culture, to make boys wait; agreeing straightaway might lead the boy to believe that one is a slapper. So, I had to play it slow and cool.

"By the way, where do you come from and who are your parents?" I inquired curiously after I realised the butterflies in my tummy were good ones and not windy ones. I felt a bit relaxed and wanted to vet Kenzo a bit.

"My parents are in Alaska mine, *baba na amai* Jamukoko - they go to the Salvation Army in Alaska," replied Kenzo.

"What, Alaska! How did you come here then, by plane or ship? And is it very cold there in Alaska?" I asked stupidly and loudly. "GOSH! You must love it here especially with this current temperature of twenty six degrees," I added.

"No dear," Kenzo laughed and explained, "Alaska is a small mine that is situated near Chinhoyi, and it is here in Zimbabwe; I came on a bus."

CHAPTER THREE

"I see, sorry dear, I thought you came from that Frozen state," I said trying to hide my embarrassment. "I will see you in a couple of weeks then - bye." I waived to him as I gave him a sideways glance of approval. Gosh, my ignorance of local geography ate my heart out, and I still relive the embarrassment whenever I have a flashback of that moment with Kenzo.

"Goodbye dear," Kenzo grinned. "See you in two weeks' time; perhaps it will be a yes, then I will take you to Alaska to meet my parents!"

I was so excited that I had finally met someone who loved me, especially after the scene which my sister Eunice had caused that made all local lads lose interest in me about stealing her bra. Meeting Kenzo just felt so good - it was like winning the lottery, especially in an environment where everyone else thought and believed that the man was the breadwinner and every young woman needed a man to survive. In those days a husband was a must-have commodity.

I felt so grown up as I was the only virgin still standing amongst my friends and was proud to be one - indeed, I was well known as the only virgin remaining amongst my friends and classmates and was considered a bit old fashioned. I made my investigations about Kenzo and found out that he was single and never been married. I bubbled with joy, thinking that all this made the two of us untouched and innocent lovers. I never wanted to lose my virginity to local lads who would end up dumping me like a heap of shit together with a fatherless child; I just wanted it to be special with a special person.

I was driven by the compelling belief that it was better to keep my virginity intact than to lose it to some college dropout and loafer; then to keep a fatherless child and become the talk of the village whilst giving my parents the burden of bringing my child up! With this mindset I hung onto my virginity for as long as it took to meet the right person. I also wanted to bring my children up differently, in a better way than I was raised.

I finally met Kenzo as planned two weeks later and we walked together from Boundary Road to Chikangwe location. I told Kenzo that it was a *yes* and that I loved him too; I did not want to play the waiting game for too long as I was scared I might lose him. Under the strict rules of my parents and respecting my culture, I made sure that Kenzo should not touch or kiss me before we were married. We immediately became friends and became more than just friends; the pair of us fell in love almost at the same time. We just wanted to get married and start a family.

We courted for a good six months without even kissing or cuddling, as intimacy before marriage was outside our culture; six months was long enough for us to get to know each other since we met regularly on a daily basis.

My Kenzo was very polite, quiet and on the shy side and

well mannered. He respected the elders and he was good at his job to the extent that he was promoted every six months. Kenzo was six feet tall, broad shouldered, attractive with nice clean teeth; he became the apple of my eye - I could not see anything bad in him. I became blinded by love as I could only see goodness in him. Most girls had a crush on him but he just wanted me, Tanaka, for a wife and to be the mother of his children. How lucky could a girl be, especially when many girls of my age carried fatherless babies on their backs! I felt very proud, like someone who had just graduated with a Master's Degree.

We fell head over heels in love and Kenzo proposed. I accepted and agreed to his proposal. Kenzo sent an elderly man on his behalf to pay *lobola*, the bride price, to my parents and we finally got married.

I felt so proud that I had preserved my virginity, and remained untouched and holy for my husband; for Kenzo, though, the wait was way too long and he lost his virginity to the local prostitutes. I did not know of this as he had kept it a secret from me. This could also be blamed on our culture, as boys didn't and still don't get enough education on puberty, lust and self-control. They were often told that masturbation was wrong, called self-abuse, hence resorting to trying it on with older women. *Please check what your culture says about this sensitive subject and educate your children according to your values and beliefs.* Girls were always taught that if you don't try it you will never miss anything not known to you. Having said that I remained faithful and never even attempted masturbation pre and post marriage - indeed I have to say it was something I never knew about. It was something I assumed and thought was not necessary and therefore never to be attempted - as attempting something might always come with some addiction of some sort. Please do what you and your heart desires in accordance with your conscience, not forgetting what your religion teaches you about the above mentioned subjects. I know that Christians are sustained by their faith that God helps them to have the wisdom to know what is right and wrong.

Since it was Kenzo's first time with a woman when he gave way to temptation and slept with a prostitute, the excitement became addictive and he got hooked on these prostitutes as someone hooked on drugs or on internet porn. He never stopped and could not help himself break free of his addiction.

Nevertheless, he waited impatiently for his bride to be delivered to him, as he had developed a habit of sneaking out for his daily or weekly fix of streetwalkers. In Zimbabwe during the early 80's prostitution was a booming business, till people started dying one by one from the thinning and immunity-destroying disease HIV and AIDs.

Kenzo knew pretty well that after marrying his wife she would not be brought to him straightaway as she had to undergo some sort of traditional training on how to become a proper wife and how to deal with the opposite sex and what to do in bed. With me as his wife, Kenzo felt complete, only to be let down by the wandering eye - an eye that kept on wandering like a chameleon's eye that can see what's behind him whilst facing the other direction, to reveal what was under every girl's petticoat and knickers. I blame it all on his parents who failed to teach their son how to respect women and not view every woman as a sex object.

When his parents heard the news that Kenzo had married, his mum Madei Jamukoko was not very pleased as she thought her son was still too young to marry and might stop paying fees for his brother. His dad Gondo Jamukoko on the other hand was very pleased that his son had done the right thing and was now a man and an adult. Kenzo explained to his parents that he felt he wanted to marry since he had fallen in love with me, Tanaka, and also that he had never lived on his own and felt very lonely, and wanted to start a family. He promised his parents that he would continue paying fees for his brother and would continue to visit them every weekend.

Kenzo waited patiently for me to be delivered to him as his new bride, as it is the tradition in Zimbabwe. He felt very mature and responsible that he had saved some money to buy cheap furniture, a bed, bedding, food, saucepans and a paraffin cooker to start with. He waited for me so that we could do the shopping together as Mr and Mrs.

CHAPTER THREE

I had taught myself how to cook and all aspects of housekeeping. When I used to cook for my family, my dad seemed very happy whilst my mother always looked at me with that "you could have done better" expression. I am sure she was just being a mother; but her critical stance made me strive to do better all the time.

MY FIRST LOVE LETTER TO KENZO

> The Greenland of Love
> PO Box mouth to mouth,
> Tummy to tummy,
> Leg to leg.
> # Couple # Mr & Mrs #

Dearest Darling Kenzo,

I have great pleasure in writing, just to tell you that I love you very much. I love every little thing about you and always will. Your beautiful and cute smile makes my heart pump faster when I see you. Your magical eyes draw me closer to you when I see you. The lovely sound of your voice makes me forget everything else on this planet earth. I love the warmth that I feel when I'm by your side as I feel loved and protected.

I think about you constantly; when we are apart and I cannot stop, the feeling is making me feel crazy about you. I want you by my side all the time and every day of my life as you make me feel complete. You mean everything to me; you are the world to me. You are the best thing that I ever had.

You are the one I hankered after for many, many months. Me,

being Tanaka the poor girl, I never thought that I would ever meet someone as special as you, who works in an office. I love each and every moment I have shared with you and will continue to share with you.

Thank you for choosing me and asking me to marry you, for loving me and for making me the proudest girl in the neighbourhood. My one and only, my hero, my Tarzan, my knight in shining armour, my prince charming and above all my partner for life. I love you very much and always will.

Love Always,
Your girlwifey,

Tanaka (aka # Mrs Jamukoko to be)

MY FIRST LOVE LETTER FROM KENZO

Love is the greatest gift of all,
P O box 2 hearts,
Beating together as 1.

My darling Tanaka,

Since the day you agreed to marry me, my heart stopped beating for a minute; and I pinched myself, to see if I was still me, Kenzo, and alive. I could not believe my luck, having you in reality, someone special that most people only dream of having. I had been searching for you all of my life, and finally I have found you and you have agreed to let me have you wrapped around my finger. You have made me the happiest man I have ever been. You are a genuine, loving and caring woman. I would not swap you for a million dollars. Grateful, pleased and blessed I am, that you loved me as much as I loved you, and that you made me your fiancé (aka husband in waiting).

We have been courting for six months, and I have cherished every moment since the day we met. I love you more and more every second, every minute, every day, every week, every month and 24/7 ever after. Contemplating on our future married life tops me with anticipation and excitement. I know and believe that we will make the perfect husband and wife partnership. I cannot wait to show you to my friends, family and to the world. Our life together and raising a family is going to be brilliant as I will work hard for you my love, to make our dreams come true, and have a happy loving family!

Money worries will not be one of our problems, as I have saved a lot and also I get a lot more from the farmers who bribe me. I shall pay everything that your parents ask for, because you are worth it. I love you, Tanaka, and I love you very much and I just love everything about you. I just can't wait to be with you in our own home. We have so much in common, the kind of food we like, the fact that we both hate cigarette smoke and alcohol, we want to be different, the type of music and films, it just make us one. I have so much to be thankful for, because having you is like winning a lottery! We shall continue to grow in love with each other. We just have to be there for each other through thick and thin; your people shall be my people, and I shall love and support you, my love.

Our life together shall be amazing, and together it will only get better and better. I will forever be grateful that you came into my life and made all my dreams come true, and I have so much to show you. You complete me and we shall be perfect together like a pair made in heaven. I am looking forward to spending the rest of my life with you. I love you more than words can say and I will always love you.

Love always,
Yours to have and to hold,
Kenzo

Some of the most frequently used expressions about love that Tanaka used throughout her married life:

- Love is wonderful thing.
- There is a fine line between love and hate.
- Love controls the world.
- I can do anything for love.
- I will always love you.
- I will take a bullet for you because I love you.
- When you're not around I do not sleep or eat.
- I think of you every second, because I love you very much and even more when the seconds tick by.
- All is fair in love and war. (Shakespeare)
- Love, love one another.
- No-one understands our love as we are one.
- Our hearts beat together as one.
- I feel your sorrow and pain from a distance.

- Your breath sustains me.
- Your arm saves me.
- The warmth of your body heals my pain.
- Your gentle touch makes my heart melt with desire.
- Your love is so genuine that I can see it through your eyes and your smile.
- My heart pounds faster the moment I see you; like someone who has just had a CPR.
- Your love is a life-supporting machine for me.

CHAPTER FOUR

THE CULTURAL MARRIAGE: 1980-1998

Tanaka and Kenzo Jamukoko's cultural marriage

TANAKA had watched some of her friends falling pregnant and the guys denying responsibility, and she vowed to be different. She just wanted to get married and be the perfect wife. Some of her friends died due to backstreet abortions performed by elderly women, and some married older men as second wives or were kept unmarried but received some money for maintenance. These older men would rent a bedsit for the girl and her child, then start treating her like a second wife. Tanaka's desire to be different grew stronger day by day, until she met her husband Kenzo who she just wanted to have and to hold.

Kenzo was young, aged nineteen, tall, fit, broad shouldered, and very attractive, erudite and worked in an office. He was such a handsome hunk that he fascinated many girls. Most of the girls wished he had married them or could just be seen walking with him. He had such a nice smile that displayed his neatly shaped white teeth. He was so good looking that every young girl had a crush on him. Indeed, the girls would wear mini-skirts to display their natural hairy legs to advantage in the hope of catching his eye. They would wash themselves and scrub their feet with a stone to give them a good pedicure; then reveal their long legs which were shiny and greasy with Vaseline that was rubbed on them as a moisturiser. Even in bright daylight, the girls would display their hairy and un-waxed legs, trying to catch Kenzo's attention. None of the girls cared that their legs looked hairy, as waxing was never heard of in their social circles. Kenzo was not really interested in lots of young girls, anyway, as he knew that if a girl lost her virginity to him, then he would be liable for damages, or he could be beaten up by her brothers.

Tanaka failed to continue with her education due to the war in the late 70's. Even though she knew that selling sex was big business, she decided to get married. The stories that were often told by older women about what prostitutes endured, and that some men had penises as long as pythons and some as long as those of donkeys, scared Tanaka and she closed the chapter on prostitution. Her younger sister Rose on the other hand decided to become a full-time prostitute and never married, had five children by five different men and later died from Aids.

Tanaka was only two years younger than her husband Kenzo. They shared the same birth month. Tanaka was born

CHAPTER FOUR

on the 28th of August 1963 whilst Kenzo was born on the 30th of August, 1961. It didn't take them long to fall in love. They were both Virgos and seemed to get on like a house on fire. The pair agreed to get married and to start a family.

Kenzo then paid *lobola* of $500.00, which was Zimbabwe dollars during the 80's when the currency was very strong, and ten herds of cattle valued at $30 per head. This was a considerable sum of money in those days. In actual fact *Kufa* did not charge Kenzo a lot of money like other families might have done, for he valued the nature of the relationship and realised that by charging too much money his daughter would find it difficult to cope financially with her husband as they were starting a family; theirs was a new relationship that would establish bonds between two families. The families had to treat each other cautiously as there would be children born to unite them and these children would need to have a better life. However, some families saw this differently, as a money-making opportunity where the son in-law might always be heard complaining to his wife that her parents had charged him an unfair burden of money. This made for a bad start for any married relationship and would cause friction in the long run; hence, Tanaka's dad chose to avoid this problem from the outset.

CHAPTER FOUR

BRIDAL MENTORING: CULTURAL BRIDAL PREPARATION OR "KURAYIWA"

After Kenzo paid *lobola* to Tanaka's parents, he waited anxiously for his wife to be delivered to him by the elderly women in accordance with the traditional custom. However, Kenzo fell to temptation and lost his virginity to local prostitutes and became hooked by these hookers, addicted to them like a drug. He would visit these hookers most days without his wife's knowledge. He never slept with one hooker twice as he was scared she might fall for him. Poor Tanaka kept her vagina as tight as possible as it was also a taboo to be married whilst not being a virgin. She did not want to be called an empty vessel.

She waited for the day to come as she had to undergo some form of training with the local elderly women on how to handle and satisfy her husband. She endured a month and some weeks without seeing Kenzo. She was taken to the villages to be taught some form of belly dancing (*Chikapa*; *shakira's* kind of dance or *Yondo* sister's sexual deviation dance or *Kwasa-kwasa* in Zambian) to perform for her husband when they got together as a married couple.

Also, these elderly women had to make sure that Tanaka's vagina was well cushioned by pulling (stretching) her labia minora (*matinji*) with black traditional medicine every morning and evening, to make it a real BADLY PACKED

CHAPTER FOUR

KEBAB, and the procedure was very painful. These thin, hair-free inner lips where pulled so hard that sometimes Tanaka found it difficult to walk and she hated the procedure. Please be advised that Tanaka had to do this herself but also had a choice not to do it if she didn't want to; but refusing to do it would only shame her and her family. For example, if her husband cheated on her, the elders would quickly blame it on lack of the basics such as missing *matinji* and an inability to perform the belly dance of womanhood for her husband. The fact Tanaka wanted to fit into her society and be able to keep her husband made her go through with the traditional wife preparation. She used Vaseline mixed with some black traditional medicine to stretch these tender bits; in the beginning it was hard since Vaseline made the bits slippery, and the bits were too small to handle; it was very painful and she had to suffer from a swollen bottom. She was encouraged by the elderly women to keep on trying as these *matinji* were supposed to be big and appear as laces for the man to play with when making love - mainly before the act as foreplay, as it was thought that once the man feels these laces he would become aroused quickly, and they also worked as extra padding for the man's testicles. Many other cultures relating to Zambians, Ugandans, Malawians, to name only a few, do the same wife preparation rituals called *Chinamwari*.

Eventually she managed to stretch them out until they were visible to the person standing in front of her, or could be seen from behind when she bent over. This was a traditional way of showing that a girl was now ready and mature. The aim of the long labia minora was to make Tanaka appear more feminine, more sexually appealing and to arouse her husband the moment he set eyes on her when she was naked; also, the man was meant to have something to explore by using his fingers, or to play with for his sexual gratification. *This is a traditional and cultural practice in Zimbabwe, though to some extent it is fading now due to the adaptation of western culture.*

FEMALE GENITAL MUTILATION: AFRICA'S SHAME AND A HEAP OF IGNORANCE!

The labia minora are also known to be hair free and homologous to the ventral penis. The labia minora flows from the clitoris, which is a small protruding structure known to be largely erectile tissue that resembles the penis and is the most sensitive part of the vagina - which helped both Tanaka and her Kenzo during foreplay. Please note that in some countries Female Genital Mutilation (FGM), otherwise known as female circumcision, takes place when the clitoris is brutally cut off using either a piece of broken glass or unsterilized equipment such as razors and knives. This barbaric practice is still practiced in some African and Asian countries where young girls have to endure the pain, and is done to innocent children without their consent. The procedure is reported being performed by elderly women where the girl child is wide awake without any anaesthetic given to numb the pain. It is just cruel, barbaric and unreasonable. It is a form of child abuse and people who put young girls through this sort of pain should be arrested and kept in prison for the rest of their lives. These women who perform the barbaric act are just as bad as paedophiles. As another writer sums it up, why change what God has created?

> "THE CLITORIS IS A GIFT FROM GOD, WHY CUT IT?" says a statement on a poster hanging by the door of Safehaven International, one of the non-governmental organizations in Nigeria working on creating awareness of the dangers of Female Genital Mutilation (FGM) and the passage of a bill to stop the barbaric practice.
>
> Margaret Onah, 48 and the founder of Safehaven International, has been through this traumatic action and has vowed to keep fighting for women's right and health. Her organization is committed both to going into various communities to enlighten women on the dangers associated with FGM as well as organizing advocacy visits with lawmakers to ensure the eradication of this traditional yet harmful practice. One of the approaches they are using to fight FGM is the Alternative rite of passage, which is a critically sensitive approach, one that respects the value of tradition but rejects the violation associated with it."[4]

---

[4]. Ifesinachi Sam-Emuwa, Project Director, Treasureland Health Builders. Extracted from her article 'Female Genital Mutilation (FGM): Pioneering Women's Nightmares...' on 30/03/12; see http://www.worldpulse.com/node/48530

CHAPTER FOUR

The good thing about the Zimbabwean culture is that this erectile tissue called the clitoris is preserved and kept intact. However, some men, like Kenzo, really don't know that it is the area that needs to be stimulated for the women to enjoy the lovemaking act and to put her in the mood together with all aspects of foreplay such as kissing, etc. Some men are concerned only with penetration. These are the people who need to attend the SEX SCHOOL.

Tanaka had to be competent in belly dancing whilst lying down and her husband on top of her (*missionary position*), to the extent that she would dance and rock and lift her husband up and down whilst making love. Tanaka was taught all the basics, like when at the end of making love she had to wipe her husband's penis and around the genitals with a soft and clean cloth; it was her responsibility to make sure her husband was sexually satisfied and never lie there like a log whilst her husband did all the work, or she could lose her husband to experienced hookers.

She was also taught how to respect her husband's parents and never to look them in the eye when they were talking to her, as well as getting up early in the morning before sunrise. Maintaining eye contact with other men was also considered taboo. She was also taught that the way to a man's heart was through his stomach and not through the vagina, so she had a duty to cook nutritious and appetising meals for her husband.

Tanaka was also taught that she should never talk to anyone

about her relationship with her husband; everything was meant to be secretive and confidential. The worst part for Tanaka was to be asked to keep quiet about her husband's extra marital affairs. She agreed and did not rebel against these teachings. She did not say anything to these women as she would have been considered rude and very disrespectful; therefore she just listened and agreed to everything that was said.

She was also taught that she should never answer back to her mum, mother-in-law, father-in-law and her father. Since she was taught that maintaining eye contact with the in-laws and other men was a taboo, it became really difficult for Tanaka as she was taught to maintain eye contact at school. Tanaka was taught how to respect her husband and never to call him by name, which she also found unacceptable. She was taught that she should kneel down when serving her husband and his relatives with food. She was taught that she should also kneel down or bend her knees when greeting her in-laws and other elderly people when talking to them. Personal hygiene was also part of the module, where she was taught to have a shower or wash every morning before dealing with food and at night before going to bed.

All the traditional values were told and taught to Tanaka. Before and after eating Tanaka was taught to put her hands together, the right hand on top of the left (*Kuombera*) and make a clasping of hands to produce a sound, which was a way of showing respect and a way of saying thank you. This was a cultural thing that impressed the elders, as they were often heard saying "*akarayiwa*", meaning she was taught and has adapted well to our culture.

Poor Tanaka was brainwashed to believe that men were like dogs that go about sniffing till they could smell a bitch that is in heat and could just have a quickie with any bitch anytime as they pleased. Yet poor Tanaka was still expected to stay faithful and loyal to her husband as much as possible. If Kenzo cheated on Tanaka, she was expected to put up with it as she was taught that all men cheated on their wives, and after all he would have paid *lobola* (Dowry) so in a sense she was obliged to be obedient and submissive to him.

This was just too much to bear for Tanaka as the thought of sharing her husband with someone else was intolerable. She was taught how to be a good wife and never to disclose any intimate problems with anyone. If her husband cheated on her, or if they were having problems in the bedroom such as penis size, erectile dysfunction, premature ejaculation or the husband being incompetent, she was taught that it should never be disclosed to anyone else and should be kept permanently under wraps.

Nevertheless, Tanaka completed her training (*Kurayiwa*) and was escorted to her husband by the elderly women who had a talk with the two of them. Kenzo had already lost his virginity to the local prostitutes, of course, so he knew what to do, even though he was not very experienced.

CHAPTER FOUR

Tanaka lost her virginity that night. It all happened very quickly and she thought that was how it was meant to be. All she remembers is the pain of the hymen breaking since there was not enough foreplay. A four-metre length of floral material was sent to her parents the following day. It was a cultural thing and is still practised in some places, that a man has to buy a length of material for the mother of the bride to express his appreciation (*jira remasungiro*). If the girl was found to have slept around, a hole was made in this material to inform her parents that their child was not a virgin. However, some people used to attach an old penny with a hole in the middle to the material rather that make a hole in the material. The mother would either make a dress from the material or use it as a wrapper. Tanaka's mum was very impressed as Tanaka was considered to be a virgin by her husband.[5]

Kenzo sent someone again to his in-laws to ask for Tanaka father's permission for them to get married at the Registry Office, to which he agreed. Kenzo and Tanaka finally got married both legally and in accordance with traditional custom. The same month Tanaka fell pregnant with their first child who was born the following year.

---

[5] Please note that due to adaptation to western culture, some people would not want to expose their future wives, but would choose to send the cloth without a hole or holes whether the bride proved to be a virgin or not.

CHAPTER FOUR

"BRIDAL LABOUR" *(HUROORA)*

The marriage opened doors to the bridal labour, where Tanaka was now expected to work very hard for Kenzo's family. The traditional bridal labour started as soon as the newly married bride entered the homestead of her parents-in-law. The bride is traditionally escorted by two elderly women. Instead of the pair going on a honeymoon, the wife is brought to the husband's family to meet everyone traditionally.

The bride and her accompanying entourage stop some twenty metres away from the husband's home. The bride is then covered with a cloth. Singing and cheering, the husband's family and neighbours then welcome the newly married woman and daughter in-law into their home.

The bride's escort will be collecting money from the in-laws and instructing the bride to walk a few steps before sitting down. The process is repeated until the bride reaches the door where she will again sit down by the door. Money will be paid by the in-laws; if it's not enough the bride will remain seated until they have paid enough when she will enter the house as a sign that the amount is acceptable. Whilst inside the house a reed mat will be laid ready for the bride to sit on. Once again she will sit on the floor and expect a payment to enable her to sit on the mat. The family and neighbours will still be singing joyous songs.

When enough money is paid the bride and her crew will be seated, the bride taking her place on the mat. The bride will remain covered under a cloth or a blanket till money is paid for the in-laws to see the bride. When enough money is agreed the cloth will be removed and the in-laws will be able to see their daughter in-law. Some will try to greet her by requesting a handshake which she will not accept till money is paid to enable the family and each individual member to come and greet the new addition to their family. They will continue with the process of paying money for everything till the bride eats a whole chicken that will be prepared for her and her crew and goes to bed afterwards.

The following morning it will be time for the bride to show her in-laws what she is made of. She and her crew will get up very early before sunrise and before anyone else and start by sweeping the yard outside, then inside the house wash and polish the floors as well as dusting the furniture and cleaning the windows; again, they will receive a payment for each individual task. Then they will boil water in a large drum. The most scary and dangerous bit is carrying hot boiling water on their heads to give to family members who live metres away from the house so they can have a bath. This will be after the husband's parents, as they will be the first in line to be given hot water for a bath. The bride will provide the soap, towels, toothpaste and toothbrushes. She and her crew will continue until every member of the family has had a bath before breakfast is prepared and served, the dishes washed, followed by the preparation for lunch, the dishes washed, and finally the process is repeated in the preparation and serving of supper.

The following day, they will continue with chores and no more money will be paid. This will now be the normal life for the bride, meaning that whenever she enters her in-law's home she has to take the role of the maid immediately. If there are any clothes to be washed or ironed, she will make sure they are done. However, those who cannot afford luxuries such as toothbrushes will omit the mouth care and concentrate on the basics.

The arrival of the son in-law at his wife's parental home is a bit different. The groom (*mukuwasha*) will have one escort, notably the person who officiated between the two when the marriage was conducted. The groom will arrive at his in-laws' home whilst they are expecting him and stay a metre away from the main gate. Together, the two men will clasp their hands to make a sound (*kuombera*) that will alert the wife's family that they have arrived whilst crouching. The father-in-law will go out to meet his son-in-law whilst crouching and clasping his hands as well. The two men will be welcomed into the family and shown where to sit. Mother-in-law, father-in-law and every member of the family will greet the new addition to the family and no monetary transactions will take place.

CHAPTER FOUR

One of the women who will have escorted the bride, normally called *tete* (aunt), will be assigned to fetch the biggest rooster and bring it to the groom and show them that as a welcome - and the family will slaughter this chicken for him. The aunt will deal with all the preparations and the cooking of the chicken, which will be served with rice or *sadza*. The two men including *tete (aunt)* and the bride will share the whole chicken. After eating, the two men will again clasp their hands to make that familiar noise as a way of appreciation. They will return all the leftovers to the mother-in-law and deposit some money on a plate. The son-in-law will now be welcome to the family and allowed to turn up any time as he will be accepted and welcomed into the family.

The son in-law will only be expected to do chores such as chopping wood and tilling the land and other manly jobs - much the same jobs he would do for his mum, really. However, in comparison it is the bride (*muroora*) who works harder than the groom. Some people with money pay other people to take part on their behalf if they were brought up in households where they did not do much work. Cultural differences can cause a lot of problems in relationships, but some people choose to ignore these factors and get on with whatever suits them at that particular time.

CHAPTER FIVE

TANAKA AND HER HUSBAND KENZO JAMUKOKO
1980-1995

"I CAN'T SEE A THING, the lady appears to have some curtains down below!" shouted Dr Maclean to the midwife.

"What curtains are you talking about?" screamed the midwife back to the expatriate doctor.

"There is a pair of some extra lace-like flesh by the entrance, so I can't feel how much the woman is dilated," shouted the expatriate doctor.

"All you have to do, doctor, is separate these lips and you will see where the fingers are supposed to go," said the midwife.

"Oh, I see," said the doctor. "Is this some sort of cancer?" he queried curiously.

"Oh, don't be silly and ridiculous!" replied the midwife.

"Oh, I do apologise, it's just that whilst working in North Africa last year I saw some women who had their bits missing and some had sutures down below," explained the doctor.

CHAPTER FIVE

"Well, in Zimbabwe you will never come across a woman who has bits that are cut off, as female circumcision or male circumcision is outside our culture - unless performed for medical reasons; however, you will see a lot of inner vaginal lips - like these ones," she said, pulling Tanaka's vaginal inner lips apart - "that are enhanced, and some women of course left their vulvas natural, as this is not enforced on anyone, being a thing of choice," explained the midwife. "These women are classified as western ladies as they are trying to preserve the western culture and they often find it difficult to keep their men who will often go chasing after the padded vaginas," added the midwife.

At this point Tanaka was in great pain. She hated the idea of being made a guinea pig. "Zimbabwe lacks ethical knowledge," the midwife continued. "No consent is sought when medical intervention is done and when students are brought in; what a shame."

"Thank you for the explanation nurse," the doctor said. "I would like to marry a black girl and she will definitely be a Zimbabwean as I love the thought of having a padded pussy instead of a wife with some of her bits missing," he concluded.

"Run quick, the baby's head is coming out!" screamed the midwife. "Bring the green cloth and catch the baby now!"

Tanaka's labour was prolonged by the lecture as she was bored being used as a guinea pig without her consent; however, the kind of nursing in Africa really lacks ethical

CHAPTER FIVE

education and it has to be pointed out - hence African nurses have to retrain when they come to work in the west.

Tanaka and Kenzo had their first daughter who was born on the same date as Tanaka's birthday, the 28th of August. Two days after the birth of their first daughter Kenzo turned twenty. Tanaka was eighteen on the day she gave birth to her daughter Patricia. This was the first time she heard her mum Kirera mention her birth date, when she said, "You have received a birthday present of a baby girl!" All the time Tanaka was growing up her birthday was never mentioned; neither did she ever receive a card or a present. Tanaka knew that her birthday did not have any significance for her parents - it was just a day when one was born, to be remembered merely for the purpose of obtaining a birth certificate or national identification card.

Nevertheless, Tanaka and her husband Kenzo were very happy that they had their own creation. Since Kenzo was the breadwinner, Tanaka stayed at home most of the time. She started buying magazines called *The Woman's Weekly* and the South African magazine *Your Family* and taught herself to knit, sew, bake, and to cook following recipes in the magazines. Tanaka started knitting following the patterns in the magazines, producing nice jumpers, cardigans, baby shawls, booties, bonnets, matinee jackets, and sewing cross-stitch table cloths and chair backs which she later sold to locals. Within no time Tanaka had her own savings account.

CHAPTER FIVE

Tanaka's desire to make it big one day did not stop. She took an interest in most of the creative ideas in magazines such as dressing, cooking, home-making and gardening. She started wearing shorts and trousers as well as her daughters. Some of Tanaka's friends started to talk about her and her husband, saying they were trying to adopt the western culture. Tanaka celebrated birthdays for her family and they were very happy. She tried everything under the sun to make her husband happy and to keep her children happy.

Since Tanaka was born under the Virgo star sign, she was very tidy, modest, meticulous, romantic, ambitious and very attractive. She tried by all means to win her children and her husband's hearts by doing the right things for them and keeping them happy. As an optimistic person with positive attitudes to life and health, she became very creative in order to become financially secure. Her weaknesses as a Virgo were based on her generous nature since she believed people easily and felt sorry for them. People often took advantage of her innocence and borrowed money from her, money which they never repaid. Little did she realise that money and friendship do not mix at any point in life. Her husband also took advantage of her loving and forgiving nature and walked all over her, by cheating on her several times and calling her nasty names such as *nymphomaniac*.

Once more Kenzo became prey to the local hookers and he started cheating on Tanaka again. It was also a norm and

CHAPTER FIVE

I think it still is within Tanaka's culture that people believed and thought that men were allowed to cheat on their wives and get away with it. The thought of her husband whom she loved very dearly sleeping with other women started to eat her away.

The men in Tanaka's culture are just like Muslims; they are allowed to marry as many wives as they like and they believe their wives should be submissive since the husband is seen as the breadwinner, the head of the family and should therefore be dominant and be allowed to do as he pleases. In actual fact some, though not all, treat women as second class citizens, and the man is often heard saying, *"Uri mukadzi wangu, ndakakuroora nemari yangu. Ndakatumira danga remombe kusha kwenyu."* ("You are my wife, I married you with my money when I paid *lobola* and I also sent a herd of cattle to your family.") In a sense he is saying, "I bought you when I paid money to your family, so you have to do as I wish." It is very sad. Having said this, it is true that the majority of Zimbabwean men treat their wives with much respect, though a few suffer from the wandering chameleon eye syndrome and have a dipstick that needs to be dipped into every available hole.

One day Tanaka was brave enough to ask Kenzo why he was sleeping around like he did. In response he was very rude; even though he loved his wife, he lacked respect for her. He never saw cheating as bad or as something that put him in the wrong.

CHAPTER FIVE

"Why are you always cheating on me, Kenzo?" Tanaka had asked.

"Variety is the spice of life my dear," Kenzo replied unkindly.

"How dare you, speak to me like that; I am your wife you know!" cried Tanaka.

"I know you are my wife because I married you! Remember I sent money to your parents, so you are my possession and I am your husband, your master and the head of the house!" He added: "Actually, you don't have to keep on reminding me that you are my wife!"

As Kenzo kept on repeating the same evil words over and over again, it pierced Tanaka's heart to the extent that she viewed marriage as a legal way of allowing men to abuse their wives emotionally. She cried and comforted herself. As she hugged herself, Tanaka just realised that her husband lacked respect for her and thought maybe it was caused by the fact that he was the breadwinner and she was only a housewife. Housewifery is a recognised job in Zimbabwe which most women wrote down as a profession on documents such as passports. Tanaka's desire to do something for herself grew even stronger. She was just waiting to hatch a plan. She just wanted to move on with life, to become very ambitious, have a vision to set goals and achieve them. She wanted to move away from the state of dependency and become fully independent.

When Tanaka had her third child in the mid-80's she

developed a desire to fly to Britain and to further her education and to gain a better profession than that of being the odd housewife. Kenzo discouraged her, giving an excuse that they could not afford the airfare. "Honestly, there *must* be ways to afford a ticket!" Tanaka declared. "I hate it when you just bleat that we can't afford it and do nothing about it; one day I will see myself in London without your help!"

Kenzo was negative and always discouraged Tanaka from doing what she wanted. Since, Tanaka was brought up in a way that valued traditional ways, she respected her husband's wishes, but deep down she just wanted to get out. She wanted to please both her husband and parents and she did not want to be seen as a prodigal daughter as she was also God fearing and a Christian; so she persevered and kept hanging on in a loveless marriage for the sake of her parents and children. She just pretended everything was okay.

She taught her children the modern ways of doing things. The children went to group A schools which were previously for whites only. Their kids had all the opportunities of playing all the sport that Tanaka could not do as a child but just observed the whites doing.

On reflection on her life as a child, Tanaka recalled the horrible white man who had made nasty comments about black people eating tripe and eating with their hands, the one who battered his son in front of onlookers. She told herself there was nothing special about holding a fork and knife, that it was not a big deal. Nevertheless she started teaching her kids to use forks and knives at an early age and to speak English...

One day she wanted to show off to her parents that she had acquired some skills from observing white people, and she asked her *amai* and *baba* to join her as she and her family sat at the table where the places were set with her cutlery. When they took their places at the table *baba* joked, grabbing the table knife in a way that made it look as though he wanted to stab someone. "*Zvava zvehondo here kana kuti zvekudya?*" he said, meaning, "Are we at war now or are we about to eat with these dangerous weapons?" The whole table burst into laughter and Tanaka's son stood up as if to help his granddad. "No *sekuru*, the knife is for cutting food and the fork is for picking up the food so you can put it into your mouth," Tanaka said patiently.

"Okay," *baba* conceded, "thank you *mufana, but tinoguta rinhi?*" - meaning, "By using the fork and knife, how long will it take us to fill our stomachs?" Tanaka made it easy for her parents and asked them to eat the way they had been doing all along as it could have been considered very disrespectful to try and encourage her parents to try using the cutlery. The most important thing was eating together as a family; above all, sitting on chairs as opposed to the floor, and having food on a table, which made them look like the queen's grandchildren or members of the extended family.

CHAPTER FIVE

I must admit that colonialism and apartheid was not a good experience, but we learnt a lot of agreeable and good things from the whites as we wanted to be like them. There were elements of bad things learnt as well, such as swearing, a lack of respect for the elders and prejudice amongst ourselves and towards other nationalities such as the people from Mozambique and Malawi. These people were called names and looked down upon. The people from Mozambique were laughed at for their inability to speak English as they could only speak Portuguese due to being under the colonial rule of the Portuguese people. They were known as poor people who came to Zimbabwe for cheap labour which only the uneducated people would do. Twenty years down the line Zimbabweans were the people who were now flocking into other countries to work as cheap labour. Today they are even found in Malawi and Mozambique as refugees and cheap migrant workers even though some have better professional jobs; the fact is they are now living in Diaspora, which was never heard of before.

CHAPTER SIX

THE CONFRONTATION

THERE WAS NO DOUBT that Tanaka and Kenzo loved each other even though Kenzo lacked respect for his wife. They were often seen holding hands and walking arm in arm which was not very common in their culture. However, their sex life was not brilliant. By the time Tanaka had a third child her husband had slept with about fifty different women, some thin, some fat, some with big bums, some pretty, and some very ugly. Honestly, no one knew why Kenzo cheated on his wife so much, even though she tried very hard to please him. Whether it was sex addiction, or a matter of status, only God knows why his willy needed to dip into every Vagina that was on offer…

One day Tanaka arranged for their housemaid to take their three kids out to Chinhoyi Caves and to have lunch at the Orange Grove Motel. They both waved goodbye to the kids and shouted, "*Muswere zvakana, musazotsuura zvamunenge maona* mumapako *monozonyan-garika!*" - in other

CHAPTER SIX

words, they wished them a nice day and reminded them to be quiet in the caves as it was always believed that people had to stay quiet and should not ask or say something bad about the caves. If they saw something unusual, they were meant to just keep quiet to acknowledge and respect the presence of the spirits or they might disappear or vanish for good! The kids enjoyed their day out at the famous Chinhoyi Caves running up and down, and they had time to swim in the swimming pool at the hotel as it was a very hot day. They had much to do and did not even think about mum and dad.

For Tanaka, the emotional incontinence of Kenzo's cheating was becoming unbearable and she just couldn't wait to confront her husband; she knew that nothing changes without confronting the problem. Thank God this was before the Internet became an established phenomenon in Zimbabwe, otherwise she would also no doubt have had to struggle with his cheating expressed through internet porn addiction.

Tanaka had grown up in a loving, well bonded household, where people never argued, had smiling dispositions and where making jokes was the norm. She was now sick and tired of playing the stupid 'everything is normal' game when actually there was something seriously wrong. It took her a while to gather her courage as she feared the confrontation might turn out wrongly and end up in chaos or total destruction. She was now at a point where she realised if they failed to reach a compromise, then so be it; if necessary, she was now prepared to opt out of her intolerable marriage.

CHAPTER SIX

She invited Kenzo into their bedroom, locked the door and threw the key outside and she stripped completely naked. She did this as Kenzo had a habit of walking out whenever his wife wanted an explanation on anything dodgy. The bedroom windows had burglar bars so there was no escape there. There was no way for Kenzo to get out and go to work. He was now a Deputy Manager at GMB Lions' Den, and as such had no choice but to respond to his wife's demands or face the consequences.

While thus incarcerated his secretary phoned, and phoned repeatedly, since he had not turned up for work. There was no response till a messenger was sent to the house to check on him. Tanaka had promised her husband that if he dared ask the messenger for the key, she would follow him to the office completely naked and embarrass him in front of his bosses and subordinates.

"Mr Jamukoko, Mr Jamukoko, are you alright?" called the messenger.

Kenzo went to the window and replied, "No, I am in here, Nhamo, I do not feel very well; maybe it's malaria since we have been to Lake Kariba for a family weekend - so I won't be coming to work today; could you let the manager and the area manager know, as I will have to go to Chinhoyi to see Dr Watson?" he lied.

"Okay sir, I will, and I wish you a speedy recovery" - and off he went back to work and reported what he had been told.

CHAPTER SIX

The manager and the area manager did not doubt Kenzo since he was a hardworking man and he was also very loyal. He never drank or smoked. His favourite hobby was sex, which didn't interfere with his work: he did it to satisfy his own ego and never bothered about the consequences to his family life.

At this point Tanaka had embraced the courage to become a real fighter and not a pushover as she had always been. She was still naked and in their bedroom during the morning and started having a good go at her husband. "Kenzo, oh Kenzo, the man of my dreams, the man in my life, my soul mate, husband and lover; the man who is in my heart, my prince charming, tell me the truth, please, for I seek an explanation!" This was met with silence and she went on: "I need to know if there is something missing on me or if there is some extra bits on my thingy. If you find me unattractive, I just want you to say so, *now*, so I can make my way out of here and leave you to enjoy the life you want of having different women!" The silence was unbearable. "I have just had enough, I have just had enough!!" I cried.

Kenzo was standing and a watching his wife crying. Tanaka walked towards him and started hitting him with her fists. "I want you to tell me, *now*!! I am fed up, sick and tired of your cheating!" she cried. She climbed onto a chair and sat on the dressing table with a mirror facing her vagina. She started pulling her bits apart one by one. "Come and inspect me now, I want you to tell me if there is something different that I have, that I shouldn't have!" she cried. "Or maybe I have a penis or a horn hidden somewhere that's pricking you when you get close to me!!!"

There was no response from him and she went on: "I need an explanation now!" she demanded. "I want to know why you keep sleeping around. If there is something that I am doing wrong, you have tell me now or I will pack my bags and go back to my parents today and start again… I don't mind starting again in a traditional round house, having to bath in the river and shitting in the bush, for there is no happiness in this house! Are you possessed with the sleeping around DEMON or something?" she queried, exasperated.

The memory of his promiscuity was overwhelming, and her words gushed out: "You slept with Magdalene, who slept with Jack, who had slept with Rose, Mildred, Jacquie and Norma, who had slept with Tim, who had slept with Rhoda, Hazel and Daisy, who had also slept with Pete who had slept with all the prostitutes around the Avenues… and with Pepetua who had slept with Jonah, the bus conductor in order for him to reserve a seat for her on the bus when she went to town, who also slept with Boyzen to avoid queuing at the bank when she went to cash her pay cheque before ATMs were hatched… who slept with the cashier for the supermarket for him to reserve all the basic commodities for her when there was the food shortage in Zimbabwe, who slept

CHAPTER SIX

with Banaye the butcher for a piece of steak…" she cried. "The women you have slept with have been represented by my fingers and toes multiplied by fifty! They can all fit into a double decker bus plus standing passengers," she wept. "I think you need medical help for this addiction of yours," she added. "It started as fantasy and now it is a very bad addiction which you cannot overcome!" She went on, her words now unstoppable, like an avalanche: "Tell me, have I ever deprived you of my womanhood? I vowed from the day of our marriage that I would do anything for you! I vowed to be your very own prostitute as long as everything was moral and holy! I am just fed up with all this cheating! It's high time I started exploring to see what other men are like out there!" She was crying bitterly as she spoke. "Don't you think that though you may find me ugly, there might be a chance that I will be able to tempt some desperate men out there?" she cried louder, desperately trying to save her marriage.

For Kenzo this was a big blow, since he loved his wife very much. It was a big shock for him to see his wife behaving like this - for until now she had just kept quiet, having put up with his cheating for a long time. He could not deny that Tanaka had been very forgiving and very faithful and loving.

Kenzo cried and cried. "My darling, oh my darling, I am so sorry." He rushed towards his wife, held her tight and said, "Please, my pretty angel, forgive me please. I don't know what got into me; it's an addiction and I can't help it. I always feel

CHAPTER SIX

guilty after doing it and I don't know why I keep on doing it," he cried.

"I just can't live without you, my love," he went on. "I love you very much and my life will be empty without you. I promise, and I promise I will never ever do it again!!"

They both cried together and Tanaka said, "You are breaking my heart apart; I have lost my self-esteem and confidence as a result of your cheating; I feel empty and naked when I walk outside, knowing that everyone is talking about your dirty habits. We live in a small village where everyone knows everyone and they know every detail and people's moves and businesses; everyone round here knows you sleep around with streetwalkers, so how can I continue to live with you as your wife, as though nothing has happened?" she lamented. "I just feel worthless and useless. I don't know if I am doing anything right at all… I feel like I have lost the plot." She took a deep breath and continued: "I try very hard to please you but it seems like it is not what you want, Kenzo; everything I do and have done for you seems to be in vain. If there is something different that these women, these prostitutes, do for you, please let me know so that I can do that for you!" Tanaka cried.

"I tell you the truth, dear," cried Kenzo, "there is nothing different whatsoever; you are the most beautiful woman that I want to be with. And I promise I will do anything, absolutely anything to please you if you forgive me!"

CHAPTER SIX

He held her really tight and started stroking her hair. "I'm really sorry, please believe me when I say I love you more than I can say," he cried.

"But you have a funny way of showing it!" protested Tanaka. "Sometimes I find it difficult to believe you when you say you love me."

"I love you and I really do; these other women mean nothing to me and there is no emotional connection whatsoever. I don't know what gets into me - please, please forgive me," emphasised Kenzo. "Streetwalkers are just like public toilets, anyone can use them anyway they want; but you are my wife, my very own wife whom I married because of the love between us, which bonds us together as one," he cried and felt guilty as charged.

Tanaka was very forgiving and loving, and just gave in.

"Don't ever cheat on me again," she implored him. "This must be the final forgiveness from me, as I can't take anymore," she cried. "I want you to know that I will be much happier in a cave with a homeless man who is faithful to me and who makes love to me and only me, than being in a mansion with a man who sleeps with half the world," she cried continuously. She went on to say, "Don't you think if you please me, I will be pleased and please you in return? If you experiment with me we will experiment and explore our bodies together, as is expected in a marriage."

After some reflection she continued: "Who am I not to

be able to forgive? Even the Bible tells us to forgive those who trespass against us." The only thing, she thought, was that once he crossed the line and cheated again, that would be it - that would be the end of their marriage. And so she forgave Kenzo as she always did.

She wanted Kenzo to understand her plight: "The fact that you had cheated on me on countless occasions made me think I was not good enough as a woman, in bed and in anything, and as a result I lost confidence and self-esteem. I wore a brave face but deep down it was killing me slowly, softly, like someone with cancer. When with other women I thought everyone could see through me and knew exactly what was going on in my life."

After the confrontation, the pair tried to rekindle their love and started kissing passionately and made love on the dressing table. Kenzo carried his wife to the bed and they made love passionately like never before, and for the first time in fifteen years Tanaka had an orgasm. She told Kenzo about this wonderful experience which she did not know about. She learned the benefits of engaging her brain in lovemaking and that the purpose of lovemaking was not just for satisfying her husband's ego but also for her own benefit - something the elderly women never mentioned.

From that day Tanaka knew that the vagina was a very powerful asset that could manipulate a man. Convincingly, Eve used her vagina to manipulate Adam as he submitted to her demands in the Garden of Eden. The majority of men might deny this, but it is a true fact that only a few heterosexuals can resist the sight of the vagina of a young woman that is put out on display.

As Tanaka discovered, making love during the day was quite different from making love in the dark. They spent the whole day, a total of twelve hours, in their bedroom drinking cold *Mazoe* orange and eating custard cream biscuits and roasted salted peanuts which they kept in their bedroom, and having steamy sessions of lovemaking till around 7 p.m. when the kids returned.

"Mum and dad, we are back!" shouted their son Ronganai (Ron).

"Okay son, we'll be out in a sec, then you can tell us all about your day out," Kenzo shouted. "I'm just in the shower and won't be long."

When they heard that the kids were back they rushed into their shower and quickly freshened up, to make themselves ready to meet their family and get ready for supper. They asked the maid to get the spare bedroom key and to unlock the door for them.

The pair sat down with their children and asked what sort of adventures they had and what they saw at Chinhoyi Caves. Since, Tanaka was very forgiving and very loving, everything appeared normal. The kids took it in turns to explain what they had done and seen at the famous Chinhoyi Caves.

CHAPTER SIX

For Tanaka, until then, lovemaking was merely a means of pleasing her husband and for child bearing. Her breasts were purely for baby feeding and nothing else. Kenzo had never bothered whether his wife climaxed or not; perhaps this was due to ignorance. Trying to reach an orgasm during lovemaking with her husband Kenzo was as hard as climbing Mount Kilimanjaro alone without any bottled water on a very sunny day - since Kenzo was unsupportive and laughed instead; all he cared for was his own satisfaction. Tanaka had spent the fifteen years of their marriage knowing that Kenzo cheated on her on several occasions but she never told her parents or best friends, yet she remained faithful to him. People used to see them as very loving and close, and as a loving family.

Tanaka tried to distract her husband from seeing other women by sending her three children to a boarding school. She planned this so that they could spend most of their quality time together, just the two of them in a three-bedroomed bungalow. They spent most of the time together, just the two of them with the kids coming home during the weekend. But you know what? Like my good old *amai* always said, "*A bird that is accustomed to its tweeting will never change its tune, and also old habits die hard.*"

One day, when Kenzo discovered that he could not cope with his wife's sexual demands anymore, since he had started sneaking out to prostitutes yet again, he just blurted out to

Tanaka's face that she was a **nymphomaniac**. Kenzo was a bookworm, well read and very educated, but for Tanaka that was just a big word that conveyed no meaning at all. Puzzled, she just smiled sweetly at her husband.

The following day when Kenzo was at work Tanaka drove to Chinhoyi town to buy a dictionary. On her way she met a local woman who told her that her husband had been sneaking into Tendai's (a local streetwalker) for sex… She thanked the woman and continued with her journey. She was shocked to discover the meaning of the word *nymphomaniac*. She did not bother to ask her husband why he had called her a nymphomaniac; instead she decided to take action and quietly planned her revenge.

"Really," she thought, "is that what Kenzo thinks about me? In that case I will have to teach him a lesson. I will go to any length to make him see sense…" The only way was to let her hair down and chill out. She hatched a plan, vowing that she would do whatever it takes to keep her *chikomba* (lover or boyfriend) happy.

Eventually, Tanaka developed a desire to be like Sharon Stone or Joan Collins, to become a *complete* bitch and *nymphomaniac* as he had labelled her. She promised herself that she would make it and as long as she had no fear and the guts to try new things, she would achieve her goal.

She made friends with local farmers and their wives. She learnt to cook western food, dress like them and started flower gardening; she joined book clubs and held coffee mornings at her house in order to meet more people and widen her circle of friends. She wanted to 'pull' someone much better than her husband, both financially and physically. Honestly, she thought vindictively, some men drive their wives to do evil things!

CHAPTER SEVEN

ROY PENDER-HURST: THE MULTI-MILLIONAIRE WITH AFRICAN VALUES

ROY PENDER-HURST was born in Surrey's Godalming area of the United Kingdom. He was from a very wealthy family. Roy was educated in a private school. According to Roy, his great grandfather acquired a piece of land in Rhodesia, which was given to him by the Queen after the Second World War as a reward for taking part in the war. Roy later inherited the farm after his grandparents' death. His grandparents died in England as they had always told Roy that they belonged to the English soil.

Life for Roy was just as good as gold, since he never had to work very much to acquire his wealth. He had a manager for his farm, another Englishman called Dick Boyle. Dick was responsible for the running of the farm whilst Roy enjoyed luxury shopping trips to New York, London and Paris. He was a man of substance. Roy chaired a lot of farmers' organisations at their local country club due to his influence and wealth.

CHAPTER SEVEN

He donated a lot of money to building private schools and clubs for farmers' families.

His mother, Mrs Margaret Pender-Hurst, was just like Mrs Bucket from the popular British Comedy 'Keeping up Appearances', according to Roy. She wanted her things to be perfectly in order and no shoes were allowed in the house during her time. She would not get into the car until her husband Dennis opened the door for her. Roy was a Cambridge graduate and had several degrees in his portfolio, which he never needed to use in his CV to look for work.

Roy lived on a large farm comprised of more than fifty acres of land and a large house whilst his parents lived in Golden Jubilee Cottage which he built for them. They had a beautiful garden that was in bloom all year round, a tennis court and a large outdoor swimming pool.

Their farm was well known by people since he had bought some wild animals such as Giraffes, Elephants, Zebras, Lions, Monkeys, Baboons, Cheetahs, Leopards and Red Water Buck that he kept in a fenced environment. He had his own truck which was white in colour with black stripes, similar to a Zebra, which he used to tour his friends around his farm on a safari treat - "*a kind of show-off thingy*," as he called it.

Life is just good for some - not for the rest of us. According to Roy, he inherited over five million pounds from his late grandparents' estates.

CHAPTER SEVEN

Sipping his red wine and with his index finger tapping on the wine glass and staring at the ceiling, he opened his mouth wide and uttered these words: "Money does not bring happiness; I have millions in Great Britain and millions in Zimbabwe, but I am not happy." He added: "I have everything I could wish for on earth, but I am not happy."

How could that be? What could be the source of the unhappiness of a man who has everything under his nose, a man who can ask someone to wipe his bum after using the loo for £100,000.00 a year, a man who can stuff his mattress with bank notes, a man who is able to live on bank interest from his savings for the rest of his life? These are the questions I asked myself. Could he be insane? "I bet he is not with it," I told myself. Perhaps, I thought, that's why *amai* and *baba* always said that too much money causes insanity and brings misery.

Honestly, there was something that was lacking in Roy's life; but no-one knew about it, since he kept his married life and matrimonial problems to himself. Roy's wife enjoyed trips to France to buy designer clothes and follow the farmers' wives' Round Table for teas and social functions. She never bothered about Roy's whereabouts or what he did with his life; it was as though they lived separate lives in spite of being married to each other.

According to Roy, his wife had a shoe collection that was almost as large as Imelda Marcos's; and if her shoe collection represented different sexual positions, perhaps their marriage might have survived! She had loads of unworn dresses in her wardrobe, still attached to their designer labels or price tags; and all the time she would be carrying thousands of dollars and pounds on her. None of their friends knew that the pair had grown apart; the chemistry of their marriage was long gone and they lived together as siblings indoors and as a couple in public, for the sake of the kids. The couple's love for each other was long dead; it was only its skeleton that people could see.

Roy eventually found solace in Kenzo and his wife Tanaka. He befriended the couple and they did almost everything together, holidays, leisure, golf, etc. He spent more time with either the wife or the husband than with his own wife. Roy's wife trusted him one hundred per cent with Tanaka, and Kenzo did the same. Friendship blossomed between them, which was very, very unusual during the Rhodesian times and early Zimbabwean days.

Roy and his wife had two adult children from their marriage, who chose to go back to England as they could not cope with their parents' differences and rowing which was constant. "I can't leave Zimbabwe, I just love it here and here I shall die," declared Roy.

"To you, the forefathers of the Zimbabwean soil, I give my life!" shouted Roy. "I dedicate my life to you as a son of the Zimbabwean soil; I am the son of the soil of Zimbabwe and will always be. My grave shall be here in Zimbabwe, Africa - the country I love, the country where the sun shines seven days a week, thirty days a month and three hundred and sixty-five days a year. I love it here and just love every moment of it. My heart belongs to Zimbabwe!" So he went on. "I am the son of the Zimbabwean soil; here I shall live, here I shall die, here I shall be buried, and here I shall be resurrected to meet my creator; on the Zimbabwean soil I shall walk again after this life." He would kneel down to pour some Zimbabwean traditional beer onto the ground as he clasped his hands together in the Zimbabwean traditional way of thanking his ancestors for the wonderful life he was enjoying on the Zimbabwean soil. "Long live the people of Zimbabwe!" he shouted. As he spoke these imposing phrases the blue skies automatically turned grey, concealing the sun, and the dark pregnant clouds hung low and it started raining heavily, with lightning and thunder. "Thank you, the forefathers of Zimbabwe, thank-you for accepting me and welcoming me into your world!" he cried with joy, his hands outstretched as if he were ready to fly.

His employees were standing by, watching him make his declaration. They clapped their hands, and some cried tears of joy. They were very impressed to see and hear their white employer acknowledging the presence of the Zimbabwean sprits in his talk, and by this gesture Roy became a favourite farmer. All local people knew him as a white man who loves the black people and some even joked with him, saying, "Boss, I think you are a black man who turned white like Michael Jackson! You are one of us, we love you very much!" After his declaration he called a local brewer to bring a tanker of *Chibuku* (local beer) for his employees and a lorry full of soft drinks for the women and children; a cow was slaughtered and cooked together with rice and *sadza*. The pheasant farmers celebrated with their employer. Roy ate with his employees, and he even washed his hands and ate *sadza* with them the same way they did. He was often heard saying the hands were created before forks and knives. Roy was one of the first farmers to build proper houses for his employees as opposed to pole and dagga huts (the traditional grass thatched round huts). He just was a giver and he loved black people with all his heart. Honestly, during colonial rule not all whites were bad, even though some were cousins and siblings of the famous P.W. Botha (the king of apartheid)[6] in their behaviour and attitude towards blacks. P.W. was the notorious President of South Africa who enjoyed watching Mandela wasting away in prison - until De Klerk came to his rescue and released him from prison.

---

6. Hendrik Verwoerd, however, was the author of Apartheid in South Africa.

CHAPTER EIGHT

WHAT GOES AROUND COMES AROUND

SINCE TANAKA had sent the kids to a boarding school she had time to do what she wanted. Kenzo became very possessive and kept on coming home to check on his wife and ringing the house phone every fifteen minutes or half hour. He would call just to say "I love you and missing you"; all the years they were married he never uttered the three little words, "I love you." However, he remembered to buy a card for his wife every St Valentine's Day and on her birthday. In reality he was starting to be a controlling husband and phoning was a way of checking on his wife as he thought that perhaps now Tanaka was the one doing what he used to do. Unfortunately for Kenzo it was already too late, for the damage he had caused was beyond repair.

Since, Kenzo had a very, very nice job which he achieved by rising through the ranks, he made friends with local white farmers. For Kenzo money was not a problem since these farmers used to bribe him in order to get good grades for their grain. At Kenzo's house a weekend at home was having a traditional barbecue (*braai* in Zimbabwe) with friends and family. Beef, lamb and chicken were available anytime since these farmers knew that they had nothing to lose, so used to bring the family a whole lamb, goat meat and special cuts of beef such as T-bone steaks and specially made sausages called *boerewors* which originated from South Africa. "Honestly," I thought again, "in life if one wants to become rich, my advice is, mingle with the rich; if you want to be poor, mingle with the poor."

Eventually one of the white farmers, Roy Pender-Hurst, befriended Tanaka. They became very close to the extent that Roy would leave his wife Ellen in charge of the farm and tell her that he was taking plants to Tanaka to help her design her garden. Even when Roy brought some grain for sale he would say to Kenzo, "I'm popping over to yours to have a laugh and a cup of tea with Tanaka - hope you don't mind." Kenzo did not mind at all about the friendship; neither did Ellen, as they often got together, the four of them, and socialised together.

Roy started developing an interest in Tanaka and they became very, very close. Since Roy was Tanaka's secret and interested admirer, he was prepared to offer anything and to lend a sympathetic ear to Tanaka whenever she needed a friend. They became very close, so much so that Tanaka ended up confiding to him about her husband's infidelity. Roy told Tanaka that Kenzo's infidelity was caused by the novels he used to read. He used to read a lot of Ian Fleming, Mickey Spillane and some of Agatha Christie's crime books, and ended up being a mini James Bond. Since Roy had fancied Tanaka for ages, he took advantage of the situation and made his move.

He sidled up to Tanaka, grabbed her bum gently and leaned forward to kiss her passionately - and it was a long lingering kiss. Indeed, it was tongues at the first go. He apologised to Tanaka, saying, "I am really sorry my love, I didn't mean to do that. I don't know what got into me - you're my best mate's wife; really, I shouldn't have done that, sorry." But Tanaka pulled Roy towards her chest, grabbed his bum in the same way he had done and held it tightly against her groin. She said, "Oh Roy, don't be silly - honestly there is nothing to apologise for, we both know what we want." She looked straight into his eyes and saw his pupils dilate, his eyes inviting - and she kissed him back passionately. Immediately the pair hit it off and they did it often.

Roy used to go round to Tanaka's and make arrangements to meet up away from home so they could talk freely. Roy also found a friend in Tanaka, and he ended up slagging his wife off by saying she was useless in bed and she was the most boring person he had ever known.

"You know what, Tanaka," Roy lamented, "having Ellen in bed is just as good as sleeping with a rough dead log."

"You lost me," said Tanaka.

"I am not saying this just because I fancy you, but it's the truth; having Ellen in my bed feels like sleeping with a rough lifeless log," he repeated.

"Oh my God!" exclaimed Tanaka, "Yet in public you two appear very close and very loving."

"It's true, babe, we do that for the sake of the outside world and our kids," he confided. "But the truth is we've drifted apart somehow. That's why our children have chosen to go back to England - because we rowed a lot in front of them."

"Oh, I see," said Tanaka, sympathising with Roy.

The two suddenly clicked; then they started having a full-blown affair and regularly confided in each other. For Tanaka it was like betraying all her family, yet deep inside she felt that she had just started on an adventure. Roy was very romantic and charming with old-fashioned values, yet very young at heart. It didn't take him long to roll his way into Tanaka's heart, and gradually the pair fell head over heels for each other.

However, the fact that Kenzo had cheated on his wife several times and called her a nymphomaniac gave Tanaka the courage and determination to break the Seventh Commandment and commit the sin of adultery. She was driven by the compelling belief that she would be much better off without Kenzo as he had cheated on her on so many

CHAPTER EIGHT

occasions and made it worse by calling her names. She did not blame herself at all for having an affair, but nevertheless wanted to make peace with her creator through *repentance*.

Tanaka and Roy Pender-Hurst became the best of friends to the extent that Roy would do anything for Tanaka whilst neglecting Ellen. For Tanaka the revenge was sour and she felt sorry for Ellen. Roy and Tanaka made passionate love to the extent that Roy wanted to divorce his wife and be with Tanaka, but it was impossible in Zimbabwe those days, since the pair had married in England. If they wanted a divorce they would have to fly to England; apart from that, Roy knew it would cost him half of his assets in the divorce settlement.

For Tanaka it was like having a replacement for Kenzo whilst he existed; it was just like replacing an old Ford with a brand new Ferrari, so much so that one day she even told her husband, "You know what, Kenzo, I don't care anymore if you cheat on me!"

"Why darling?" demanded Kenzo. "Don't you love me anymore?" he queried.

"I do love you, dear, very much; it's just because I am now used to your cheating and it doesn't hurt me anymore, and I have fallen in love with my knitting needles: every night and every minute what I think about most is KNIT ONE, PURL TWO, my love," she said tongue-in-cheek. Kenzo did not get the joke at all - that Tanaka was actually saying the 'knit one' was herself while 'the purl two' was Kenzo and Roy - *lol*.

CHAPTER EIGHT

She poured herself a non- alcoholic drink which she sipped whilst listening to Beyoncé's 'Best Thing I Never Had' and singing along loudly and happily. "Come and join me, my love, let's dance to this song and I want you to listen to the lyrics." Together they danced happily, but Tanaka imagined she was dancing with Roy:

What goes around comes back around (hey my baby)
What goes around comes back around (hey my baby)
What goes around comes back around (hey my baby)
What goes around comes back around

There was a time I thought, that you did everything right
No lies, no wrong
Boy I, must've been outta my mind
So when I think of the time that I almost loved you
You showed your mask and I saw the real you

Thank God you blew it
Thank God I dodged the bullet.
I'm so over you
So baby go lookin' out!

I wanted you bad
I'm so through with it
Cuz honestly you turned out to be the best thing I never had,
And I'm gon' always be the best thing you never had
Oh yeah, I bet it sucks to be you right now…

CHAPTER EIGHT

Kenzo just looked at his wife and shook his head. He could not figure out why she was so excited. What he did not realise was the fact that it was not enough to be married, and that marriage needed to be sustained and love between the two has to be unconditional. Love is not love until it is expressed.

The word of Almighty God says, "For out of the abundance of the heart the mouth speaketh" (Matt 12.13). If a man like Kenzo uses abusive words to his wife, he is speaking out of the abundance of his heart. Men initiate things, and women respond to them. Thus, as husbands initiate the loving relationships between themselves and their wives, there is no woman who hates being loved. When a woman is loved and respected the man will easily win the woman's submission.

Tanaka yearned for a deeper, fulfilling relationship, and she craved sexual fulfilment from Kenzo which she did not get. Kenzo had forgotten his role as a husband and that God did not make provision for spiritual needs of men only but also physical needs as well, which is why it says in the Bible both shall leave their parents when married and become one flesh. Kenzo had forgotten that Tanaka was a wonderful woman who was efficient in her housewifery duties and was pleasant and dutiful to his parents, elders and neighbours. Housekeeping books were part and parcel of her life as she struggled to self-educate herself on the modern ways of living to match their friends' lifestyles.

CHAPTER EIGHT

Kenzo and Tanaka had grown apart but still no one knew about it since it was a taboo subject to talk or seek counselling about a relationship. Tanaka used to stay up late at night knitting and watching television instead of joining her husband in bed. Neighbours and family viewed their relationship as just perfect and they compared them to couples like Posh and Beck and Jay-Z and Beyoncé, yet in bed the pair weren't so good together.

Tanaka was a tall attractive girl, who had a lovely model's figure. She had natural curves, a nice round bottom, large breasts that most women would die for. Although she had French manicures regularly she had natural long nails that were always painted in red nail varnish. Nothing was fake on her body except for the Brazilian hair extensions which changed several times. She had lush sensuous lips and natural big boobs, and her bum was not unlike that of Jennifer Lopez or Beyoncé's. The girl was most attractive but unlucky in love, especially in her married life. She wore very rich sweet-scented perfumes.

Two other white farmers, Nicholas Bronkhorst and Jim Brown started to develop an interest in Tanaka, but she kept her distance. Nick offered Tanaka a big financial leg-up in exchange for sexual favours, but Tanaka kept him waiting by saying she would think about it and he had to consider that she was someone's wife in as much as he was someone else's husband. He tried everything under the sun to lure her into

CHAPTER EIGHT

bed and insinuate himself into her heart. Jim Brown showered her with gifts and played the waiting game. He was a slow mover.

All this time the relationship between Tanaka and Roy blossomed and became completely full blown, though it was done secretly. The pair could not spend a day away from each other, which forced the two couples to go on holidays together and to plan their activities together. Roy and Tanaka became more than friends as they grew closer and shared confidences.

As time progressed Roy Pender-Hurst bought a very big house which they called The Roy-Tan Grange in Harare's Mount Pleasant low density area, for Tanaka as a birthday present, but without either of their partner's knowledge. Roy told Tanaka that he wanted to start distributing his wealth and give away as much as possible before he started divorce proceedings with his wife. Tanaka kept a low profile and kept the title deeds of the house at her parent's home. Roy was very rich since he had inherited loads of money from his late grand mum who had died five years before in England. During that time the economy of Zimbabwe was very strong and everyone just wanted to live there. The house was built in a mansion style, with a tennis court and a swimming pool. The market value of the house at the time of writing this book is $480,000.00 US dollars. We are talking about Obama's US dollar which has been adopted in Zimbabwe after the collapse of the Zimbabwean Trillions to inflation. The house was bought at a price of around £20,000 in the mid-90's when Zimbabwe was still a little heaven on earth.

It was overwhelmingly luxurious, with its own swimming pool, a four-poster bed with luxurious Egyptian cotton bedding, continental pillows, standard pillows and beautiful bedspreads and cushions. The moment one took a glance at the bed, one instinctively wanted to spread one's wings: the beauty was beyond imagination, breathtakingly attractive and with much evidence of quality and class. The things that some men will do for the sake of one hundred per cent sexual satisfaction are beyond belief!

Roy furnished the house in such a beautiful way that it looked like a five-star hotel or a royal palace, and it became his and Tanaka's secret meeting place. They hired a guard who lived in the staff quarters. The guard provided twenty-four hour security for the house, cleaned and maintained the garden. Since Tanaka wore a wedding ring from her husband Kenzo, the guard Vincent Banda assumed Roy and Tanaka were husband and wife who lived at their farm in Chinhoyi, but wanted to stay away from the majority of people since they were in a mixed relationship. The pair agreed that no-one else should know about their hideout where they shared and lived out their fantasies; it was a best kept secret, another Garden of Eden.

Just a message for men here: women constitute a very smart species that can tolerate much pain such as childbirth as well as putting up with lying and cheating partners; but when they choose to retaliate, they can be very, very deadly, just like a poisonous viper - so ne warned! Treat them with care since they are fragile and break easily.

Honestly, when a woman cheats, particularly in retaliation, no-one will easily scent something fishy about anything, especially when she can sustain her sense of joy and keep herself busy; so guys, know that being forewarned is to be forearmed; treat women with extra care as they are fragile and break easily - yet deadly, just like broken glass that can stab you when broken. Trying to pick up the broken pieces and put them back together is a time consuming and dangerous endeavour; so it is better to protect than to break and then try to mend.

CHAPTER NINE

THE AFFAIR

AS NICK'S DESIRE for getting Tanaka into bed grew stronger, he started to stalk her. Tanaka did not realise she had a stalker and continued to do her normal things freely without any fear whatsoever. As she was continuing to be popular among the white farming population, she began to feel uneasy and intimidated by Nick's charms. One day as they were having a *braai* (barbecue) at Roy's place, Nick walked briskly up to Tanaka and gave her a hug and a kiss on the cheek, which made her feel very uncomfortable.

Someone who was standing nearby asked if there was something going on between the pair. Tanaka just blurted out so loudly that everyone else turned around to stare: *"Are you kidding me! He is old enough to be my dad and, after all, I am a married woman!"* Nick was not impressed by the response and because of this set out on a mission to strike back.

Tanaka used to buy her clothes from a small designer boutique called Lily's and Marloons, situated in the high street of Chinhoyi town which was close to the motorway that ran from Harare to Kariba. Not very many people bought from that shop since it was considered very expensive. Essentially it was a shop exclusively for posh people. One day Nick followed Tanaka as she drove to Chinhoyi for her clothes shopping and weekly hairdo. After shopping she was meant to meet up with Roy for a drink at the Orange Grove Motel. Nick could hardly believe his eyes when he saw Tanaka swinging and wiggling her waist in a sexual and provocative way whilst walking towards Roy, who was sitting on a high stool at a bar. He watched in disbelief as he saw Roy open his legs wide, his arms outstretched suggestively and invitingly as he whispered "Welcome, my beautiful angel" to Tanaka, who slowly sandwiched herself between Roy's legs and arms. Roy gave Tanaka a warm embrace as she fitted perfectly between his legs. Roy had his right hand clenched on Tanaka's bum and whispered, "*Je t'aime bebe, tu es tout moi*" (I love you babe, you are everything to me).

"*Je t'aime moi aussi*," Tanaka replied with a broad smile.

This was the only French they could string together, from a perfume advert that used to appear on the local television. But it worked for poor Tanaka who could not remember the last time Kenzo used the phrase 'I love you' when addressing his wife.

Tanaka and Roy started kissing passionately in the Moonlight Bar, which surprised Nick to the extent that he opened his mouth wide like a crocodile lying on a river bank waiting patiently to catch flies. This was a bar that was mostly dominated by whites only.

Nick kept his distance and watched the pair from afar as he pinched himself. "Am I dreaming?" he asked himself. "Have I gone insane, have I lost my marbles? Have my eyes given way? No please, tell me my eyes have not betrayed me!" he said as he approached the barman.

"How can I help sir?" asked the barman.

"Is what I am seeing correct?" asked Nick.

"What do you mean sir?" asked the barman.

"I mean, the couple I am seeing in my head displaying public affection over there; are they real?" he asked, rolling his eyes towards Roy and Tanaka.

"Oh, you mean that couple over there?" said the bar man quietly. "They are regulars here, and they're well known to our staff; are they your friends?" the barman queried.

"No, no, I don't even know them," he replied quickly. "I just thought they were a bit over the top displaying affection publicly like that."

"We don't mind as we often have newly married couples who stay for their honeymoon," the barman explained. "We have seen a bit more than that and we are accustomed to that kind of behaviour anyway."

Nick did not quite like the answer he got; he bought himself a drink and continued to disguise himself by sitting behind one of the wooden pillars in the bar.

CHAPTER NINE

The pair later booked a room to have a quickie at the motel before going back to their partners.

"Would you like a gin and tonic, gorgeous?" Roy asked.

"No thanks babe, I'm not sipping gin and talking shit with you, my love, and I never will; it has to be red wine when I'm with you, babe, and orange juice when Kenzo is around," she whispered. They ordered a bottle of red wine which was to be delivered to the room by a waiter and off they went to the room. They had also agreed that neither Tanaka nor Roy should bring their partners to the Moonlight Bar. Since the couple were so happy together they never bothered to look around and check who was in the bar. They just concentrated on each other, gazing in each other's eyes and kissing and sipping their wine as if they were teenagers again, and continued to exchange the words *Je t'aime, Je t'aime…* repeatedly.

Just the tongue wagging and fondling was enough to arouse Roy before seeing Tanaka's naked body. He just felt like a bull that had been starved from the cows for a decade. Indeed, there was nothing to suggest that Roy was a married man, for he behaved as though sexually starved and sexually dehydrated. He was definitely gagging for it.

Nick followed them, crawling behind a hedge to avoid being seen; he finally stood by the window of room 69 which the pair had chosen and peeped through the windowpane and pried on them. The two lovers were so excited that they did not even notice Nick in the bar or at the window. As Nick peeped through the window he could not believe what he saw, which was unambiguous and very apparent. He never thought a black girl was able to do what he observed. He saw the pair ripping each other's clothes off, kissing passionately and pouring golden syrup and ice cream onto each other's bodies, licking and sucking each other to climax. It was just jaw dropping and bloody fantastic to watch, and he touched himself with desire.

Tanaka had big seductive eyes that gazed into Roy's blue eyes and told him she was bursting with desire. She grabbed Roy's finger, scooped ice cream with it and licked and sucked his finger before finally guiding his finger down to feel her erect clitoris. Within no time the pair engaged in a perfect 69 position. Tanaka reached for Roy's dick; she licked and sucked it to the extent that Roy groaned with excitement and as he reached orgasm, he moaned, "Oh, oh, this is a highway to heaven, GOSH!!!!... it just feels like I'm in paradise already... I will buy you another house tomorrow, oh!! Oh!!! Oh *je t'aime bebe*!! My head is spinning with excitement... I think I am going bonkers, I love you to the bone... Tan, you are simply the best and you are driving me crazy... THIS IS WHAT I CALL A NEATLY PACKED KEBAB, A SOFT CUSHIONED, PUFFY PUSSY!" he shouted. "I love you very much, gorgeous, no one else has ever made me feel like this before! Everything that you do for me is completely out of this world and yet to be discovered, you are just so good…" Roy continued to shout: "Babe, you make my heart sing and my eyes water with excitement, *je t'aime bebe, je t'aime*…"

Roy was very well endowed and he lasted very long; though he was a sexually starved beast, he had the *vavavoom*. Honestly, the guy had balls for ten men, if not two dozen. Probably he had taken the Zimbabwean Viagra mixed with the crushed black Rhino horn, also mixed with some Chinese herbs. The act was very long, but not without excitement. It sounds too good to be true, but that's exactly what transpired. Roy was just that kind of guy who knew the purpose of lovemaking and he never suffered a brewer's droop with Tanaka, and his nine-inch prick was as hard a Rhino Horn when aroused. I assumed that with other women he had bonked off before it was the same. He always told Tanaka that there is a difference between making love and having sex. Roy was just a thirty-something-year-old guy with his thingy that never let him down. There was never a dull moment for the two when they were together.

Unlike Kenzo, Roy stroked and sucked Tanaka's boobs and licked, stroked her clitoris with his tongue until Tanaka reached multiple orgasms and she declared her love for him and said she would die for him. Roy's tongue was just as a good as the vibrator known as The Rabbit powered by Duracell batteries… Their lovemaking was out of this world,

CHAPTER NINE

totally insane, it was... Tanaka giggled and cried with excitement as this was an adventure for her which she never wanted to end.

It was a high adrenaline moment. It was just so incredible and exciting. Tanaka's restless energy kept its pace in pleasing Roy, to the extent that he even told her that if she ever asked for the moon or stars, he would die in space trying to get them for her. Roy certainly did his best to satisfy Tanaka sexually. When the pair finished their foreplay they went to the real thing, starting with Tanaka on top of Roy; then finally Roy took his turn to please his girl in the missionary position. He kissed her, licked and sucked her boobs several times and fucked her till she reached the peak of Mount Kilimanjaro. Tanaka changed tremendously from the way she did it with Kenzo and become a real "BITCH". It was too late to introduce what she did with Roy to Kenzo as it would be a cause for divorce. Tanaka kept all the pornographic magazines and videos which she had smuggled from South Africa in her Harare Mount Pleasant house which Roy had bought for her. *These constituted a deadly possession in Zimbabwe, for one could face a long jail term for possessing pornographic material - worse than having a gun! This is due to the influence and after effects that were believed to be the result of being exposed to porn material, which it was believed could lead people to raping minors or innocent girls and all the evil deeds associated with the exposure to the material.* According to

CHAPTER NINE

hearsay pornographic material is now plentiful in Zimbabwe, with some locals even recording themselves and uploading videos to the internet. Surely, times have changed, but it nevertheless remains illegal to be in possession of pornographic material In Zimbabwe.

As for Tanaka and Roy, if the pair had recorded their act then in the 80's it would have surpassed the offings of playboy by far. Nick thought, "I must make sure that I get some of that treatment too, though not today." He reassured himself of this as he battled with desire to join them. No doubt if their performance was videoed and uploaded to YouTube, it would achieve over a trillion hits - but this was before the era of YouTube! Nick managed to take several photographs of the pair in several compromising positions. The scene had an inflammatory effect on Nick and he kept on thinking of Tanaka every minute thereafter.

After their steamy session Roy and Tanaka had a shower and kissed passionately as they listened to Lionel Richie's 'Stuck on You' playing in the background. It was Roy's favourite song and he always played it when he was with Tanaka. As the pair sang along they kept on gazing into each other's eyes and cuddled and kissed over and over again.

They finished showering and took it in turns to dry each other's backs, still kissing and singing along: *"Stuck on you, I've got this feeling down deep in my soul, that I can't lose…"* Lionel Ritchie's lyrics had the effect of bringing the pair even closer together, bonding them together as though their hearts were glued together with super glue! Honestly, their two hearts just beat together as one. The pair towelled each other dry, then dabbed on their favourite deodorants and Tanaka used her favourite Coco Channel brand which Nick always brought her from his trips abroad. They planned their next meeting and kissed goodbye. Surely, the former poor girl who used to have natural scents and odours had been introduced to some highly reputable perfumes on the market. She felt exceedingly posh, especially when people told her she smelt heavenly.

They left quickly and went straight to their cars; they waved goodbye to each other. Roy winked at Tanaka and she smiled as she drove off in her convertible BMW with her big Gucci sunglasses on. Roy drove in the other direction as he pulled his large Land Rover out of the Motel. He went into a large supermarket to buy a few things so that his wife would assume he had just been drinking with his mates and ended up doing the shopping! What a thoughtful husband he was. He also bought a nice bunch of pink Carnations for his wife. Again, what a thoughtful husband - who bought FLOWERS for his WIFE and INVESTED in PROPERTY for his mistress!

Nick crawled out of his hiding place under the window and ran back to the bar, ordered a drink, drank it quickly and drove off to Lion's Den - still with a hard on; he could not believe what he had seen and pinched himself as he thought he must have been dreaming. He just thought if all black girls

CHAPTER NINE

were like that, then he was missing out. He packed his car at a lay-by, undid his trouser zip, pulled out his cock and gave himself a good hand job as he imagined Tanaka riding on him. He exploded with relief in no time, breathing heavily towards the end, shouting "Tanaka, oh Tanaka!" with excitement.

"Phew!" he sighed as he splashed his face with cum. "That was a relief; otherwise I might have committed rape!"

He quickly wiped himself clean. "That black bitch is now under my control with all this data," he reassured himself.

He drove to nearest music shop and bought himself Clarence Carter's 1977 'I Got Caught' tape - there were no DVDs at that time. He kept on playing and singing to the lyrics again and again, *"I got caught, making love to another man's wife... Yes, I did... and before I knew what was happening she was in my arms..."* He thought, *"I never knew a woman in Africa could do what she did..."* Then his conscience said, *"Clearance Carter, don't you know this is another man's wife..."*

This became Nick's favourite song and he was often heard humming it when playing golf, feeding his cattle or on the field. In the bar he would pay money into the music box so that it played the song repeatedly until he left the bar. No-one would dare confront him or tell him that the music was boring since he was well known for his anger and boxing ability, and people were scared of him. They were often seen giving him dirty looks but that was about it - until one day another farmer called Henry Wilkinson thought the repetition of the same song was becoming unbearably tedious.

Henry walked up to Nick and said, "Hey man, whatever you're going through, just fucking keep it to yourself! If you were caught making love to another man's wife, it's not something you have to BLOODY BOAST ABOUT! YOU NEED TO BLOODY GO HOME!"

Nick was pissed already and drunk so he struggled to stand up, and said to Henry using the words from Clarence Carter's song, "OH YEAH MAN, I GOT CAUGHT BLOODY FUCKING YOUR WIFE!" Henry lost his temper and punched Nick so hard that he fell onto the floor. "THIS AIN'T GONNA CHANGE ANYTHING MAN, YES I GOT SUCKED BY YOUR BLOODY WIFE!" Nick sang whilst struggling to stand up. The two men continued fighting with Nick receiving most of the blows, till the barman called the police. The police came in quickly and stopped the fight. Both men were taken to the police station and charged with causing disorderly and public fighting. They were both asked to pay for the damages caused to the Bar which they duly paid on a fifty-fifty basis to defray the cost of the damages. Nick was kept in custody until his wife came to pick him up as he had drunk excessively and was too drunk to drive himself home safely.

CHAPTER TEN

THE SOCIAL LIFE OF BLACK AND WHITE MEN IN THE EARLY 80'S

THE FOLLOWING DAY when Nick had sobered up a bit, he went straight to Kenzo and asked him to come and have a drink with him at a local pub where most farmers met. Kenzo did not refuse as he assumed Nick might have a good business proposal for him, and he was also bored being alone waiting for Tanaka's return from Chinhoyi where she said she was going to meet an old friend for coffee. Kenzo was not surprised to see Nick with a black eye, since he was well known for his violent behaviour, but he bit his tongue and did not bother to ask.

Partially, Nick and Kenzo became good friends. Nick did not betray his feelings for Tanaka to Kenzo or reveal that he knew anything about her affair with Roy. They started hanging around together and playing golf together during the weekends. When they met in a bar they were often seen enjoying and singing along to 'The boys are back in town'

CHAPTER TEN

and 'Jailbreak' by Thin Lizzy - two of the songs of that time. The men were often seen dancing and pretending they were playing guitars as they enjoyed each other's company. They danced and sang the lyrics very loudly, like a couple of crazy teenagers.

Nick started to resent Roy after the discovery of his affair with Tanaka. Roy just thought that maybe Nick hated him because he was richer than him. Nick used to go round to Kenzo's house for a cup of tea but their wives never got on. Nick's wife Anthea was the sort of person who did not like black people at all and did not feel comfortable around them. So, their friendship did not become as strong as Roy and Ellen's with Kenzo and Tanaka. This did not stop Nick befriending Kenzo though, since he had his own private agenda.

One day as Kenzo and Roy were having a drink, Nick turned up unexpectedly.

"Do you mind if I join you guys?" Nick asked.

"Come and join us - as long as you don't smoke your pipe near me," Kenzo joked.

"Oh no, I won't," Nick laughed. "I'm trying to catch a black girl. I've been told they dislike cigarette smoke as they get enough oral satisfaction from giving a bloke a BJ!!"

"*Catch* a black girl - you mean *pull*, don't you!" joked Kenzo.

"Yeah, man, I'm trying to speak the local jingo," laughed Nick.

CHAPTER TEN

"You are dead right man, some black girls hate cigarette smoke, but definitely not all!" said Kenzo.

"I've been told that some hate cigarette smoke as much as they hate giving a bloke a blow job!" said Nick.

"What are you talking about!" laughed Kenzo. "What have you been drinking today - *Kachasu*?" (*Kachasu* is Zimbabwean traditional Spirit.) "I have never heard you talk like this before…"

"I just fancy having a quickie with a black girl," grinned Nick. "I certainly have never tried *Kachasu* since I've been told it burns one's liver."

The three men started talking about black girls. Kenzo told them what he thought he knew about Zimbabwean women. He told them that he had read in a novel that white women can suck a man's cock till it ejaculates. They all laughed, since it sounded very funny to them.

"What about black girls?" Roy asked. "Don't they do that?"

"No way, Roy man," Kenzo said, "the mouth is for eating and praying to God. That is a no-no for black girls." Basically Kenzo was talking from his own experience; even though he had slept with a lot of prostitutes, none of them had done that for him; neither did he know that his wife was actually doing it to Roy, though Nick of course knew it.

"How about you, man?" Nick asked Kenzo. "Would you lick your wife's pussy?"

CHAPTER TEN

"No way," replied Kenzo, "I don't think she will even allow me to do it as this is outside our culture." Kenzo continued with emphasis: "Man, you don't do such things! You will get cancers in your mouth from down below; that thingy only tastes good for your Dipstick, the PENIS - it smells, it bleeds and it spits and it discharges!"

Nick continued in an attempt to provoke Roy: "I have never had a black girl - I would buy her a house if I find one that sucked my cock!" Nick said this staring at Roy and giving him a very dirty look.

"You will be very lucky to find a black girl that does that for you," said Kenzo. Poor Kenzo had never had his cock sucked; neither did he know that Tanaka was an expert in that department.

"So, if I want to find a black girl, where do I find her?" asked Nick.

"I'm told if you go to Harare's second street extension area during the night you will find yourself one." Kenzo was trying to let Nick know that only hookers in Harare's Avenues area were keen on white men and were likely to be submissive, since they were after money. "They will do anything for money, those girls, because the majority of them go to the streets *when everything else has failed for them*, as a way of rejecting poverty," said Kenzo.

The three men laughed as they thought, gosh, imagine driving all the way to Harare for an hour plus, just to have

CHAPTER TEN

one's cock sucked! "That would be absolute craziness," added Roy.

Kenzo went on to explain to his friends that he was told that these girls targeted tourists, and they would wear a bikini and a bra, then a white coat on top; they would flash open the coat as soon as a car flashed lights at them - then you would know they are available and on a mission.

"Thanks Kenzo, next time I'll know where to go when I'm in Harare," said Nick.

Kenzo warned Nick to be very careful when he visited these girls since the government was trying to keep them off the streets by arresting them, although the girls kept on going back. In actual fact, the Zimbabwean policemen used to go to the Avenues to plot a raid on the prostitutes. They would arrest them and gang rape these poor women. Some of these men from the ZRP (Zimbabwe Republic Police) would bribe the prostitutes for money or sexual favours, then allow them back on the streets. These prostitutes also used to fight amongst themselves if one operated within someone else's zone.

Nick kept on asking Kenzo, "There must be local ones who do that, man! Find me one around here please."

"I will ask around, mate, but can't promise," said Kenzo.

"How about your wife, mate?" Nick probed. "Does she know or have any single female friends that I might teach?" Nick was giving Roy dirty looks as he said this.

"I don't think this is a subject that's open for discussion in my house, or I will get a red card!" Kenzo said.

CHAPTER TEN

Roy hardly said a word during this conversation, since he thought Nick was being sarcastic. As the saying goes, the guilty are always afraid. Roy shrank from the conversation, making himself as inconspicuous as possible, as though he were not there. He kept sipping his Lion Lager, the local popular beer. The truth is he was fed up with the conversation, but could not go, leaving Kenzo alone with Nick. He started to resent Nick, and did not feel at all comfortable when he went to Kenzo's house.

The two farmers lived as if they were in competition with each other. However, Roy always won because he had money and his wife got on so well with Kenzo and Tanaka. Roy took the trouble to pay an annual membership for Kenzo and Tanaka at the local Country Club so that he could keep any eye on Tanaka, especially since Nick was prowling like a hungry dog in search of a black bitch on heat.

One day Roy warned Kenzo to watch out for Nick as he seemed to have gone crazy for black girls. "Not my wife, I doubt that very much," Kenzo said," black women do not cheat on their husbands!" He laughed and continued boastfully, "I also trust Tanaka so much - I don't think she would do anything like that." Kenzo seriously believed that Tanaka was very loyal, albeit daft to remain so, and therefore would never ever cheat on him - especially since she continued to live with him after 15 years of his cheating. Kenzo did not know that Roy and his wife were seeing each other any time they desired. This was KARMA, in so far as Tanaka had planned that once Kenzo found out what she had been up to, he would stop in his tracks and reflect on his behaviour. It was meant to be a learning curve, but it seemed to be dragging on and on before the time came for him to find out and learn from the experience.

They still lived together as husband and wife and still put up a show that they loved each other. Unfortunately, Roy's dad passed away in a London hospital, which meant that he had to go to England to sort out his father's funeral and to manage his estate. Surely, money always goes where there is more money, for Roy inherited even more money. One might say his money attracted more money.

Whilst Roy was in England Tanaka fell pregnant with her fourth child by her husband - a tool which some Zimbabwean men used to keep the wife at home. Local men were often heard shouting, "Give her a baby!" They encouraged each other in this way, for a wife who began to dress up nicely and walk about without a baby strapped on her back was considered a warning sign. "It's high time you fill her up!" they would say, meaning, "Make her pregnant!" They might add, "The kids will drain the life out of their mother, and the beauty and energy will be drained too!" and argue that "The more kids the woman has, the less active, less attractive and less energetic she will become". In their view a wife was for staying at home to perform her housewifery duties, making

CHAPTER TEN

babies and not dressing up and walking about the neighbourhood like a single woman; if a wife walked about for many years without a baby, it proved her husband had been firing blanks! "Generous and intelligent is a husband who gives his wife a child on a yearly basis, as he shall be rich, for his children shall bring him wealth because they shall work on his farm," they echoed again. Surely, these men must have thought that children were conceived in order to work for their parents and not to fulfil their own lives as adults.

Having children was seen as a symbol that the girl is taken since the majority of them did not know the benefits and meaning of a wedding ring; but a group of children revealed there must be a man at work who had fathered the lot. It was life that was lived on someone else's terms, mainly the husband as the head of the house. Sometimes the influence would come from the husband's mother (*mamazala*) who would suggest to the daughter in-law that the last child seemed to have grown old enough to have a younger sibling. Surely, some cultures still view women as second-class citizens; adding another baby is something the husband and wife should agree upon; while the wife may be married not only to her husband but in effect to his mother or siblings, the choice should really be between the two.

Kenzo's bosses became jealous of his friendship with white farmers. They promoted him to the post of Depot Manager and sent him to the rural areas so that he could spend more

CHAPTER TEN

time serving poor African farmers. No more white farmer friends for him, they thought and laughed as they rejoiced.

However, this did not stop Tanaka and Roy seeing each other when Roy returned from Britain. The plan of Kenzo's bosses seemed to be thwarted, because on his return Roy had even more money than before, since he had inherited money from his dad's estate. He therefore was able to set some money aside so that Tanaka could afford a nanny as they continued with their affair. When, on his return, he learned that Tanaka and her husband had been transferred to Karoi, it did not take him long to find the family and decide to buy a large farm in the Karoi area which he named 'The Garden of Eden Farm'. He could not resist the urge of seeing his lover; he just wanted to be near to Tanaka as much as possible so he could get a fix whenever he wanted. With money one can apparently do absolutely anything, though surely money chatters and brings speculation.

Since Roy had two large farms to deal with he started to neglect the other farm and concentrated on only one. He started growing tobacco that hit record sales in the 90's and he won several awards as the best tobacco grower in his region. He became very well-known and active in Zimbabwean politics, since he was into black people in a big way. He blended in very well with everyone, up to the top political officials and the CIOs. He had learned the way to survive and to live safely in Zimbabwe, since living in

CHAPTER TEN

Zimbabwe was about adopting the law of the jungle where the huge ones ate the little ones, the fierce ones ate the submissive, the wild ate the tame and the cruel ate the kind - you know what I mean.

When The Zimbabweans held celebrations such as the Independence Day celebrations on the 18th of April, Roy used to give the local Zanu PF people several whole cows, if not four or five, or six goats or lambs that could be slaughtered and cooked and served to the locals. Tanaka taught Roy all these tricks of the trade, never to go against or oppose the ruling party or he would be killed. He also brought bags of maize meal for the people to cook *sadza* as they celebrated. The locals were often heard saying "*Murungu akanaka uyu ari mushe siteriki!*" - meaning, "This white man is really good, generous and he is a very nice person!"

He wasn't daft. He knew what he wanted and had learnt how to survive in Zimbabwe.

CHAPTER ELEVEN

THE BEAUTIFUL ZIMBABWE AND HER SECRETS

ZIMBABWE is such a beautiful country with its capital city Harare, formerly known as Salisbury, also known as the Sunshine City. Harare is situated on the central plateau of the country. The city was named after Chief *Neharawa* who was nicknamed *HAARARI* ('the one who does not sleep') because none of his enemies managed to play tricks or attack his kraal day or night.

Life in Harare is fast and similar to that of London, with the exception of the underground and the freedom of the gays and human rights and the fact that the streets of LONDON ARE PAVED WITH GOLD which makes it a Gold Paved Paradise whilst the streets of HARARE ARE PAVED WITH POVERTY… This could also be proven wrong as Zimbabwe is a country that is very RICH in minerals. Recently, at the time of writing this book, diamonds were discovered in Zimbabwe. Someone told me before that GOLD is everywhere on this planet, and one only needs the correct vision to be able to see the GOLD. That is, if one is lucky to find the gold, of course, because I have been doing gold panning along the River Thames for the past 15 years but haven't found an ounce of GOLD yet!

The name Harare means 'they don't sleep'. Otherwise, Harare herself is the home of prostitution and they certainly don't sleep, roaming around the streets of the city looking for men, God help us! The Avenues area is a well-known area for the vagina-selling business. *This book will hopefully* annoy a few Zimbabweans if not all, but the truth should be told as it is so that souls can be saved.

HETEROSEXUALITY AND HOMOSEXUALITY

In London at places like Trafalgar Square and in Brighton, Sussex, the sight of two men kissing or two girls kissing is an everyday thing. In Harare this sort of behaviour is illegal. I am not saying there are no gays in Zimbabwe but it is something which is swept under the carpet and considered taboo, as in most of African, Asian and Muslim countries.

Life in Zimbabwe has always been a matter of the survival of the fittest, which is known as the law of the jungle. Those with money continue to make more and those without continue to get poorer. One good thing about Zimbabweans is that they try by all means to stick to their culture, remain positive and stay very happy even if the going gets tough.

Women still accept their cheating husbands and stick to their marriages for the sake of their children. It is high time that people stand up for their rights and women should accept that times are changing and start challenging their unfaithful husbands. During my research on cheating partners, 80% of women in developed countries said they would leave their cheating partner whilst 15% said they might give their partners another chance, but that if they did it again they would be ready to walk out, and 5% said they would go with the flow, meaning the situation would force them to make a decision whether to remain or take action. Amazingly the same survey was carried out in Zimbabwe where 70% of women who participated said they would give their cheating husband another chance, forget everything and move on for the sake of the children, while 10% said they would seek revenge and 5% said they would leave them; 15% did not know what to do but would either go with the flow or let nature take its course. I am positive that if the survey were to be done on men 90% of them would tick the box that says 'leave them' and 5% would forgive while the other 5% would go with the flow - because a high number of men would prefer a faithful partner whilst they would be cheating on their faithful partner or wife.

When HIV and AIDs was first spoken of in the mid-80's, the majority of people in Zimbabwe thought it was a joke as people were often heard saying that there was nothing like

CHAPTER ELEVEN

that. It was often joked as the **A**mericans' **I**dea of **D**iscouraging **s**ex, till the majority of people started dying. Sex seems to be the most readily available activity in Zimbabwe. Most married women in Zimbabwe have known only one penis in their lives, never done drugs, and yet found themselves HIV positive.

During the mid-80's, some people deliberately ignored the advice from health advisors to use condoms, saying, "*Kudyira siwiti mupepa aiwa?*" - meaning, "Why eat or suck a sweet that is wrapped in a plastic paper?" and preferred to have unprotected sex. AIDs, which has been labelled by some people as "the gay plague", killed and is still killing a lot of heterosexuals worldwide, even in Zimbabwe where gay relationships are illegal; so how is it passed on and by whom? According to the World Health Organisation, the Sub-Sahara is the most affected part of the world. To label AIDs as a gay disease is very wrong since the majority of heterosexuals are dying from it.

Zimbabwe's beauty made her a target as far as this deadly disease is concerned. The economy was very strong, the beauty of the Victoria Falls, Lake Kariba, the Inyangani mountains, safaris at the Hwange National Park, the sights of animals roaming free in their natural habitats, the real jungle, so different from seeing animals in a Zoo, brought in a lot of tourists. Zimbabwe attracts a lot of tourists which brought a lot of foreign currency into the country as well as AIDs.

CHAPTER ELEVEN

On the south east of Harare is the famous Inyanga Mountains which is Zimbabwe's largest mountain range. This is yet another popular tourist attraction, with famous hotels such as the Troutbec Inn. The Inyanga Mountain range is well known for its ability to draw people and make them disappear if they have foul mouths. Tourists and local people are expected to be quiet and not say anything bad on this mountain as they might vanish. Several people have been reported missing and have vanished on the mountain, especially children. These mysteries remain unsolved and untold. I personally, being a Zimbabwean, would not dare say anything bad about this mysterious mountain. The remains of the Iron Age have also been reported to have been seen on this mountain.

Some people in Zimbabwe are reported to have magic that can make a man's penis get stuck in a woman's vagina. If the woman is married this is known as *Runyoka* or *Rukahwo*. Some people believe that the man who has cheated with someone's wife will have a swollen tummy and swollen legs or will behave like a snake and will often find his skin starting to peel off like a snake, which will only heal after he admits to his actions and pays compensation to the wife's husband. Other people are believed to have magic that can cause any culprit to be struck by lightning or thunderbolts known as *mheni*. Most types of demons are believed to live amongst Zimbabweans and other nationalities.

CHAPTER ELEVEN

The mysteries of Zimbabwe herself are many. The Chinhoyi Caves which are located along the Harare to Kariba road are believed by the locals to be mysterious. Inside these caves there is a beautiful pool which is always blue. It is very lovely to see. According to stories and myths about this pool, divers who have explored the pool could not find where it ends; and some people have disappeared in the caves, hence the name CHIRORODZIVA. People also believe that if one should throw a stone into the opening of the caves it will never cross the pool to hit the other side of the caves. There is also a story of a long snake that took about twelve hours to cross the road around the Chinhoyi Caves area and it is assumed to have come from the caves.

In the Kariba dam which is the biggest lake in the country and part of the Zambezi River, there is believed to be a snake called *Nyaminyani*. When the bridge was built a lot of people died in the process; it is believed that all the disasters were caused by *Nyaminyami*, the River God, who was angry because he was separated from his wife when the bridge was erected. There are episodes when Kariba gets earth tremors which are like minor earthquakes that last for a few seconds yet cause no damage. The locals are often heard saying *Nyaminyami* is really angry today; for scientists this is just an earth tremor or a minor earthquake.

In the olden days it was believed that if travellers went under a tree, clasped their hands and asked their ancestors

CHAPTER ELEVEN

for food, the food would just appear under the tree. They would eat, then thank the ancestors and the plates would just disappear. Please note that there is no evidence to prove these happenings as they are merely hearsay though also documented in some of Zimbabwean history books.

While Zimbabwe was colonised by Britain, the people were also highly influenced by the Americans as a result of the film industry. 'Dynasty' was screened in Zimbabwe and every young woman just wanted to be like Joan Collins, Linda Evans, and so on. Sharon Stone and Sylvester Stallone also became significant role models for the young and middle-aged after the release of films like 'Basic Instinct' and 'The Specialist'. Some young men also wanted to play hard like James Bond who was played by Roger Moore.

The British TV comedy that was shown in Zimbabwe, 'Keeping up Appearances', had no scenes of a sexual nature at all, but the characters became endeared to many, characters such as our lovely Mrs Bucket and her husband Richard; it was a good, inoffensive comedy that every member of the family could watch together. Honestly, there was nothing to criticise in this comedy - it was just good fun to watch.

My question remains, since Zimbabwe is a gay-free country, where did this deadly and very contagious disease of AIDs come from? Some Zimbabweans claim that they would not change, but no one knows what one does behind closed doors. Then there is the likes of the late President Canaan Banana who was charged with sodomy. He was also known to be a church minister, who was reported to have abused his political position to do what he did - raping his bodyguards and team players from the football team which he coached. Therefore, if a top political official was labelled gay and charged with sodomy, what about Tom, Dick and Harry? They would surely do it and keep their status secret. The truth is, homosexuality is practised in Zimbabwe and in many countries in Africa and Asia by some political people and some ordinary people, yet it will be swept under the carpet - and these countries will continue to portray themselves as very strict on gays. It is practised in Zimbabwe, but the people concerned prefer to keep their sexual orientation private. Some even go to the extent of marrying women to cover up their homosexuality and so avoid any suspicions. Many men in Zimbabwe get involved in homosexual activities with foreigners to earn money in order to make a living due to poverty and desperation.

"*Hatidi ngochani mu Zimbabwe*" - "We don't want gay people in Zimbabwe"; "*Pasi nengochani*" - "Down with Gays!" declared President Mugabe; yet the former President Banana was accused of sexually molesting the innocent men of Zimbabwe. Some were being raped, some did it for money, some did it because they enjoyed it, whilst some were experimenting and some wanted to gain favours from the highly respected members of the party. The truth is homosexuality is practised in Zimbabwe yet swept under the carpet. Robert Mugabe disallows and will continue to disallow gays in Zimbabwe; but people will continue to practice homosexuality against his will as it has been done previously in the White House by the former president; which also the famous and wonderful CIOs failed to find out until the victims spoke out.

Young people of the modern age are bound to experiment on a lot of things due to exposure to the media such as the internet, television, magazines, as well as peer pressure, especially in schools. Some young men and women have sexual fantasies which are seen as taboo in their culture, such as having oral sex that goes beyond just kissing. A young Zimbabwean woman I know and will not name for legal reasons once rowed with her husband who had cheated on her in London. She told her husband: *"Enda unosvisvinwa mboro yako ikoko, kwete neni"* - *"Well, if you have found a new woman who is now sucking your cock, go back and get sucked by whoever that is, for I have to tell you I will never ever do that!"* That was something that took place in broad daylight in the streets of London. I am sure some cock suckers must have heard her; within a week, the husband met a black Zimbabwean woman who was willing to suck his cock and the street shouter was left miserable, sucking her pen and fingers instead of her husband's cock.

CHAPTER ELEVEN

Perhaps, having his cock sucked was the husband's fantasy due to the society he is now living in. Many Zimbabweans are now living in Diaspora where they are seeing a lot of things that they have never seen before. The same attitude will influence married men and women to cheat on their partners as they might enjoy the novelty of being sucked or licked elsewhere. Similarly, there might be some men who fancy sleeping with other men and women, known as bisexuals, and women who have sexual relations with other women, or lesbians. This is when most people's faith is sorely tested.

The majority of Zimbabweans who have left their country and are living abroad are now mixing with other cultures. Some go home on a regular basis and some don't go back at all, depending on individual circumstances. People are of course entitled to make their own choices; when Judgement Day comes, God will not destroy those who listen to and obey his commands, bearing in mind that he saved Lot and his family (though not his wife!). People who have heard the Word of God and have chosen to follow his commandments will be blessed; and those who have accepted his unconditional invitation to receive the gift of eternal life and who have surrendered their lives to him will be forgiven and live forever. Who are we to judge others? That is indeed God Almighty's prerogative.

The good reputation of Zimbabwe encouraged some

CHAPTER ELEVEN

directors to shoot their films in the country - films such as 'King Solomon's Mines' based on the book by the same title by H. Rider Haggard in the mid-80's. This then brought in a lot of tourists into the country. The tourism industry is very rich in Zimbabwe due to its natural wonders, heritage and safaris. The beautiful Victoria Falls is a must-visit for anyone who chooses to visit Zimbabwe.

At the same time Zimbabwe suffered a massive drought and maize was imported from neighbouring countries such as Zambia, Tanzania and Malawi to name a few. This was the first time for Zimbabweans to eat yellow *sadza* made from yellow maize meal which the Zimbabweans labelled *Kenya* which was a stock feed.

Prostitution became a major business for the girls who sold their bodies to the truck drivers, who were on transit from South Africa to other African counties such as Zambia, Malawi and Tanzania. These truck drivers made sure they slept with a different woman at every place they stayed the night, hence the Sub Sahara become the biggest hit area by HIV and Aids.

Since prostitution has always been on the high in Zimbabwe, people should be allowed to make their own choices. Pornographic material is not allowed in Zimbabwe, yet video and DVDs and magazines are available in some places. The truth is that since these materials are illegal and not available to adults, they have the appeal of forbidden fruits, which drives people into wanting to know the contents of these forbidden videos, CDs and magazines; as the saying goes, curiosity killed the cat. People of all ages become very curious and want to know why they are being forbidden to view or buy the pornographic material.

These materials have been smuggled and will continue to be smuggled into the countries where they are not allowed, such as some African countries and Muslim countries. Zimbabwe is a *damn* strict country yet Tanaka managed to smuggle sex videos and pornographic magazines from the neighbouring country South Africa during the 80's. Adam and Eve were allowed to eat every fruit that was in the Garden of Eden, but were forbidden to eat the fruit from the tree which stood in the middle of the garden, which was having sex. All the years they walked about naked they were without shame, but the day they ate the fruit they realised that they were naked and wanted to cover themselves up with leaves.

The availability of these sex tapes does not mean that they will be shown or sold to everyone including children. The adults will have a responsibility to protect their kids from these materials, in as much as they themselves would hate to be caught by a child whilst having sex. In Europe and the US and other developed counties, the population has the benefit of observing the law of the country regarding the ages that can purchase such material. Therefore, other countries should follow suit and make this material available to adults with the stipulation that it should not be sold to people of certain ages, e.g. those under 18.

In countries like the USA, UK and some other European countries people don't seem to be bothered at all about the contents of phonographic tapes since they are available to those who want to buy them and are made available to people who are above a certain age. Some married couples who have had time to watch these films together have confessed to having their sexual relationship enhanced. For those who are of a stricter disposition, like me, who prefer to stick to their cultural background and values, may well have ended up being sad and lonely. However, whatever one does in life, one has to condition and programme one's mind to use caution and moderation, as most things have a potential for addiction of some sort, so be warned.

The truth is, there are those who are bound to over-indulge in whatever they do, and will indulge in pornography or illicit sex behind the backs of those who practice caution and toe the line. The choice is yours, guys. The truth is about trying to help each other to come out and be as open as possible in relationships to avoid... well, you all know what. In most boring relationships the other party will end up having an extra marital affair regardless of which country he or she lives in. *Marriage is a "to have and hold"* thing, a bond that brings two people together in holy matrimony. I think growing old together and getting to know each other better, and being creative whilst exploring each other's fantasies, is the only remedy to a long and lasting relationship. This will help the majority of people to stay faithful and happy throughout their married lives.

The likes of Kenzo and Tanaka are spread all over the world. These are the people that end up cheating on each other, yet giving the wrong impression to people that they are happy together when indeed they are not.

WHY DO MEN AND WOMEN CHEAT?

Cheating or being unfaithful has been taking place for as long as humans have lived. The question is, what causes infidelity? Why do partners cheat on their wives or husbands?

Some people say partners cheat to fill the gap created by something that has not been happening in their relationships. If we go back to Chapters 4, 5 and 6, you will be reminded that Kenzo started sleeping around before even sleeping with his wife; and when Tanaka started living with him, he continued with his game, since he had become addicted.

In Zimbabwe it is a very common thing for some men to cheat on their wives as a way of status. They think that they are entitled to cheat as they have married their wives by paying the bride price, which means they think the wife should submit to everything and is expected to put up with their cheating.

Some people say they cheat because their relationship has turned a bit boring and lifeless. This can even apply to newlyweds. I have known people who have cheated on their partners on their wedding day.

Some people define cheating men and women as those with wandering eyes, as they feel that every woman or man was created to serve that purpose (i.e. copulation), except for family members.

There are some men and women who have never cheated in their lives. For example, in Zimbabwe the majority of women have died and are still dying innocently whilst they have known only one penis in their lives, never had a blood transfusion or used contaminated needles - yet found themselves with Aids; for the sake of the children and being honest wives, they put up with their cheating husbands, mostly because the husband is the breadwinner.

Cheating might apply to anyone, men or women, but when a woman cheats the man feels much pain, such as shame and a sense of a lack regarding his manhood. WHY? When a man cheats on his wife he expects her to take the event lightly and easily, and then be forgiven. However, if a woman cheats the man feels as if his heart has been pierced and ripped open. Some of them will choose to end their relationship with that woman and go about telling everyone they meet that she is a slapper. Why?

Life is not fair at all. All my life I have never heard of a male slapper; even after bedding a full double decker busload of women, including the standing passengers, the man will never be called a slapper or be regarded loose. Why??

Does this mean that man has the right to sleep around - and if so, who gives him the right?

If a woman cheats, men are often heard saying, "She disrespected me and she made me feel useless!" Honestly, that is the same way the woman feels when her partner cheats on her. She feels empty, useless, lifeless and incompetent.

It is also very easy to know if a man has cheated, whereas in the case of a woman it will be very, very difficult unless someone sees her or if she confesses. So men need to be very careful with this species called women. Handle them with the back of your hands and you will get the same in return.

Some God-fearing women will always stand by their men through thick and thin and this type of woman is hard to find these days. If you are lucky to have one of these women, please, my brother, take good care of her.

Cheating is a result of LUST. If we all renounce Lust and view every member of the opposite sex as a relative, no one would cheat. Learning to respect women is an art that is learned and learning to respect men is also an art that is learned.

Viewing every member of the opposite sex as a sex symbol is wrong. People need to condition their minds and learn the art of self-control.

CHAPTER TWELVE

SEX AND MONEY

MONEY AND SEX go hand in hand and they bond in most situations and are mostly the top subjects in most places, and have always been branded the root of most evil and wickedness; and are also known as the best means of leisure and happiness by some. Young guys might say, "I need a girl, haven't had one for a week" - especially when they have been drinking; the next thing you might hear is, "I need to go to work to get some money." People hardly talk about food or clothes, but SEX and MONEY are recurring topics. Some guys I know live off one-pound ready meals and make sure they have enough to pay an escort when they visit one, and they do this on a weekly basis! They may have no money in a bank account or insufficient money to buy healthy food, yet will have enough to pay a streetwalker. Addiction of any sort is a very difficult thing to overcome, honestly, God help us!

In Zimbabwe poverty has led a lot of young women to sleep with wealthy people whilst knowing their HIV status to be positive, saying "*Kusiri kufa ndekupi*" - meaning, "Whether I catch the virus or not, I will still die of hunger." Either way, they will die. So they have unprotected sex with infected persons knowingly in order to earn a living. The main reason for doing this is lack of proper education on how to earn money - but the majority think they can use their sexual appeal for money. These are the people who have been brought up thinking only men can be breadwinners and that women should be provided for by men. It is not bad to be in a relationship but not for the wrong reasons such as marrying for money or being trapped in a loveless relationship for money.

The strangest thing that I have discovered during my research is that most parents do not teach their children about money or sex. They don't feel very comfortable talking about these subjects; even in schools they touch only briefly on sex and never on money - WHY?? I think parents should teach their children about sex and money rather than allowing them to find out the facts the hard way.

Male and female prostitution, regardless of which country it is in, has always been seen as a dangerous but lucrative business. During my research I discovered that in some countries escorts are highly paid and do not have to do a 9 to 5 job. They only work when they want to work. They do not pay tax at all. This clearly shows that this world is not fair in many ways. Doctors and nurses who save people's lives earn far less than the top class hookers, who do not even pay taxes. I am not against hookers at all, as it takes two to tango, and

CHAPTER TWELVE

it is also their chosen lifestyle, and that's who they want to be and what they want to do. But there is an undeniable dark side to this lifestyle.

People who engage in girl trafficking, and those who operate brothels, become millionaires quickly until they are found out, as we often hear on the news. Businesses that sell sex lingerie and sex toys, magazines and videos hardly get affected by the recession. This shows that the Vagina is a powerful asset for a lady, though it needs regular maintenance and to be used as the other party expects... Men might say "the thingy smells; the thingy bleeds and the thingy discharges" - surely, it needs high maintenance and one man should be enough for one thingy, end of story, not the whole territory. God forbid!

I am sure that if most governments legalise prostitution and start taxing male and female prostitutes, the world will come out of the recession without any struggle. It is all about MONEY, MONEY and SEX. For example, if someone who is famous is caught by the paparazzi guys coming out of a prostitute's house, the newspapers will sell billions if not zillions of copies, because of that particular story. Likewise, the prostitute will have been paid a fortune to shut up. WHY?

My question is, what is it that these so called *mahure*, *pfambi* - hookers, streetwalkers or escorts - do that married woman cannot do? Some typical Zimbabwean women might speak with their mouths and hands, like a Nigerian woman, trying to emphasise the point that they will never do what prostitutes do, since they are married woman - acts *such as performing oral sex on their husbands*.

Since Tanaka wanted to get rich quickly, she had a dream in which she launched her Sex School business. This school was launched to enable people who believe in certain traditional values to bring their partners and learn from the sex experts what to do to turn a partner on, how to perform oral sex and how to make sure the other partner has climaxed and reached orgasm. The charges were very high, yet people afforded to come to the sex school either as a couple or alone. This is a place where modern couples and those who have old-fashioned values should go to learn new skills that could save their marriages. Everything is private and confidential.

In this modern world we often hear about some celebrities who have it all - money: you know what I mean, have regular Botox injections, lip fillers, boob jobs, plastic surgery, designer vaginas, buy expensive clothes, wear nice perfume and jewellery; yet they struggle to keep their partners happy. Some even afford to have designer vaginas but still don't know how to use them and struggle to keep their man happy. WHY?? The likes of Kettle Parish aka River Jayden has all the money imaginable, big melons, large lips, just to name a few of her assets, yet I pity her for she can't keep a man: the papers have repeatedly mentioned her failed marriages as well as the failed relationship with her toy boy.

CHAPTER TWELVE

Some marry every year and divorce the next - *hoo la la!* Honestly, the saying 'we can't have everything in life' is true. It is important to know what the other partner likes, and then to go to the extra lengths and make all the effort to keep your loved one happy. In my own experience, I discovered that lack of communication and lack of openness of sexual desires and fantasies lies at the root of all problems. Even though every girl has a vagina, the way these vaginas are shaped is different. Similarly, every man has a dick but they are shaped, formed and sized differently. Here again at Tanaka's School of Sex every size of penis in dildo form is available, as well as rubber vaginas and boobs for demonstration.

In her dream, Tanaka designed her business in such a way that a partner would come and explain to Tanaka exactly how they would like to be touched or treated or stroked. Tanaka will then invite the other partner to attend and ask him or her how they think they are doing and make a suggestion on what to try, based on what the other partner has said.

The other partner will also be given the opportunity to say exactly how he or she expects their partner to perform, whatever floats the boat for them. This is specifically for helping couples who experience difficulties in communicating about their sex life. Once all parties know what to do they will be in a position to perform the sex act according to their requests, then report back to Tanaka's

CHAPTER TWELVE

school of sex to explain their experiences. The idea for Tanaka's dream business is to enhance sex lives and improve relationships.

Most men agree with me that looks alone are not very important but mutual satisfaction *is* more important. Some women spend a lot of money on make-up, fake eyelashes, fake nails, fake bums and perfumes to smell nice, and fake tans, and on cosmetic surgery and boob jobs - yet in bed they are totally useless. The truth is, if a woman is not adventurous in bed she is bound to be left for an ugly yet adventurous girl who charges £1,000.00 or more per night! I am sure that Tanaka's School of Sex is the only place to go and get the necessary education. I would rather go than lose someone I really love and care about.

Here's a funny thing, guys - I have never seen a vagina that has lipstick on it, yet it has lips, WHY?? And you know what? The thingy's lips are always sad by being squashed by G-STRINGS, the most uncomfortable piece of apparel I have ever known to be worn by women.

I am sure that sex is not a subject that is open for discussion for many people. SEX is not something that we can learn, from our parents for instance - but maybe from friends and distant relatives, DVDs and books. Therefore, the majority would agree with me that young men like Kenzo often experimented with older women who were likely to charge for their services, and as a result were in high risk of catching all types of sexually transmitted diseases under the sun, moon and stars.

Since Tanaka was really good using her hands, lips, body and vagina, she dreamt about Roy and herself being the main characters who often demonstrated to their clients how to give good blow jobs and how to make the woman climb Mount Kilimanjaro with just the tongue (aka *mini and natural rabbit*), which is priceless and needs no batteries. Men, you have to teach your tongue to vibrate more than a battery-changed vibrator, as this is natural and original.

During the demonstration Tanaka would see couples holding hands and starting to give each other passionate kisses and leaving the room to go and do it at their house or in their cars. Tanaka's business blossomed to the extent that she became a multi-zillionaire within a year! It was a really good dream which later turned into reality.

Some people often travel as far as Amsterdam for sex *hooo-la-la* - why? Because the male and female hookers display themselves behind glass windows and in bars? Certainly they are there for a purpose. Some people save up money just to go to Amsterdam for drugs and sex. This is a place where any kind of sexual activity can be seen. It is all to do with SEX, drugs and money! It is just like Sodom and Gomorrah! God helps us!! The world we live in is corrupted by Information and Technology. Indeed, there is too much information for our small brains to take in.

CHAPTER THIRTEEN

THE STALKER AND THE MURDERER

AS TIME WENT BY, Tanaka enjoyed life to the full, except for the time she used to receive anonymous calls at night - when a male voice would say, "I know what you did at the Orange Grove Motel" - then hang up. Sometimes the voice on the phone would say, "I know what you did at the Orange Grove Motel with Roy; if you do the same for me I will buy you three bungalows" - and hang up. The voice haunted her for a long time, causing her to become emotionally drained until she decided to move from the company house to a private house in Karoi's low density suburbs. She never told Kenzo but said she fancied a change of location; however, she confided in her lover Roy. Roy warned Tanaka to be very careful when she went out and never to trust anyone. When she moved from the company house the telephone calls ceased as the perpetrator of the calls did not have her new number - and eventually the spectre of this dark time faded.

CHAPTER THIRTEEN

Tanaka did not have the slightest clue as to who her stalker was, but Roy had guessed and suspected Nick to be the culprit. Roy feared for Tanaka's life and he thought of employing a group of black youths to keep an eye on Tanaka whilst Kenzo was away working in the rural area. Roy went to meet Mujibha and his gang at a local motel. He bought them the famous Castle and Lion Lagers to drink. This was a complete luxury for Mujibha and his friend, to be able to drink in a pub from a bottle as opposed to a plastic mug shared between the two men whereby they had to take turns to drink, the one passing the mug to the other after each mouthful!

As the guys sipped their drinks Roy whispered to Mujibha, "I need your help, guys."

"What sort of help do you want sir?" Mujibha asked.

"I have one particular enemy I want out of my way, or see him disappear for good; I think you might be the guys to help me," Roy said in a barely audible voice. For the young youths of Zimbabwe this was a very good job for them, especially given the opportunity to be able to speak to a *murungu* (a white man). Those days brushing shoulders with a *murungu* gave people a noteworthy status, worth much respect.

"Since you don't do politics, I thought you might not have any enemies," whispered Mujibha.

"I have one particular enemy; he seems to have let his cattle or about to let his cattle into my field of sweet corn," said Roy. "We need to exterminate and obliterate him and we

CHAPTER THIRTEEN

shall not put our feet up till we are triumphant," added Roy. "I shall rest when his body has been eaten and digested by the vultures and his bones grated to make fine bone china mugs."

"That's not a problem, man," grinned Mujibha. "We can get the job done before sunset; what are you offering as settlement for the deal, or what is the compensation for the damage?" the young man queried.

"Name your price, because the sky is the limit for me when it comes to brass; get the job done and you will be laughing all the way to the bank; and the bank manager will offer to meet you personally in a private room for all your services and never over the counter - that's the kind of respect you will have." Roy looked pleased with his rhetoric.

"How about a cool dwelling, a nice homestead, three bedrooms maybe or four if the job is exceptionally well done, and a few thousand bucks for the lads?" suggested Mujibha.

"Okay, deal," said Roy, shaking hands with Mujibha.

"Right, now name the target," said Mujibha.

"I want you to watch over my best friend's wife - Tanaka is her name; her husband Kenzo gives me very good grades for my grain, he is a good manager; so I am doing him a favour, so not a word to anyone." Roy tapped the side of his nose.

"Deal," said Mujibha.

The boys watched Tanaka very closely and one of these boys asked for a job from Tanaka as a gardener and a private eye. Not surprisingly this guy was called Mujibha.

CHAPTER THIRTEEN

Mujibha enjoyed trips to Chinhoyi and Harare for free with Tanaka. He felt very honoured as he had never been to Harare before. When Tanaka went into the shops, he would look after the car, even paying for the parking. He also directed Tanaka when she had to do parallel parking in the city; all this careful attention spoiled Tanaka to the extent that she forgot to use the mirrors and relied heavily on the street kids and Mujibha's directions when parking.

One day when Tanaka made her trip to Chinhoyi, she stopped at a service station at Lion's Den to refill and to say hello to some of her friends. This is when Mujibha spotted Nick following Tanaka but pretending to be reading his *Zimbabwean Herald*. He did not tell Tanaka and just watched from a distance.

When Tanaka walked out of the supermarket, Nick pulled his white sun hat over his eyes so that Tanaka would not recognise him. She went straight into her BMW (which the young boys called '**B**lack **M**an's **W**illy or **B**e **M**y **W**ife) and drove to Chinhoyi. Nick quickly jumped into his black Land Rover and followed Tanaka. As Tanaka went into her favourite boutique she left Mujibha looking after the car. Mujibha saw a large black Land Rover Discovery pulling up next to Tanaka's car.

He recognized Nick straightaway but didn't know who he was.

"You got a nice *mota mufana*," Nick said to Mujibha. (Meaning, "You got a nice car, young man.")

CHAPTER THIRTEEN

"No, it's not mine sir," replied Mujibha with his lips trembling with fear.

"Is it your dad's?" queried Nick.

Tanaka had forgotten her cheque book in the car, so she came out of the shop and shouted, "Mujibha, bring my cheque book please!"

Mujibha grabbed the cheque book, crossed the road safely and handed the cheque book to Tanaka. "Here you are mam," he said.

"Thank you, I shan't be long since I have already tried on the clothes I need. Here, take this and get yourself something to eat whilst you wait." Tanaka handed a red ten-dollar note to Mujibha so that he could buy himself a drink and a couple of buns whilst he waited.

"*Maita henyu*" ("Thank you"), said Mujibha, clasping his hands as he accepted and pocketed his tenner.

He walked back to the car and he noticed that the *murungu* (white man) in the Land Rover was still there waiting for him to return and continue the conversation from where they had left off.

"Beautiful wife you got, *mufana* (young man)," said Nick.

"No, she is not my wife sir, she is my boss's wife. I work in her garden."

"Married is she?" asked Nick.

"Yes sir, she is married - why do you ask?" queried Mujibha with his trembling lips. "She is married to a black guy but the couple have a lot of white friends, sir," he added.

CHAPTER THIRTEEN

"Oh I see, no big deal, it's just that the girl is very attractive - I thought she might be single," said Nick "One of their friends is Roy Pender-Hurst, isn't he?" he added.

Mujibha's heart started pounding with fear and his lips trembled quite visibly.

"I think so, but I am not sure sir," said Mujibha.

"Where are they living now?" Nick queried.

"Somewhere in the Tengwe area sir, I am not sure of the address," lied Mujibha.

When Nick saw Tanaka coming, he drove away without even saying goodbye to Mujibha. Luckily, Mujibha did not give away much information. He had scribbled down Nick's car registration number at Lion's Den service station when he saw him acting suspiciously. They drove back home and Mujibha rushed to find Roy who was drinking at a local club. He quickly spotted Roy and walked up to him.

"Can I have a quick word with you please sir?" said Mujibha to Roy. "I have seen some oil underneath your car; it looks like oil is leaking," he added. Mujibha's idea was just to get Roy to come out so he could tell him about his findings.

Pointing under the car to mislead people, Mujibha quickly passed on Nick's car's registration to Roy who had sent him on a mission. Immediately after Mujibha's description of the suspicious man and his Land Rover Discovery with its black-tinted windows, Roy knew his suspicions were right and that he had confirmed the identity of the stalker.

CHAPTER THIRTEEN

"Okay, jump in and let's go and talk about this in more detail at a private location," said Roy. They drove for a few miles and stopped in a secluded area. They jumped out of the car and started plotting their game.

"I knew it was Nick, fucking hell!" he shouted. "I will bloody kill him and I shall throttle him; his dead body shall become food for hungry vultures," he declared.

"Why do you want to kill and throttle him?" asked a small squeaky voice in his head.

"For the VAGINA," replied another squeaky voice in his head.

"Go ahead, do it or pay someone to do it, then it won't be your fault," said the other horrible squeaky voice again.

"Come on, pay someone and play safe and smart," the horrible squeaky voice added.

On hearing the last sentence from his vindictive conscience Roy smiled. He took out a bundle of Zimbabwean dollars and handed it over to Mujibha in appreciation for what he had found out. He told him to stay alert all the time and not to get drunk. Roy gave Mujibha a small black pistol and one bullet. "He is the culprit and he has to go to the world of no return. Make sure you get your aim correct, and don't miss because if you do, he will get you and you will become a dead man; if that happens or if he catches you, I will deny responsibility and any involvement. Deal?" said Roy.

"Sure, it's a deal," said Mujibha as they shook hands on

the agreement, his left hand pocketing the bundle of notes in his left pocket. "Consider the job done, sir," concluded the smiling Mujibha.

"Now, go and get him, he is our man!" commanded Roy. "Beef him up for the vultures; don't leave him kissing the dust - let him face the sky so the greenflies can find their way into his mouth and nostrils so that they can quickly lay maggots on him and let him became manure!"

"Sure, sir, consider it done," replied Mujibha.

Honestly, a VAGINA is a powerful female asset that can make men commit murder, as someone said.

Roy asked Mujibha to keep the gun safely and he would pay him loads of money when he used the bullet on the right target. He told him to let him know when he had done the deed and never to tell anyone that he had a gun. Mujibha did as he was told and kept the gun safely and continued his job as Tanaka's gardener, bodyguard and private eye. They drove back to the compound and Mujibha went home to hide his bundle of cash. Roy went back to try and convince his friends that there was indeed something wrong with his car, and that he had taken it to the garage to have it looked at.

When Tanaka returned home from Chinhoyi she and Mujibha did not notice Nick following them as he had gone to a friend's to borrow a small car which he used to drive behind Tanaka's car. He followed her till she reached her house and Nick drove past them and pretended not to look at them.

CHAPTER THIRTEEN

When Nick discovered Tanaka's address he started writing to her, threatening to tell Kenzo about her affair with Roy. He demanded that he wanted a steamy session at the same place that she used to go with Roy. Tanaka feared for her life and told Roy about it.

It was a lovely Friday evening the following day; most farmers where gathered at the local Country Club, drinking, catching up on the latest gossip, playing, snooker, table-tennis, pool, darts, and those who liked lively loud music were in the disco. The Country Club was humming with people.

Rumour started to circulate that Nick had been reported missing by his wife.

"Maybe Anthea hit him on the head with a saucepan and dragged his body into the septic tank so that she could enjoy the fool's money whilst she is still young!" joked one of the farmers.

"I will not be surprised if I heard that he was killed in the African *Shabeen*[4] in Harare, as he had grown fond or had developed a strong urge of having a leg over with black girls!"

"Surely not!" exclaimed another farmer.

"Oh yes, he was often heard saying he would buy her a bungalow if she went down on him," said another farmer.

"You must be kidding!" said another farmer.

"True, very true, he had developed a very bad crush on a certain married black girl, but nobody knows which one," volunteered another farmer.

CHAPTER THIRTEEN

"That explains why he became friends with Kenzo, that black guy, a manager for the Grain Marketing Board; he has a very pretty wife," said another.

"You are right!" another agreed. "There was a time he slept in the stocks after a terrible fight with someone, after repeatedly singing along to Clarence Carter's 'I got Caught' - to the extent that someone got bored and challenged him."

As they were talking the waiter came to collect the empty glasses and bottles and he overheard the conversation. "Who is the guy you are talking about, if you don't mind me asking?" asked the waiter.

"Oh, we mean Nick, the one who has been reported missing," said one farmer.

"I just heard one of the guys sitting on the opposite table, that one in the white shirt" - he pointed at Roy - "saying that Nick's body has been found dead in his own tobacco field. He said he died from a gun-shot!" Having delivered this astonishing news, he walked away.

"Oh my God!" the first farmer exclaimed. "Guys, this isn't a joke, it's a WHUDUNNIT! So I wonder who did it?!"

"Well, Nick had a few enemies and it may be Mugabe's land grabbers," suggested another farmer.

A farmer shook his head. "I don't think it was Mugabe's land grabbers, because by now they would have helped themselves to all the goodies on the farm; don't forget that Nick had plenty-plus enemies - why shouldn't it be one of them?"

CHAPTER THIRTEEN

Nick was certainly killed under suspicious circumstances, and in his own tobacco field. The bullet had been aimed straight for the heart - and there Nick's body lay in a pool of blood, apparently shot in cold blood.

There was no evidence and no clues as to the identity of the killer at the crime scene, since the killer had apparently worn gumboots like anyone else who worked on the farm. Within no time the vultures had started helping themselves to Nick's body.

Since Nick was known for violence and disruptive behaviour, his wife thought he might have been the victim of an attack as a result of causing a fight, or for causing disorder in his local pub and delayed calling the police. The police checked with all the police stations and none of them had made an arrest or given a caution to Nick. The following day in the afternoon one of the farm security guards spotted Nick's Land Rover and went straight to report his findings to Nick's wife. The wife called the police who then made a search on the farm with helicopters and dogs and men on foot, some in trucks. Nick's body was found that day with some parts missing. Wild animals had helped themselves already. The sun was piping hot; it was not good for a corpse to be left exposed, and maggots, flies, ants, you name it, were already feasting on Nick's body. The news was passed to the farmers around the area. All the farmers where really upset as their dear friend had died. Even if he was violent, he didn't deserve to die that way, the local farmers lamented.

CHAPTER THIRTEEN

Roy played an active role in the inquest since he was chairman of the farmers' association. A post mortem was carried out and confirmed that Nick was shot at very close range with a silencer and that he had died instantly as the bullet went through the most vital organ, the heart. Funeral arrangements were delayed for a while, pending investigations, but nothing seemed to throw any further light on his death and the body was handed over to the funeral directors that were chosen by the family.

Nick was buried in the Chinhoyi cemetery. After the funeral a lot of suspects were called in including the deceased's wife. They were questioned and interrogated. No clues were found as Nick's body was found holding the murder weapon; no other fingerprints except his were on the gun.

Murder was then ruled out and no foul play was suspected. The irrigation pipe had watered most of the footprints so no clues were left.

As time went by rumours started circulating about Mujibha in his neighbourhood about how his life had changed suddenly from rugs to riches. Most people wondered what business venture he had gone into; some thought he might be selling hard drugs and some thought that perhaps he had discovered a Gold or Silver mine, whilst others thought he might have stumbled on a *marijuana* field or found Diamonds. He started dressing up nicely, living in a three bedroomed bungalow.

"He is a true flamboyant, isn't he?" asked one of the local girls.

"Be careful, don't go out with him, I think he has got Aids," warned one of the girls in an African pub known as *Bawa*.

"I have been told that he sleeps with white men - foreign men - for money," laughed another. "His asshole is a gold mine, that's why he is the richest black guy in our area!"

"What!!" exclaimed the former girl, "you mean he is a male hooker or a male streetwalker?"

"Yes," replied the other girl.

"Oh my God!" her friend exclaimed. "He is a poof; look at the way he walks, just like a lady with loads of money!"

"The only thing that's missing is a handbag," laughed the other girl.

The change in Mujibha's appearance sent all the gossipers' tongues wagging. They never stopped - it was wag-wag-wag every time they saw him! No one's tongue wagged in murder accusations, but it was all about homosexuality, since Mujibha had started to dress up nicely.

"Then we need to make sure that he is out of this area because he is taking our customers," said another girl, who was a streetwalker.

"No, darling, they are not *our* customers, because these men who have sex with men do not like women at all," explained the other girl.

"He disgusts me!" said the other, "He should be killed!"

"How can one prove that he is sleeping with men? It's

difficult, and I don't think he is stupid - he knows what he is doing, and whatever he is doing has landed him in money, big money, of course," concluded the other girl.

"I have been told that some of them are bi-sexual though," said another girl.

"Bi-sexual! What does that mean? Does it mean he has both a VAGINA and a PENIS?" asked the second girl.

"I am not quite sure but I think he has one of each bits," laughed another.

"Wow!" her friend exclaimed. "So that means he can be a boy or a girl?"

"Then he must be disabled," said the first girl.

They remained without a clue as such terms as bi-sexual were never heard of in the then Zimbabwe; however, people were partially aware that GAYS existed though rarely spoken about.

Mujibha got his reward of a three-bedroomed bungalow which was bought for him by Roy, and an undisclosed amount of money for a job well done. All the people just wondered where Mujibha got the money from and some even thought that he was sleeping with *varungu* (gay white men) for money. Locals were often heard calling Mujibha names such as *ingochani iyi* (meaning "This one is gay"). The locals believed he was gay because they wondered how he could afford money to buy such an expensive house when he did not have a job or business. No one ever suspected that Mujibha was a cold blooded killer.

CHAPTER THIRTEEN

Roy confided in Tanaka what he had done. Tanaka was not bothered as she knew that her stalker was no more, but had to ask Roy a few questions to see if he was in the clear. She wanted to know how much Mujibha was paid.

"How much did his action and silence cost you?" queried Tanaka.

"I bought him a bungalow and a couple of grand, but the bungalow remains in my name as I hold the title deeds," replied Roy. "Mujibha is just happy showing off to his friends that he is now living in the white neighbourhood."

"Don't you think he might come back for more helpings later on?" asked Tanaka.

"How?" queried Roy.

"In the form of emotional or financial blackmail," added Tanaka.

"Well, I will deny responsibility and he knows he will be landing himself into trouble as I will threaten him that he was the actual murderer; moreover, the lad is not smart," Roy grinned.

"Just keep close to Mujibha and know what he is up to all the time," advised Tanaka.

"I will keep him within arms-length," added Roy.

"Oh, people will end up thinking you are gay," joked Tanaka.

"It's better to be seen as a pillow biter than a murderer," laughed Roy.

CHAPTER THIRTEEN

All the people just thought that Nick's death was politically motivated, yet in truth it was a result of *murungu* versus *murungu* (white man versus white man), where killing someone was for the Vagina... the badly packed kebab with lips without lipstick on. What a shame! Nick's killer was never found. Indeed, it has always been easy to kill in Zimbabwe and get away with murder.

CHAPTER FOURTEEN

TANAKA'S SMUGGLING ADVENTURES

MY DESIRE to make it big in life continued. I became very creative and worked tirelessly. I wished I lived a life like Roy's and other wealthy white farmers. Unfortunately, when my grandparents died they left me nothing except for the round clay pots (*Hari* or *chirongo*). I wished my parents knew about life insurance and investments, for they, too, left me nothing except for the family house which is still in *baba*'s name and my brother Petros claims it's his since he is the only boy in the family. In life we can never choose our families but our friends. I had to put up with my non-supportive family who depended on me for everything. If someone died in the family, I had to take the full responsibility of funding the funeral and then inherit their children, pay their school fees and all that a child needed to grow up.

I started to befriend airhostesses who worked for Air Zimbabwe so that I could travel abroad with them. However, I needed to raise enough money to do this. I started crocheting some nice summer tops, tablecloths and chair backs which I sold in South Africa. The business blossomed and I realised that I needed help with the crocheting. I organised a group of rural women who did the crocheting for me. I filled loads and loads of suitcases.

I then realised that I had loads of stuff and needed help to sell them. I recruited four girls from Harare who sold the products to South African locals and tourists. Two girls were based in Cape Town and two in Port Elizabeth. I then stopped selling and my job was to travel between South Africa and Zimbabwe to deliver the goods and to collect thousands of South African Rands.

I still remember the time when Zimbabwean teachers were earning about $3,000.00 per month, when I was earning $15,000.00 to $20,000.00. Since Kenzo and I were separated, I moved to Harare. I didn't want to live in my big house which Roy had bought for me to avoid conflict of interests and suspicions; therefore I rented a medium sized three bed-roomed bungalow. Kenzo refused to divorce me. I ordered a local estate agency called Fadzi and Corry to let and manage my property which Roy bought for me on my behalf.

Kenzo said to me, "Tanaka, if you are thinking that I will divorce you, forget it; come hell or thunder, I will not do it!"

He took everything that we had bought together, including my knickers and clothes.

This was just great, I thought! Men, ha! They think

CHAPTER FOURTEEN

material things can bring you together when love has actually ended. No, I wanted to show Kenzo that I could work and replace everything, most likely with much better things.

I was now back to basics with no knickers and no clothes. Once again Every Thing Else Had Failed, but I said NO TO POVERTY! It was not a joke or a laughing matter. Since I had money in my savings account it did not take me long to replace everything. I continued with my business, though having to replace everything I had lost was a painful experience.

One beautiful summer's day the weather was just fine; the sun was excreting Vitamin D through its rays at the rate of 29 degree Celsius in Lusaka, Zambia; it was absolutely roasting! My sister and I took a taxi from Kamwala market where we had bought bales and bales of used clothes for resale in Zimbabwe, since it was booming business then. We had help from a group of youths to load the bales of clothes onto a truck and we headed for a place called *Kwa Gula's* where cross-border trucks congregated, in search of a truck to smuggle the goods into Zimbabwe for us. Some of my colleagues were green with envy as they could not afford as many bales as I bought, let alone the amount of money to pay the drivers to smuggle the stuff; which means they had to go home the long way via *Kanyemba* on canoe boats over the Zambezi River, which was also very dangerous.

As the sun continued to excrete hot rays, we had to be

very careful what we wore. We wore these summery sandals and nice see-through blouses to suit the weather. It's true that money talks, as the saying goes, because it was as easy as ABC for me to find a driver or drivers who were willing to smuggle the bales of used clothes for me. I found one particular driver who was not Zambian; he sounded South African or Namibian. I wanted to avoid Zambian drivers as they were becoming suspects on the Zimbabwean border side. The Zambians were becoming popular for corruption and well known for smuggling while South Africans were considered okay and honest.

When I had agreed the deal with the driver he wanted to see proof of payment before loading the goods. I looked around for my handbag but it was nowhere to be found. I wondered where on earth I might have left it, since it contained all the cash as well as my passport. I sat down and started crying buckets! My cousin Seria realised that crying would not help at all and she said, "Sis, let's have a cold drink and think about what to do, as crying will not help." She bought two bottles of half frozen Fanta and we drank it very quickly, since we were thirsty. As we drank I thought about how I might have lost the handbag, as it is very unusual for a lady to lose a handbag. I recalled that I had paid the taxi driver but from there I hadn't bought anything else, which meant my handbag must still be in the taxi.

We went straight to the place where the taxis parked and

CHAPTER FOURTEEN

luckily enough the taxi which we had used was still there and clearly marked, *Lusaka Cars taxi 800*. We saw the driver and heard him bragging that he had stumbled on a lot of cash. We headed straight for the taxi, sat in like customers and *there* my bag was, right on the pedals of the taxi! I grabbed my bag and stood outside the taxi, checking to see if all the contents were in the bag. In fact, the cash was one grand down. The driver saw us and came running and said, "I am sorry, I was just about to come and find you, but I was chatting to my friends." We did not want to show him that we had heard him bragging that he had stumbled on a lot of cash, so thanked him and left. I just thought, gosh, that was too close!

We went back to continue to close our deal with the truck driver, showed him the cash and he took care of our stuff. He gave us his contact details in South Africa as well as in Zimbabwe, and the name of the company he worked for. He then loaded our bales and lifted the copper bars he was transporting, making sure our bales were completely concealed. At around 5 p.m. the truck driver came to fetch us as we stood outside the Truck Inn watching some female belly dancers who danced outside the Inn so they could let the truck drivers know they were available on a take-away basis! We responded to his call and off we went to start our journey home.

As we drove home just after *Siyavonga* in Zambia, the driver insisted that he was tired and needed to sleep as it was very risky for him to carry on, for he was beginning to fall asleep at the wheel. It was in the middle of nowhere, no villages that could be seen anywhere. It was by a lay-by. As it was very hot my cousin and I decided to sleep out of the lorry to get some fresh air. We felt comfortable sleeping in the open as we were told that Zambia did not have any wild or dangerous animals along the Lusaka to Chirundu road.

Everything was dead quiet - not even birds were heard tweeting. Since we were tired it did not take us long to fall asleep. As we slept the moon started to peep out, giving us a bit of light. As we lay half dead, we heard footsteps of a group of either animals or human-beings. We looked into the distance and with the help of the moonlight we saw a group of tribesmen heading towards us. My cousin and I did not know what to do as we froze with fear. We held each other tightly and stuffed all our cash and passports into our knickers though we left a few dollars in our handbags.

"Sis, we are finished, I think we are going to die!" whispered my cousin.

"Stop it - and no, we are not going to die," I reassured my cousin. "Have faith and stop drawing negative spirits, we will survive!" The group of barely visible strangers kept on advancing towards us. "Whoever they are, let them not harm us," I prayed. "Father God, I know that our lives belong to you - if this is the way you have chosen for us to come to you, let your wish be fulfilled, but we truly wish and beg you for your protection. I have four children who love me dearly and whom I love too. You gave me these children and they need their mum and love her dearly. My cousin has two boys who mean the world to her; please, Father God, help us please to get through this. Amen."

As we were saying this prayer we hurried to the other side and climbed into the truck. We had no mobile phones and had absolutely nothing to protect ourselves with. At first we could not do anything due to fear. When fear strikes it can freeze both your mind and body. We could not move for a few minutes due to fear. When we had conquered the fear, we eventually managed to jump into the truck and started to take action: we locked the truck and woke the driver up. The moon was now high up and we could see a bit clearer that the strangers were fierce, masked men who wore animal heads or pretty white women's faces, dragons or baboon heads, carrying spears, machetes, bows and arrows and axes. I think they were performing some ritual and thought maybe we were spying on them.

The driver was rather confused as he had woken up from a deep sleep, and being South African, his understanding of English was not very good as he had been brought up speaking Zulu and Afrikaans.

The strangers kept on coming towards the truck. "Start the truck and drive!" I shouted to the driver. He thought I was calling him when he heard the word drive.

CHAPTER FOURTEEN

"*Yebo* sis," he replied.

I pointed to the window and shouted, "*Hona!*" in my language, meaning, "Look!" This made sense as in his language look is *bona*, so it sounded alike and he responded. Since he was half asleep he struggled to remember where the keys were.

By the time he had found the keys the suspicious strangers had surrounded the truck. Some had climbed on the back in search of food and goods for re-sale. The driver could not understand their foreign language and neither could any of us. "*Tifuna ndalama*" (we want money) or you are all dead!" shouted one of them. "No Zambian Kwacha, we want Dollars, Rands, Pulas and Pounds, then you can go!" they shouted.

We did not want to appear as smugglers, as smugglers were always thought to have loads of money everywhere. My cousin quickly jumped onto the driver's lap and said, "This is my boyfriend and this is my sis. We are not on business but had come to visit your country and to see how beautiful it is; we've only got a few dollars on us!"

My cousin pinched the driver and said, "Talk to them, you are the man!" They were about four men who wore artificial legs that made them look very tall as they peeped through the windows. We gathered a few dollars and gave them to the leader. One of them was on long artificial legs, demanding to inspect the insides our handbags and we showed him - and he was convinced we did not have any money on us. The ones who were at the back of the truck later realised they were wasting time for nothing because the lumps of copper were very heavy that they needed machines to lift them up.

The ones who stood next to the truck where shouting and singing, *"Ponya, ndichiponya"*, meaning, "I will throw this spear or axe at you!" Also, "M*enya, ndikumenya ine"* - meaning, "We want to hit or hammer you!" It was a very frightening experience. When they mentioned *menya, ndikumenya*, I thought they were going to peel us, as *menya* in Shona which is my language means, "Peel the skin off"; it could be the skin of anything, a fruit or an animal. We later discovered that they were some *Nyau* dancers or *Gule wamukulu*, otherwise known as African *Nyau Ritual Dancers* from Malawi, Zambia and Zimbabwe.

After collecting a few bucks from us, they danced the *nyau* dance for us and finally allowed us to go straight away as they thought there might be some of us in the bush somewhere. They warned us never to stop over at that particular lay-by ever again as it was their territory where they performed their rituals and practiced their dance moves.

"*Phew*, I will never sleep anywhere where there is no hotel ever again!" I cried; and off we set for the Chirundu border. "I am sure it must have been Friday the 13th," I said. "No sis, it's not Friday the 13th - not all bad things happen on that day, it can be anytime," emphasised Seria. "We really

CHAPTER FOURTEEN

need to thank God Almighty for deliverance!" she added with feeling.

After this trip I had some hard thinking to do on my way home *about smuggling*.

When we reached the Chirundu border we crossed over the Chirundu Bridge on foot looking at the deep waters of the Zambezi River. It was just so fantastic to watch men's creation. Even if the bridge is very long it did not take us much time to cross the bridge; but there were so many things to watch, such as men in canoes and elephants swimming near the banks of the river; they just drew and stole our attention completely.

Our driver had already crossed the bridge but was still in a long, long queue of trucks, waiting to be cleared. We joined the queue for those travelling on foot but on the 'nothing to declare' side. It did not take us half an hour as we did not have anything that required any sight.

We stood by the shops and waited for the truck to cross the customs border. It took the driver more than an hour in the queue and he finally made it. I'm sure if he had paid some money to be let through… You know, the customs people back home are very corrupt and also two-faced; one needs to know who one is dealing with before offering a bribe. Anyway, for our driver I assume it went well. We had to wait for him to have a shower and to have something to eat. It was now past midday and the sun was extremely hot at

CHAPTER FOURTEEN

Chirundu. When the driver had finished showering and eating we returned to the truck.

On arrival, the sight was unbelievable - we saw two dozen monkeys on board! They sat proudly and carefree on the back of the truck as if they were on some hill or mountain. They protested and refused to jump off the truck as they were feasting on loaves of bread they had snatched off people. We had no choice but to sit down and watch them eat as the driver was not allowed to drive with wildlife on board. We were tired and felt roasted enough by the hot weather; we just wanted to go home. I realised we were wasting time, so I walked to the market where the ladies sold cooked corn on the cob; I bought a dozen cobs and went back to the truck. I threw one of the sweet corn cobs at the back of the truck. One mother monkey grabbed it and she started fighting with another mother monkey.

I pretended to throw another cob, trying to catch the animals' attention. When they noticed and saw that I had more and had unshelled two of the sweet corn cobs, I threw them onto the hot tarmac. They all jumped heading for the cobs. I later threw the remainder to them. I walked briskly towards the truck and jumped in, followed by my cousin and finally the driver.

"Oh, what a day!" sighed the driver.

"That's Zim for you," snarled my cousin.

"We are not there yet," I said, "we've still got a long way to go."

CHAPTER FOURTEEN

We were excited that finally we had won the battle and managed to smuggle twenty bales of used clothes into Zimbabwe. As we had driven halfway toward Clouds End, Makuti, just before the junction to Kariba, we saw a heard of elephant totally blocking the road. Some of them were sitting on the tarmac to soak up the heat as the sun was about to go down to its mum.

We stopped and just had to watch the animals. On the other side of the road was a Land Rover that was carrying two white men and two white women. I guess they were tourists because any locals would not have made the kind of mistake they were about to make. The driver of the Land Rover was bored of waiting, and started hooting loudly. The locals who were driving behind the Land Rover started making U-turns and going back in the direction they had come from - whilst the four tourists just sat there and enjoyed taking pictures of the elephants as they rose onto their four legs and started charging towards the Land Rover.

It was a real stampede as the elephants were angered by the noise; they started flapping their ears and lumbering fiercely towards the Land Rover. They started bashing the truck with their trunks and heads as well as using their hind legs to kick the Land Rover as they were retaliating on account of the noise of the car horn. It was very distressing to watch the vehicle being pushed and pulled with four people in it. The elephants continued with their stampede

CHAPTER FOURTEEN

till the vehicle was turned onto its side. The game people were called and they drove the herd away successfully.

I was pissed off, but the truck driver was furious. He vowed that he would never ever work for anyone again in his life; he was upset and just blurted out the words: *"Uboss wami ulele ngoku, mina ndiya sebenza kodhwa ndiya sokola! I mali yakhe iya ngena ibanki account eyake every minute even ulele nge mufazi wakhe"* - meaning, "My boss is sleeping now whilst I am going through all this, also working which is not changing my life for the better: money goes into my boss's account every minute, even when he is sleeping with his wife! I give up!" emphasised the driver.

The four tourists were helped out. They had fortunately sustained only minor injuries. Honestly, they had no idea how lucky they were. We offered them some cold drinks from our cool box and chatted to them till their Land Rover was towed off the road. They drove to the nearest hotel as we headed for Karoi. It was one of those days when one could just give up easily on life, saying everything else has failed; amazingly, it was not Friday the 13th either! We saw a lot more animals along the way, giraffes, zebras and lions; luckily they were not on the road.

We finally arrived at home around 8 p.m., feeling tubed (tired), drained, dehydrated, exhausted, sweating buckets and starving. I got all my stuff from the driver and paid him. I thanked him for his kindness, asked him for his contact

CHAPTER FOURTEEN

details just in case we needed help to smuggle more stuff. He replied in plain English, "I think I have had enough for a lifetime in one day; this is a lesson for me that I should do something for myself which is safer, such as making money whilst sleeping with my wife. Goodbye ladies, I don't think you will ever see me again." We waved goodbye to him and off he went. I was very surprised that the truck driver felt so pissed off with his job; aided no doubt by his exasperation, he certainly managed to string together a very good sentence in English.

What the truck driver had said about making money whilst he slept kept on coming back to my mind, but I could not figure out what he meant and how to make money whist I slept.

I went to bed feeling very tired and within seconds I was fast asleep, dead to the world. I slept for the whole population of Zimbabwe as I did not even want to get up for a drink!

It only took the girl who worked at the market a week to sell the clothes; as soon as the girls sold the clothes I was busy preparing for my next trip. I had loads and loads of pairs of shoes and bags of flour; I smuggled them into Zambia again and got loads and loads of cash.

On this occasion I bought some African attire for resale in South Africa as opposed to the second-hand clothes because almost everyone in my town was now selling second-hand clothes. It was no longer a niche market.

CHAPTER FOURTEEN

Instead of selling them myself, I employed some Zimbabwean women who sold my stuff at the beaches in Port Elizabeth, East London, Cape Town and Durban. They would deposit thousands of Rands into my account before the month-end, which I would later withdraw and order more stuff, paid the workers and burnt the rest of it since I was scared of hoarding money - lack of money education, hey?! The business boomed and I started importing electrical goods such as fridges, TVs, welding machines, compressors, solar panels, used cars and vans for resale in Zimbabwe, but still I didn't know how to invest my money. I made it and blew it. The only good thing was that I knew how to make money and still do. Reflecting on my own childhood at this point, I realised that money attracts more money, and that lack of money attracts no money and eventually poverty.

The demand for Zimbabwean shoes made by *BATA* remained high in Zambia. I smuggled more shoes and bags of flour into Zambia by using truck drivers who were exporting maize to Zambia repeatedly and paying them, and I made massive profits; this was to my advantage as Zambia's economy was in a shambles then, just after Dr Kenneth Kaunda's downfall.

On one occasion I had sold several pairs of shoes to an Indian shop in Lusaka together with bags of flour for making bread. I had loads of money that made me feel too scared to cross the Chirundu border with it in my handbag. I decided to buy some handbags from Zambia which were being imported from Italy. I decided to hide some of the money in one of the bags and waited to find a truck driver who was willing to smuggle the handbags and ties and dyed clothes for me to the Zimbabwean side. I must admit I slept rough, I went hungry and I went without a shower for a few days as we had to wait by the roadside to find willing drivers. I had to carry water in a large bottle and have enough to wash my private bits, face, armpits and teeth every morning. I finally found a driver who was willing to smuggle the stuff for me; we agreed on payment terms and off we went on the journey home.

* * *

I dealt with large sums of money which I didn't know what to do with. My culture was against having loads of money as we often heard the elders saying that too much money can make one insane. I started giving money and goods to my family members and extended family members as well as friends and neighbours. When my parents taught me about entrepreneurial skills they never taught me about investment and even about saving for a rainy day, hence Africa is the richest continent in minerals but has the poorest people. My brain was programmed as a child that too much money was not good, and money was the root of all evil. I managed to put a little bit of my money in a fixed savings account on a monthly basis which was then swallowed by Mugabe's Zimbabwean massive inflation where we held trillions in savings that bought nothing. If I had invested that money property, I would be saying something quite different now.

Reflecting on what *baba* had done previously, when he had a little bit of money, sleeping around with prostitutes and finally divorcing mum, made me resent keeping too much money; having said that, I discovered that I was one of the chosen few and a money magnet; money kept on coming from all angles, rubbish paper money which was used as tissues in the end. One million Zimbabwean dollars was worth nothing then - it could not even buy a loaf of bread.

Making money has always been very easy for me but I needed education on how to keep a cool head, attract more and even more and how to handle it and keep it. Due to my experience of what happened in my country of birth, I shall never horde but buy assets that appreciate in value instead. This sort of education was not available in my country, from my parents or at school. My God Almighty has always blessed me with money, for when I sell anything the demand always gets high and higher; and it was all down to 'give and you shall receive', as I gave and still give to the church and to those in need. I learnt the benefits of giving from an early age. My brother would never ever give anything to anyone and his life has always been that of a dependent. He has always been mean and stingy. He blames everyone for his life's failure and I blame no one but myself; we are the offspring of the same people, yet totally different people in comparison.

I have always built and my brother has always destroyed. It was tough as window frames and door frames where removed from the house which I had built for *amai* to be sold for cash that was just blown away. I left some herds of cattle before *amai* passed away; all these were either slaughtered for meat or sold for less than the market value. These are all the things that were done by someone who has never worked in his life or done anything to help himself and his children. He has been a dependant and will always be. They say we can choose our friends but never our families.

* * *

As I continued travelling on a lorry down the narrow gauge mountain roads and steep hills in Zambia, I enjoyed the beautiful views though I held my heart in my hands with fear, wondering when this taxing lifestyle would end. Halfway through our journey the driver decided to park the lorry by the road and said, "We are going to sleep here as I am tired." I insisted on him driving to Chirundu so that I could find somewhere safe to sleep. "You can sleep with me in the driver's cabin," said the driver. I thought, what! Sleep where and sleep with whom? I said, "No, I am not sleeping anywhere on this lorry!" He actually meant me sleeping with

CHAPTER FOURTEEN

him, of course. The truth is I had never wanted any man other than Kenzo. The fact that I had cheated with Roy was because he was classy and he was my heart's desire and he was loaded, and I did it in anger and in retaliation. I refused to sleep with the lorry driver who slept with women in South Africa, Zimbabwe, Botswana, Namibia, Zambia, Zaire, Tanzania and Malawi, as I had my pride.

Honestly, I wasn't that thick and stupid! I just told myself, "Thou shalt not shove thy womanly assets and thy lovely lady humps at any male baboon that sniffs around!" My "no" had to be a firm "no"! I knew these drivers travelled across Africa and I knew pretty well the results of sleeping with them. So a *no* was a firm *no* and I *meant* no. I was too smart for that. I told him that I did not mix business with pleasure and never would; he would have to name his fee and I would pay him for smuggling my goods for me - and that was as far as it went.

When he realised I was not interested, he grabbed me by the upper arm, pulled me towards him and held me tightly. With his right hand grabbing my clothes from the back he tried to reach for my knickers and pressed me against the cabin bed. He managed to pull my knickers down and ripped them. There was no point in shouting as this was an isolated spot. I tried to reason with him and said, "Please don't hurt me, let's be friends and I will cooperate." I told him there must be a nice man inside him who I wanted to know and not the beast who was hurting me. The driver was sweating

CHAPTER FOURTEEN

as if he had seen a lion. I had to use psychology to achieve my freedom. I told him if he went on to do what he wanted to do, I would not resist but warned him that he would be stuck in my VAGINA till my husband came to release him as I had been given African magic known as *Runyoka*. He still would not let go of me and I was about to rip his face off with my teeth. I had made up mind up that I was going to use my teeth for survival as Everything Else Had Failed - once again. But on reflecting on what I had said, he suddenly let go of me and said, "I think it's better to do it properly; give me a chance to know you."

"Sure," I said sweetly, "I would like to know the better person in you, not the devil I have just witnessed."

"Sure, we have to do it properly… *haa*, you are a real fighter, aren't you?" he added.

"I don't know about that," I replied, feeling relieved.

Once again I thanked my God for deliverance. I did not say a word till we got to the Chirundu border. I just kept praying quietly that he should not touch me again.

Instead of trying it on again, the truck driver developed a hump and drove all the way to Chirundu without saying any more words to me. I found a hotel to sleep and have a shower and a nice meal. In the morning my friend who had travelled on another truck and I crossed the Chirundu border on foot as we did not want to be seen with the truck driver; most of the custom officers had always suspected that we were big smugglers as we always had nothing to declare. The truck driver went past us and managed to cross the border with the smuggled goods well before us. When he was on the Zimbabwean side he did not bother to wait for us but drove away with our goods and loads of my cash stacked in one bag. I tracked him down through my friends as I had written down his truck registration number and the name of his company.

I waited in the queue on the Zambian customs side. There was a long queue, mainly women who were travelling on cross-country buses. I waited in the queue as Zimbabwean women were asked to strip and bare it all in front of the Zambian customs officers. I just thought, there is no way I am going to be humiliated in front of male and female customs officers. If I am carrying something that is illegal, what the damn, I was only a few metres away from my home country and was heading home, not into their country. I expected this type of search at the Zimbabwean side but *no-oo*, it was on the opposite side.

I left the queue and without a gate pass went straight past the guard and ran as fast as I could. The guard saw this and ran after me. "Hey *vapongozi* (a way of respecting ladies), come back... *Va-sister* (sister), come back!" called the Zambian guard who was an elderly man. I ran as fast I could, even though I knew my legs could not perform miracles; I just pleaded for my two legs to carry me to my destination and not to give way. Indeed, I outran the gate man. As I was

CHAPTER FOURTEEN

halfway across the Chirundu Border I reached the middle of the bridge and shouted, "Hurrraaaaay, home, here I come!" The Zambian official called the Zimbabwean authorities to inform them about me. I did not panic when I was met by two Zimbabwean Border Giants who demanded to know what I had done. I explained to them what was happening, that women were being humiliated and being stripped naked and that I did not want to give them the satisfaction of seeing me stripping and baring it all to them. I did not have anything illegal on my body or in my handbag. I was assigned to a lady customs officer to check on me and my handbag; she found nothing and they allowed me to pass; actually, this helped as I was made to jump the queue as a priority case.

I later made a search for the driver who had my smuggled goods and found him after a long while. I asked him why he had behaved in such a manner and he replied that he did it because I had refused to sleep with him. I told him that I was a married woman but he was one of those men who think every woman constitutes valid sex material - those men who totally lack any kind of respect for women. Despite the fact that Kenzo had cheated on me with several women, I did not want to reduce myself to his level by sleeping with every Tom, Dick and Harry - in other words *Tafara*, *Dodhi* and *Hwindi*, meaning *Tafara* (Happiness: the James Bond type), *Dhodhi* (Poo, the gay or bi-sexual man) and *Hwindi* (a cheap guy with nothing). I could have done it if I wanted to, but the thought of it just made me sick. I recovered all my stuff and money. I then decided to put an end to smuggling and turn to flying, which was a bit smarter.

The pain of leaving Kenzo was healed by making money and I never looked back. In 1991 I discovered the island of Mauritius. It was just so wonderful and so beautiful. I loved every minute of my life there and enjoyed everything that I did. I ate well and slept well. I loved and still love travelling but there is nothing better than being home surrounded by those who love me and those whom I love dearly, my family.

I extended my business to Mauritius where I sold the crocheted tops to tourists in Port Luis. With my baby Lolo strapped on my back I sold the crocheted tops at the beach. It used to take me two days to sell the products. After selling my products I would sunbathe and swim in the Indian Ocean. This is where I started wearing bikinis, you know. Granddad Robert Mugabe was very strict; the first Miss Zimbabwe contest had girls wearing swimming costumes on the stage, but granddad Bob discouraged even that. That amounted to treating women as second class citizens, you know - not allowing women the freedom of choice or a say is utterly cruel to them.

In the evening I would leave my daughter with a babysitter amongst other fellow Zimbabwean women and attend several nights of clubbing in the tourist area of Port Luis. I had just started living again. On the beach I would just say, "Bollocks to you, Robert Mugabe, here I am, a Zimbabwean in my bikini and enjoying sunbathing!" Back home I would be expected to be wrapped up, concealing even my clothes, not just at funerals but when I had in-laws around. I know that as an African I was expected to behave with absolute decorum; but I hated the idea of the long wrappers. I really hated wearing long wrappers that covered my legs, even though I was not forced to do it, but this cultural thing just made one look like an outsider or someone who lacks respect for the culture of the country one was in.

The Zimbabwean gays would say the same thing and get laid in broad daylight in countries like South Africa and in the West; the truth is they would be working in those countries - if you can call prostitution working - since there were no jobs in Zimbabwe; and there still aren't any, for it's even worse now as I write. The majority of Zimbabweans have claimed asylum based on homosexuality due to the current economic climate; some basically grabbed the opportunity to get out; while some Zimbabweans seeking asylum are genuine political refugees, the rest are simply economic migrants.

I made several friends from different countries who were holidaying in Mauritius. I had loads of fun; you know, that kind of fun an ex-inmate has when he or she is released. I did all the things that people at home would whisper and laugh about. I did not care because I had to live my life the way I wanted it, because it was my life and not anyone else's.

CHAPTER FOURTEEN

My baby Lolo was potty trained at six months and there was no longer a need for me to wash towel napkins. My friends used to call my daughter Lolo Potty as they found it quite hilarious for a kid of her age to hold on till she got her potty!

Due to my regular commuting, I did not see much of Roy apart from once or twice a month. Roy was heartbroken and asked, "How would you like me to help you, my love? You are working far too hard." He went on: "What can I do to stop you from all this travelling? *Je t'aime bebe*, *Ndakupenda* - you know I love you with all my heart and can do absolutely anything for you!" He insisted, "Please let me help you." He expressed his love for me in three different languages, in French, Swahili and English, to try and convince me, but I refused to depend on him financially. I asked myself, what would happen if the relationship were to end? Go back to square one and start again? No way! So I dismissed the opportunity of being looked after, which would have amounted to being a kept woman.

I told Roy not to worry as I was on a mission and enjoyed my adventures. *What more is there for a girl to do when everything else fails*, I thought? *She has to do something, take action and help herself!* I just had to lift my chin up and smile to the world and pretend everything was okay - and me being me, I had always wanted to achieve something for myself and never wanted a man for financial independence. I just wanted to build my own empire with my own achievements.

CHAPTER FOURTEEN

The Sheraton hotel in Harare became our new meeting place, when Roy visited Harare. We really enjoyed each other's company in the luxurious 5***** Hotel. We would watch the videos which I had smuggled into Zimbabwe from South Africa. Life was just so good with Roy and he was a 50-50 man. He never domineered in our relationship and always gave me time to say something, not to listen to his orders all the time. We ate and drank together and spent some quiet nights together. Roy gave me the impression that all Englishmen are very nice, very loving, caring, considerate and generous human beings. Roy was my soul mate and no word in the dictionary and under the sun could describe him. I loved him dearly and he loved me very much.

According to Roy, he and his wife were just living together - their relationship was already dead. His two children Megan and Michael could not stand them arguing most of the time, so they decided to return to England. They held both Zimbabwean and British passports. Since they were adults they wanted their space. Roy kept his marriage for the sake of his two children. According to him, he was trapped in a loveless marriage in which he slept with a lifeless log at night.

I also had kept my marriage for the sake of my children, and felt nothing for Kenzo due to his multiple cheatings. One day prior to our separation, I decided to visit Kenzo in the rural areas where he was working. I did not alert him of my visit and just turned up. I was surprised at what I saw. I caught my husband doing it - I mean, having sex with another woman! I just opened the door and said, "If the girl had been classy enough and knew what she was doing, I might have joined you in a threesome; anyway, carry on - enjoy yourselves and, by the way, sorry for disturbing you guys; just ignore me and carry on!" With that Parthian shot I walked out.

Kenzo did not wait to finish the act and started shouting at the girl: "Go now, I do not ever want to see you again - you arranged this so that my wife finds me!" In actual fact the poor girl was innocent. The couple had been sleeping together for some time and the poor girl was pregnant and did not even know me. She was kicked and punched - that's the way some men behave when caught doing it. They blame the victim to make her take the blame. He tried to apologise and explain to me; but I showed him that I was not bothered at all; all I wanted was to deliver the message that we were finished, not just separated. I spoke my mind and drove back to town.

I just thought, even though children were involved, if the marriage wasn't working it was time to move on; and there was no need to stay in a loveless marriage. Kenzo followed me but I refused to speak to him till the day he died. I still feel guilty for holding a grudge, mind you. Until today none of our friends knows exactly what happened between me and my late husband, especially the fact that he was a womaniser and I had caught him red handed doing it with someone else

CHAPTER FOURTEEN

- except for Roy, of course, in whom I had confided. I just thought TIT for TAT is a fair game, since he was the one who had told me that "Variety is the SPICE of life" and who called me a NYMPHOMANIAC when I was purely innocent; but it appeared that in the long run he was hurt more than me as I retaliated and he started spreading rumours about my infidelity before he passed away. I know and admit that I had cheated on my husband - I didn't mean to but he called me nasty names and drove me to it.

Since Kenzo was an introvert, people believed him and blamed me for the failure of our marriage. Culturally I was considered the bad one, for it was never heard of or supported that a woman should walk out of her marriage because of a husband's infidelity. I couldn't bare it or keep pretending, but walked out and accepted the blame instead of blaming my ex-husband. Everyone turned against me, even some of my own children, but I did not fancy living a lie. I earned myself names such as 'bad wife', 'good-girl turned bad', '*wannabe* prostitute'; I did not care as I had my whole life ahead of me and I just wanted to live my life to the full and not spend the rest of my life cuddling a pillow and crying on account of an unfaithful husband; hence I walked out on him, and out of my marriage.

In my country it was a very common thing that when a woman is divorced or separated, she goes straight into the nearest beer garden (pub) to tell men that now she was available as a badly packed kebab seller, or streetwalker (prostitute). I did not want to go down that route! I wanted to earn money in an altogether different way, and not by selling my bits!

I just thought, "What more is there to tell the world in order to prove my innocence? The only fact that remains is that God is a silent listener to every conversation and the silent observer; therefore he knows what transpired and what is yet to take place in my life. This I know: big, very big things are going to happen now that I have taken a step forward and left him!"

CHAPTER FIFTEEN

A FOOL IN LONDON

AFTER KENZO was killed suspiciously in a hit and run car accident, I decided to bury my estranged husband and fled from Zimbabwe. Even if Kenzo and I were separated, it still hurt me to the bone since he was my first love and the father of my children - and he certainly did not deserve to die in the way that he did.

Before he died he was living with another woman who, after his death, was not recognised by anyone; even the GMB could not give her any money from his pension as she was not included or listed as a beneficiary. Despite what had happened between Kenzo and me, I still had a legal and moral right to make sure he had a good send off. My in-laws took everything that Kenzo had left behind. I mean, *everything* down to the teaspoon. I was not bothered at all as I did not want anything at all. I just wished them good luck.

Since Kenzo's death was suspicious due to his involvement with white farmers, I had no option but to flee

CHAPTER FIFTEEN

and save my life as I had started being talked about. It was a difficult time as I had lost my sister to HIV and Aids seven months before, with my dad following her within the next two months. I did not say goodbye to any of my family members except for my children. My children thought I was flying to London for a week or a month. As I boarded the Kenya Airways, I climbed up the stairs and stood by the doorway. I waved at my children and crossed my arms to make an X sign to show that now I was crossing to another country in a different continent. I saw my kids crying, even though they continued to wave; it was a painful and heartbreaking experience. I cried on the plane nonstop till I reached Nairobi. I just couldn't stop crying, as I thought, what else could I have done, especially WHEN EVERYTHING ELSE HAD FAILED? I had to take action and help my children and myself - and reject poverty.

My children had watched me flying to Mauritius and coming back within a week but on this occasion it felt very different as they knew that their dad had died. The pain of leaving my children behind was unbearable, but I had no choice. I had to seek safety and greener pastures and work for my children to have all they wanted and to be able to put food on their plates. Whilst I was on the plane, after having two sips of refreshing tea, I thought, "Now this is the end to poverty! I will work hard and provide for my children." My intentions were to work and return home after six months

CHAPTER FIFTEEN

when it was all peaceful and quiet. However, things did not turn out that way. The political situation in Zimbabwe worsened to the extent that the white farmers lost their farms. I lost contact with my best friend and lover, Roy, who lost one of his farms. A lot of innocent people died. I just feared for my children every day and night. It was ever so scary. I did not know what to do. I had been actively involved in ZANU PF and supported President Mugabe so much that I voted for him twice, if not thrice; I am sure everyone did at some point, but it turned out nasty.

When I first arrived in London, I had the impression that things would be easy for me. I expected to collect gold from the pavements of London.... then go and sell it to the GOLDSMITHS, you see, and acquire some wealth; then my family and I would be secure and posh.

Arriving at London Heathrow airport was just so fascinating - but I could not believe my eyes when I saw the number of people flocking into the country. Honestly, London's streets *must* be paved with gold, I thought! I had never seen such long queues at an airport before. The United Kingdom is only an island but hey, it was welcoming loads and loads of migrants as if it were the size of mother Africa! This was also the same time that the news on television was showing loads and loads of asylum seekers flocking in via France and being smuggled into the country in the back of lorries. I thought, maybe this London was another heaven on

CHAPTER FIFTEEN

earth - I should definitely make my way in or else I would burn and rot in the Zimbabwean hell on earth. I held my head high and forced a smile, just to be allowed in. I would have done anything to be allowed into the United Kingdom, if necessary submitting to x-raying, anal poking or even the strip search which I had refused at the Zambian border. I just wanted to go to London, the city that is famously known for being paved with GOLD.

When my turn came, I walked up to the counter with my head as high as an ostrich and a smile that lacked emotion as I was saying my prayers quietly. I bit the corner of my bottom lip, ready with my memorised words.

"Hello ma'am," came the voice from the white gentleman behind the counter.

"I beg your pardon?" I replied.

His greeting did not make sense to me as no-one had ever called me Ma'am before! Neither did I realise that he was saying "Hello madam" to me! In the colonial Rhodesia 'madam' was a term used to address every white woman or young white girls. Sometimes the young girls were referred to as *pikinini madam"* - this was a language that was created by the whites called *chilapa-lapa*, broken English mixed with broken Shona and Ndebele. 'Madam' was never used to address a black woman!

I had memorised, "Good Morning sir/Madam, How are you?" - but it all went wrong as the psychology was reversed.

CHAPTER FIFTEEN

Me being called madam! I pinched myself a bit to make sure I wasn't dreaming. I took a quick glance behind me but there was a white man. So, he is calling *me* madam? Well, I stood tall and braved it; immediately I pictured the late Princess Diana, how she used to walk and talk; I was in England - perhaps we should all behave English when in England! I quickly adjusted to a ladylike posture and way of speaking, imitating the Princess; little did I know I was making a fool of myself!

The gentleman repeated again, more slowly, "I said, Hello madam, and how are you?" This time I managed to understand him and knew he was talking to me as his eyes were focused on me.

"I am very well, thank you sir, and how are you?" I replied. (People in the queues within earshot turned to eyeball me as I imitated the English accent in a squeaky voice - you know what I mean, speaking through the nose in order to sound posh like a real English madam!)

"Not bad thanks," the gentleman replied, "Can I have your passport please?"

Oh God, please make me understand this gentleman, I prayed quietly and quickly. I did not pray to be allowed into the country, as I never thought people could be returned home, but to be able to understand this new accent called Cockney...

"Are you visiting someone or are you coming for a holiday?" asked the gentleman again. I did not understand a

CHAPTER FIFTEEN

word he said and I again begged his pardon and asked him to repeat what he had said.

He felt sorry for me, as he must have thought I might have a hearing impediment. The truth is, I was struggling to understand his accent. The English accent was totally different from that of our Zimbabwean and South African whites back home. Hey, I did not want to appear stupid even though I did, so I continued to hold my head high and a fake smile to cover my uneasiness. I held my black handbag which matched my semi-high heeled shoes right on the centre of my left arm as I tilted my wrist and spread my fingers apart to reveal the French Manicure and my yellow metal wedding ring and a three-diamond engagement ring. This was done on purpose, just to show off to the Immigration Officer; so he could see that he was dealing with a mini-posh madam.

"I can see you are a traveller and are on your last page of the passport, married and have four children." This time he spoke very slowly and very clearly and I understood every word.

"Yes sir," I replied quickly, with a smile that said, "You see, I have just showed you who I am and am glad you understood and are convinced."

"How much money have you got on you?" he asked again, very slowly.

"Oh," I said, "I have five hundred Zimbabwean dollars and three hundred pounds' worth of travellers' cheques as well as two five-pound notes which a friend gave to me."

CHAPTER FIFTEEN

"Can I have a look at your money and travellers' cheques please, as well as your return ticket?" said the immigration controller. I quickly took everything out from my waist bag that was hidden under my jumper. He went through every little piece of paper that I had and counted the money and travellers' cheques.

"You have one hundred pounds in cash and three hundred pounds worth of travellers' cheques. I won't include the Zimbabwean dollars as I think you will not be able to use them here," said the immigration man.

I was surprised to learn that the two red notes which Roy had given to me two years ago were actually fifty-pound notes. I thought they were five-pound notes as in Zimbabwe the largest note at the time was a twenty-dollar note.

"I have given you six months on your visitor's visa - enjoy your stay, madam."

"Thank you sir," I said as I walked out, slowly, and so excited deep down that I felt butterflies flying in my tummy. I walked straight to my friend whom I had met earlier on the plane, whilst I waited for my colleague whom I had arranged the trip with to be cleared. When I looked back I saw my friend Maggie being escorted to a secluded room. I was getting worried but did not have a clue what was happening. Our plane had arrived at six in the morning and the time was already approaching midday. I was through and still waiting for my friend. I started feeling scared as I did not know where

CHAPTER FIFTEEN

to go or how to get to my destination. London appeared very different from other African cities I had visited, and in my imagination I thought there was an underground city as well as an overhead level. I didn't know that the underground was just for train lines. What a fool I was!

My friend whom I had met on the plane came from Uganda and was a student. She told me that she lived in Manchester. She was very kind and she promised to wait for me till my friend was cleared. I never thought that it would be difficult for me to find my way to London as I thought that Heathrow was ten minutes away from London. I did not have a clue where I was going to go since my friend Maggie had been to the UK before and had a sister and cousins living in London.

My new friend Mwandi seemed to know what was happening. "Do you know what your friend was carrying in her luggage?" she asked me.

"No," I replied. "She asked me to carry most of her stuff, but I did not have any of my luggage searched."

"I think she must have overstayed her visa last time she was here, or maybe she was carrying some illegal stuff, or maybe she did not have enough money to live on," suggested Mwandi.

"She never told me how much she had on her," I replied. I also did not know what she was carrying, I told Mwandi. "So what will happen to her?" I asked, as it was already past midday without any sign of Maggie.

"Chances are she will be returned home on the next

flight; if she was carrying something illegal she could be detained," said Mwandi. My heart started pounding, fearing for the worst. I did not have a clue where to go and how to use the phones in London. As you know, London is a world in its own right; it was a terrifying thought which turned out to be true.

"By the way, was there someone who was supposed to meet you?" asked Mwandi.

"I have a telephone number here for Maggie's cousin who she said was going to clear me; I don't know if she lives in the underground city or the overhead city."

"What are you trying to say?" asked Mwandi.

"I mean, I do not know where this lady, who was supposed to speak to immigration and with whom I am visiting London, lives - on the underground or the overhead city."

My friend did not want to laugh at me but the look on her face made me feel stupid. "You know what, Tanaka," she explained, "the underground is not a city; it is where the underground rail operates. Nobody lives there. People live overheard," she added.

"It's just because back home we often heard people saying that in London there are two cities, the overhead and the underground," I replied.

"I see," said Mwandi. "The reason is because there are trains that run underground and overhead in London; thus you have London Underground Trains and The British Rail."

Thanks dear," I said as I quickly brushed the subject away

CHAPTER FIFTEEN

to avoid further embarrassment. "I did not tell the immigration man I was going to visit Maggie's cousin because I don't know her," I told Mwandi as I quickly resumed the previous conversation.

"Okay, give me her number and let me phone her," said Mwandi. "If she is not prepared to take you in then you will have to come with me to Manchester," she said.

"Manchester? No, no, no!" I declared. "I have to be in London, not Manchester or anywhere else."

"I can't leave you here or else you will be on the streets wondering when your money runs out; you will have to come with me," she insisted. Mwandi meant well, but I was told that money and gold was to be found in LONDON and not anywhere else!

I am not going anywhere, I thought. I came to London and I must stay in London.

I battled with my thoughts; it *has* to be London, where the money is, I told myself. I had heard that the streets are paved with gold, so what was the matter with this girl?

We quickly walked to the payphone. She dialled the number I gave her. She spoke to the lady on the other side, who appeared to be Maggie's cousin. Margaret's cousin was reluctant to speak to Mwandi so my friend passed the phone to me and said, "Speak to her in your language so that she feels comfortable."

"Hello," I said, "Sheila."

CHAPTER FIFTEEN

"*Makadini henyu?*" (How are you?)

"*Ndinonzi Tanaka, ndabva ku Harare!*" (My name is Tanaka, I have come from Harare.) "*Munoziva Maggie Goremusandu?*" (Do you know Maggie Goremusandu?)

"Yes, I do," replied the voice on the phone. "She is my cousin; our mothers are sisters; is she okay?"

"No," I replied. "We arrived at six in the morning and she is still in there - I don't know what is happening to her."

"Oh my God!" said the lady. "Honestly, I don't want to get involved or they will come for me as well."

Then she hung up without even saying goodbye. We rang her again and asked, "How do we find Maggie's sister?"

"Her sister is there at the airport waiting," said Maggie's cousin.

"So how do we find her sister?" I asked.

"Go to the information desk and ask for them to call out for Sheila Mare Masamba. Then if she is still around she will come to you," said the lady on the phone.

"*Maita henyu*, bye" ("Thank you, bye"), I said and replaced the receiver.

We quickly walked to the information desk and passed the details and asked for the call out. Thank heavens for Mwandi, I really didn't know what was going to happen to me if she did not hang around.

Within no time the call for Sheila was broadcast. A very loud voice came over the loudspeakers: "Sheila Mare

CHAPTER FIFTEEN

Masamba - come to the information desk please!" - repeated four times. That's how I heard it.

We waited patiently but Sheila did not come to the information desk. Thankfully Mwandi spotted a lady walking up and down and past the information desk looking at us.

"I think that lady must be Sheila," said Mwandi. "Let's walk up to her and remember to speak to her in your language," Mwandi added.

"*Mhoroi, ndimi Sheila here?*" (Hello, are you Sheila?)

"*Hongu ndini Sheila, ndimi aniko?*" ("Yes, I am Sheila, who are you?") she asked.

"My name is Tanaka MuZimba *aka* Zibigihauzi. I came from Harare, with your sister, Maggie. We left Harare via Nairobi yesterday afternoon. Your sister Maggie has been detained, I think, because it's been a long time since we arrived and she is still in there."

"Okay, she told me that she was coming with a friend - not friends," said Sheila.

"Sorry," I explained, "I forgot to tell you that this is my friend Mwandi. We met in Nairobi. She is from Uganda and she lives in Manchester. She waited with me because she knew I did not know anyone in the UK."

On hearing this, Mwandi did not want to wait. She whispered in my ear, "It's all up to you now dear; if you want to come with me to Manchester you are welcome, or you can go with Sheila."

CHAPTER FIFTEEN

I whispered back, "Thank you very much my dear, for your help! I will always appreciate it."

Mwandi gave me a hug and said, "Goodbye dear, it's been nice meeting you; I hope it will all work for you" - and off she went. I did not ask for my friend's telephone number or address but I still think of her and the kindness that she showed me.

Sheila did not want to wait any longer. She asked me to come home with her and said, "Let's go, I do not need to wait here any longer as I do not know what Maggie has said to the immigration people. If her information differs from that of the person she said she is visiting, then she could be sent home as well as myself if I try to help her - since I have overstayed my visa."

We left quickly to catch the underground train. Everything looked very different to me. I had not seen so many people in my life! Every nationality was on the train and some people spoke in languages I had never heard before. All I could hear was the sound "*tili tili tili*" as they spoke very fast.

This was the first time I saw women dressed in long black gowns with their heads and faces covered except for their eyes. These women must have been talking about me as they kept on staring at my chest. I wore a V-neck jumper and my cleavage was visible. This was not a problem in Zimbabwe since we had adapted to the western culture. Sheila whispered in our language, saying that these women dressed like that no matter how hot the weather might be. I asked why they did that. She replied that it was their religion that required them to dress like that. I just looked at them and felt sorry for them; yet they seemed happy and viewed me as the stupid one.

GOSH!! Honestly, I thought, there must be a lot of gold in London. If anyone asked me today what my journey from Heathrow to Streatham High Street was like, and how I travelled to get to Sheila's flat, I would be lying if I said anything. I don't remember a thing at all; even if I look at the map I still cannot figure out how we connected with the trains and buses and how we travelled to reach our destination. The only thing I still remember is that we got our last train from Victoria station where I saw a world of trains to Norbury in South West London - and the rest is history. The station was packed with people; I got smashed into and smashed against several people several times as I kept staring at things I had never seen before. I saw trains of all colours and sorts. "Wow!" I exclaimed quietly as I kept on staring at these very long trains. I saw people of different sorts, some with tribal marks, some with large lips, some with big noses. I am pretty sure that at that station every country, city, town, village and island had a representative. So, what brings so many people to London, I wondered? Surely by now the GOLD must have run out, I thought, because of all these masses of people. Immediately, I recalled a Zimbabwean guy who had gone to England to study but turned beggar. He pretended to be blind, sitting in the street to collect the loose

CHAPTER FIFTEEN

change people might throw at him. I was told he became one of the richest people in Zimbabwe! I just thought, no wonder people were flocking in, as I stared at bins full of food that appeared fresh but had gone past their sell-by-date. In Zimbabwe I had never known food to expire the sell-by-date! I knew that bread would dry up if left exposed and milk would go sour if not refrigerated, but cheese, fruits, biscuits and absolutely anything else would be devoured long before they showed any signs of going off. For once in my life I wished I could export all the food they were throwing away to save the masses and masses of people starving in Africa.

London, hey! The CITY THAT IS PAVED WITH GOLD and The CITY that throws TONS and TONS of FOOD away while some folk go hungry in Africa... I asked myself, why on earth does God keep on blessing people who waste so much?!!

CHAPTER SIXTEEN

LOOKING FOR GOLD IN THE STREETS OF LONDON

The Gold Paved Paradise

WHEN I ARRIVED at Streatham, I was very disappointed as we entered a small corridor, walking past black bags of rubbish, treading over dog poo. I did not believe my eyes at all. Maybe this area is for poor people, I thought: I still have to go to the places that are paved with gold, the real London. We finally reached our flat which was located on the second floor and the lifts were not working that day. When I got into the flat, I expected it to be huge as I had the impression that people in London lived in big houses and had loads of money. It was a two-bedroomed flat which Sheila shared with her husband and her friend Marcia. This meant that I had to crash in the living room, on the couch or on the floor. Back to basics, I thought!

At approximately seven past midnight, Maggie called to let her sister know that she was coming home and she had been allowed to come in. Since she had been to London before she knew her way home. It took Maggie about an hour to reach her sister's flat. She sat down and explained why she had been detained. It was because her cousin Tara who worked as a staff nurse at St George's hospital in Tooting had forgotten the date when Maggie said she would be coming to London. So there was a bit of a mix up, till she and her English husband drove to Heathrow to collect her; otherwise she was set to go back the following morning or on the next flight.

When Maggie arrived she cuddled her sister and the pair cried together with happiness.

"So, Tanaka, how come they let you in so quickly?" asked Maggie.

I replied, "The immigration officer felt sorry for me as I struggled to understand him."

They both laughed out loud (lol!), and very loudly indeed! "It happens to everyone on their first visit," Sheila said. "You don't understand a thing, it's called Cockney."

The girls started imitating the accent, asking me what I thought, still laughing. Sheila was the one who knew most of the words, since she had been in London the longest. She said to her husband, "Could you make us cheese, ham and toma'o sandwiches please?" She then asked me what I thought she said. I told her that she had asked her husband to make her something called "sa-ngwe jies" with cheese, ham and "toma'o".

CHAPTER SIXTEEN

Sheila asked again if I knew what it was. I said no, except for the ham and cheese and maybe some mayonnaise called "toma'o".

GOSH, they all burst into loud laughter again - you know, the kind that makes you feel stupid or appear as an idiot or like someone who has shit or a vagina on their forehead!

Then her husband finished making the "sa-ngwe-jies" and cups of tea and brought them on a tray to the living room. I looked on the plate and laughed at myself. "Did you mean the sandy witches (sandwiches) - are they called sa-ngwe-jies here?"

"Yes dear," said Sheila.

"Then what is called toma'o?" I asked.

"Toma'o is tomato, dear," explained Sheila. "You will come across people who swallow the T's when they speak to you." She added, "Some will say, 'Innii?' meaning 'Isn't it?' 'It is' will be pronounced as TEEs here, my luv."

"Gosh," I said, "I thought they spoke proper Cambridge English or Oxford English in London."

"No ma luv, there is a difference between spoken English and written here. Even if we bump into Aussies, or Americans, or the Irish and the Scottish, we know them through their accents," said Sheila.

That was a good lecture for me as I never thought of these things. "So what jobs do you do here, or have you collected much gold yet?" I asked patiently.

CHAPTER SIXTEEN

"Gold!!!" exclaimed Sheila. "There is no Gold here; we bloody work hard like bloody donkeys here!"

I tell you, she scared me a bit. Working hard like bloody donkeys, in London? No, they must be mistaken, I thought.

"Wait till tomorrow, dear," Sheila said, "we will take you to central London, then hopefully we can get you a job."

"What kind of job?" I asked patiently, as I thought it would be some typing work or filing.

"To start with, cleaning will be fine for you or being a porter, or a chambermaid in one of the posh hotels in central London," said Sheila.

Oh, it sounded all posh for me as I assumed it would be easy. The thought of crashing on a two-seater couch just did me in on the day of my arrival, since I was used to spreading my wings on a therapeutic bed back home in my lovely sexy and silky nighties which I bought from Meikles and H.M. Barbours of First Street, Harare. It was a complete shock for me. I never slept at all that night, wondering why I had come to London. I still cherished the belief that I was not in the *real* London. Roy always brought loads of money and nice things from London, so I thought there must be another London somewhere, not this one.

The following morning I woke up looking forward to going into central London to see the streets that where paved with gold and to collect some gold for myself.

"First of all," Sheila smiled, "I will have to show you the

CHAPTER SIXTEEN

REAL LONDON before I can take you to where the streets are paved in GOLD!"

I felt very excited, like a ten-year-old! Finally I was in LONDON and now I was going to see the Real London! We boarded the BIG RED DOUBLE DECKER BUS (no 133) to Brixton. I made sure that I remembered the bus number for future reference, but what I did not know was that the bus would have the same number whether going into or out of the city - *ouuuch*! When I arrived at Brixton, what I saw was not what I expected at all! I saw some street adults sitting by the cash point, asking for cash.

"What!! Street fathers, begging in London, noooo!!!!" I exclaimed very loudly. Nooo, I thought, it can't be like MBARE *musika* (Harare's biggest Market). I never expected to see white men begging, let alone smelling like they had never been near a shower for the whole year. I did not laugh but felt tears rolling down my cheeks. "Poverty is everywhere in the world," I cried. If one works hard and says 'NO' TO POVERTY, is this what happens to one when EVERYTHINGS ELSE HAS FAILED? This really pierced my heart as I grew up being made to believe that all white people were rich.

In Harare we were used to seeing blind people boarding buses and singing, asking for money. I could understand this because in Zimbabwe there was no Social Security or benefits. People do not get benefits at all. Mind you, I left

CHAPTER SIXTEEN

Zimbabwe when it was still Zimbabwe, a little heaven on earth, before all the problems began.

"Don't feel sorry for them!" shouted Sheila. "They chose to be like this."

I didn't quite understand what she meant.

"I mean, these people made themselves homeless; they are alcoholics and drug addicts and if you are not very careful in this country you could end up like them," said Sheila. "They receive money every week as benefits, but they choose to buy beer or drugs instead of food; hence they are on the streets..."

I just wondered and wondered how people in a rich country like England end up being homeless; I could not get an answer. I recalled when I used to watch programmes from England, it was all rosy - we were never shown places like Brixton on the BBC News whilst back home. PROPAGAGANDA! We were only shown the best parts of England and never Brixton, Peckham and so on.

"This is the reason I brought you here," Sheila said, "so that you can see for yourself and never accept anything from anyone you don't know in this country, not even a lift or that might be the end of you, or a drink which might be spiked."

My hopes for collecting GOLD sank as I knew that the streets of LONDON were not paved with GOLD after all. As we walked along the market stalls we saw different types of meat being exposed in the open air, being sold to people: GOAT HEADS, LAMB heads, COW FEET, PIG HEADS,

CHAPTER SIXTEEN

Pig Trotters, all types of fish under the sun, huge snails, crabs, prawns, absolutely anything, and I was shocked. I saw some of the things I had never seen in my life before.

When I left Zimbabwe, I had never seen meat being sold at market places but in supermarkets or a butcher's shop, neatly displayed in a glass display fridge. Markets in Zimbabwe were for selling things like vegetables, fruits and crafted items, not raw meat.

"Can we go to central London please?" I asked Sheila, as I did not want to continue with the market tour. We saw some men selling marijuana in broad daylight and I thought never again will I set my foot in BRIXTON - and this was years before the Brixton nail bomb which was deposited in an Iceland store on Sunday 18th of April 1999; the news report of that event made it even scarier for me to visit Brixton market.

We went for the underground to catch a train to central London. We got off at Charing Cross and Sheila walked us to the Zimbabwean Embassy. She said, "If anything goes wrong or if you lose your passport, this is where you will need to come to obtain a travel document to go back home."

I smiled when I saw the Zimbabwean flag flying in central London and seeing the pictures of the famous Zimbabwe Ruins and the Victoria Falls displayed inside the embassy. We did not spend much time there and we walked to Trafalgar Square.

What a beautiful place, I thought. I loved the sight of the

water fountains and the huge statues at Trafalgar Square. I climbed up onto a plinth with the help of some guys. I managed to have some photos with the huge lion statues. Now I am in London, I thought; this is now the *real* London. We boarded a sight-seeing bus and I could understand the guy who was doing the commentary very well. He was well spoken, loud and clear. I just fell in love with London. It was beautiful!

We drove by Grosvenor square - I just loved the place. The commentator informed us that some famous people live or may have lived here, people like Margaret Thatcher and James Bond! It felt really great to know that some famous people live or lived there. We headed to Buckingham Palace and I waited in much anticipation of seeing the Queen, but all we saw was the changing of the guards. "This is where the GOLD is," said Sheila, "take a look on the gates."

I looked at the GATES and the Statues - indeed, that is where the GOLD is, and the diamonds are on the Queen's Tiaras. It was just so beautiful to watch. I was finally happy that I was now in London. We went to see Kensington Palace. The gold-wrought iron gates looked stunning.

"This is where Princess Diana lives," we were told. It was purely beautiful. "It is a Palace as well as a museum," said Sheila.

When went back to Buckingham Palace to watch the last bit of the changing of the guards, we walked across the famous Green Park. We went into the RITZ Hotel and

CHAPTER SIXTEEN

bought some drinks. Now I have started living again, I thought. We visited all the places of interest and finally went on a RIVER CRUISE on the River THAMES. Life will be really good here, I thought.

It never crossed my mind that life could be both sweet and sour in London; neither did I know about the phenomenon called stress and depression... Fucking hell, it's a very bad thing that affects a lot of people in their lifetime, due to too much pressure in life, brought about by having to pay the so-called bills which I had never experienced before. All the houses I had lived in before were mainly company houses where ten per cent of my husband's salary was deducted to pay for everything, including the telephone bill. If I had to live in our own house it was bought outright and all we paid for was the electricity and water; rates were paid annually and there was nothing called Council Tax!

CHAPTER SEVENTEEN

GOLD PANNING ALONG THE RIVER THAMES

AT THE END of the day Sheila took us to see one of the Indian guys whom she knew. We saw this tall Asian man who had the longest nose I had ever seen. I am sure Pinocchio's nose was not as long as Amish's.

Amish ran an employment agency and had several contracts with top hotels for which he employed people to clean.

"Hey Amish, I have some girls who are looking for work," said Sheila.

"I have plenty of work," Amish said and asked, "When can they start?"

"Anytime," replied Sheila.

"Is there anyone who is geared up to start this evening?" asked Amish.

"What kind of job?" I asked with interest, as I was keen to get myself out of poverty. I shall work hard, earn some money, go back home looking like one of the white people loaded with cash, I thought quietly as I smiled to Amish.

CHAPTER SEVENTEEN

"Porter," replied Amish.

"What kind of work is that?" I queried as I had never heard that word before.

"Washing up dishes," he replied.

"I can do that," I replied quickly. "How much does it pay?" I asked.

"Five pounds per hour," replied Amish, smiling at me. "Usually it's the boys who do this kind of job," he added.

"No dear, in Zimbabwe it's the girls who do the washing up," I replied stupidly, not realising that the dishes were those of a very busy London restaurant.

"We'll see," said Amish, "I don't want you to charge me with sex discrimination. Come along," he added.

I followed Amish, smiling. I did not worry about how I was to get back to Streatham. I did not even ask for phone numbers - how clever is that? I quickly converted the currency into my Zimbabwean dollars. The five pounds per hour appeared to be a lot of money to me. It was more than a teacher, nurse and some managers earned in Zimbabwe.

I was told where to catch the NIGHT BUS back to Streatham. Amish felt sorry for me and said, "If you are new here you will never get back home." I thought he was lying.

"I am well-travelled, you know," I pointed out. "I have been to Mauritius, South Africa, Zambia, Botswana and Namibia, so I will find my way home easily."

"Okay, that's fine," replied Amish.

CHAPTER SEVENTEEN

As I started washing up, I noticed the plates and pans kept on coming like diarrhoea. "Holy shit!" I swore, "I will not come back here again!" Before I finished loading the dishwasher there were loads more. You can imagine the hectic pace - this was the Tamarind Restaurant, a Michelin restaurant not very far away from the Ritz and the Queen's residency, just 0.2 miles from Green Tube station. There were piles and piles of plates, pans, woks and cutlery, as well as some small bowls. I told Amish that I could not cope.

He promised to take me to a better place the following evening. When I finished washing up my back started hurting - to the extent that I had my period the following day. Amish just said, "I did try to warn you but you told me that the girls did this sort of work in Zimbabwe." He drove me to Trafalgar square from Green Park where I waited for my No. 133 bus. As I waited I watched two gay middle-aged men kissing. I had never seen anything like that happening before; though I knew homosexuality existed, I could not believe my eyes. My bus finally arrived before I finished watching my free romantic movie of the middle-aged gay guys. I threw myself onto the seat and I don't remember falling asleep but woke when the bus reached the last stop. The bus driver woke me up and asked me where I was going. I told him that I wanted to go to Streatham High Road.

"Oh my God," sighed the driver, "we are in Morden."

I told him I didn't know where I was and where I was going, and how to get back to Streatham.

CHAPTER SEVENTEEN

"What number in Streatham High Road?" he asked.

"1223," I said quickly.

"Take a seat. I am going back that way. I will show you where it is."

I tried to stay awake, but hey, everything looked just the same. I wondered how people found their way round London. Finally, we arrived at a service station nearer to 1123 Streatham High Road.

"The number that you want should be somewhere here," he said. "Next time ask for the house phone number and mobile phone numbers for the people you live with. You also need to get yourself a mobile phone and an A-Z." The bus driver also taught me to time my journey in future to see how long it took me to get home and to take note of landmarks. He was such a nice man, bless him. He told me that the trick was to carry a pocket A-Z and a mobile phone. The time I left Zimbabwe mobile phones were not very common, so I wondered how an ordinary girl like me could have a mobile phone in London.

I could not remember the number to ring on the intercom at the entrance to the building where Maggie lived. Gosh! I had to go round to the back to pick up some mud and small stones. I threw them onto the window and shouted the way we did back home. I called out loud, "*Maaaaaaaaaggie!!!!!*" loud and louder, "*Maaaaaaaaaaaaaaggie!!!!!!!!!*" and even louder: "*Maaaaaaaaaaaaaaaaggie!!!!!!!!!!!*" Honestly, I was just like a father baboon that was screeching in the middle of the city. I didn't even realise that it was late at night and past midnight, till someone heard me. They let me in and I was so tired that I just wanted to go to sleep. I got laughed at and talked about. But I didn't care, it was an adventure. It was my experience in a very large city in which I had never been before. All I wanted was to go to sleep as I felt very tired.

My housemates kept on talking and talking till I fell back to sleep on the couch. Life in London, hey! It's a dream for some but it was definitely not funny or a joke for me. The sight of very similar houses shocked me. I had never seen terraced housed before. In my country the white people built bungalows and mansions; when I left Zimbabwe I was living in a bungalow on a one-acre plot.

The experience frightened me, as there was a high chance that I could miss the right door and try to unlock a neighbour's door, especially if I didn't check the house number... London, ha! A dream for every African who was colonised by the BRITISH!!! Everyone thinks life is as easy as ABC in London, but believe me it is not!

London's dirty jobs for foreigners

The following day Amish offered to come and pick me up. I thought he was very kind. The truth is he was struggling to find staff since the work was very hard yet not rewarding and none of the British people could be seen doing that kind of

CHAPTER SEVENTEEN

job. Those who did not have jobs had their rent and council tax paid for by the government and they also received income support - what a luxury the British people have, I thought. Amish asked me about my trip back home. I told him everything, and that I got lost. He again offered to drive me back after work. He started showing an interest in me but I turned him down point blank. I couldn't stand his very large nose and the smell of garlic coming from his breath. It was quite obvious that Amish had sex with his foreign employees.

"This evening I will take you to SAROVA HOTEL," Amish said, "that is where you will be working." I was introduced to a Nigerian boy called Gbenga and a girl called Ola. I was shown around the place and had my job delegated. I could not believe it - it was a cleaning job! I had to clean the toilets of SAROVA HOTEL in Knightsbridge. Just between you and me, can you imagine that at home I used to have a maid, a gardener, body guards and electric gates! Now here I was, reduced to level zero, cleaning toilets and all the large mirrors. I had never seen such long mirrors in my life. After that we had to clean the swimming pool area and the Sauna which was very hot. I sweated buckets and vowed never to return again. I also had to clean the swimming pool area every half hour.

It was terrible - even the prisoners in a maximum prison called Chikurubhi in Zimbabwe did not work this hard, I thought.

I told Amish that I did not want the job anymore. He

CHAPTER SEVENTEEN

pleaded with me to complete the whole week then he would pay me.

"Jobs are very difficult to get in London," he said. "Foreigners are the ones that do all the dirty job and this job is much better than garbage collection or working as a sewer attendant." He added confidently, "You will come back since you do not have a work permit."

"I don't think so," I replied. "If the going gets tough, I will go back home," I declared. I thought, why would anyone want to be a garbage collector and sewer attendant? I had assumed that machines and robots did jobs like that. "I would rather go back home," I declared.

"We'll see," said Amish. "London is very addictive. Once people come here they hardly go back." He drove me back to Streatham after work. I did not return to work for Amish - I had had enough in one evening! A colleague brought my wages for me. Sheila demanded that I paid thirty-five pounds per week towards bills. She said, five pounds per week was for gas and electricity, ten pounds for food and twenty pounds for accommodation. I just wondered, as this sort of thing is not practised in Zimbabwe. I just wondered about paying all that amount of money whilst I slept on the sofa. She went on to say, "You turned the job down - you will see how hard it is here!" I replied, "My ticket is still valid, so I will use my travellers' cheques to do some shopping then I will go back home."

CHAPTER SEVENTEEN

They all laughed. This is what every Zimbabwean was doing here, I was told. People have bought large houses this way. NO, I thought, I bought my large bungalow by just using my VAGINA. I never worked that hard for it!

Nevertheless, the following week I found a job at the Cookie and Chocolate factory in Esher. The working conditions were much better than doing the dirty jobs in central London. I used to work ten hours a day, starting at seven in the morning and finishing at five in the evening. I did not know anything about alarm clocks and one day I turned up late for work as I had overslept.

"I guess the dog has swallowed the alarm clock," my manager, Raymond, said fiercely.

"I don't have one, sir," I replied.

"Get yourself one then!" he shouted. "They are very cheap from the pound shop - they cost only one pound."

I was surprised to find out that in this factory, no-one else spoke English except Maggie, Shamiso, Helen and myself. The majority of whites spoke Portuguese and some difficult to understand European languages. I thought, something was not right, as I wondered where the English people were. Some could not communicate, even in broken English but could sing a racist song over and over: "*Marikinya marikumiki ku Angola!*" I just assumed they were name calling us black girls, saying go back to Angola. All I could hear most of the time was the word *Preto*, meaning blacks! It did not bother me much because I was after money, not friendship with these migrants like me! The owner of the factory was Jewish who had brought his idea from the US. It was a busy factory - we packed for J. Sainsbury's, Tesco's, Blake Brothers and a few more.

We ate muffins, flapjacks, cookies, and chocolate brownies all day long. I needed to subsidise my money before I got myself a second job at a binding factory. This place paid much better than the cookie factory, where I earned five pounds per hour. I was earning one pound fifty pence more per hour than I was earning at the cookie factory. My second job started at half past five in the evening, finishing at half past ten at night.

I was so pleased that finally I was earning between three hundred and fifty and four hundred and fifty pounds per week from my two jobs. Every Saturday, without fail, I would go to Western Union to send money home. Since I was not happy with the idea of sleeping on the couch, I started asking people about accommodation to rent so that I could have my own space. Sheila had started complaining about knickers that I washed and put on the bathroom radiator to dry, saying she was not happy seeing the knickers in the bathroom as we lived with her husband. I became totally confused as I didn't know what to do.

My workmates told me that they knew of a place where I could get a room for myself for twenty pounds per week. I went to view the room in Tooting and paid a deposit. I moved

CHAPTER SEVENTEEN

in on a Sunday; it was much better than having to crash on the sofa and the rent was much cheaper at £20 per week and £5 for bills. Sheila was not happy with this. She came to my workplace at the cookie factory with my money, about one thousand pounds which was in her account. I had used her account as I did not have a bank account of my own. Since, I did not have a lot of bills to pay the money mounted up quickly. I used to send my children about sixty pounds per week, then about eight hundred pounds at the end of the month to pay for rates, telephone bills, mum's monthly shopping and money towards building mum's house.

Sheila told me to ask my employers to stop depositing my salary into her account. They told me that the arrangements to have my money for that week deposited into her account had already been made, and that it was therefore too late to stop it. I went to Sheila and asked her for my four hundred and fifty pounds, and she replied, "I asked you to tell your employers *not* to deposit any more money in my account," and she added, "I have since closed that account."

Both my employers checked with the bank and were told that the money had gone into Sheila's account and the account was still open. She did all this because she wanted me to continue staying in her house, sleeping on the sofa. God bless her, I prayed. I will earn more, I reassured myself. It just taught me how my fellow people could be mean, especially in a foreign country.

CHAPTER SEVENTEEN

As time went on, I started buying newspapers. I bought the *Surrey Advertiser*, where I saw loads of jobs advertised. I called a number from my large black mobile phone that I had purchased. This was a nursing home that was looking for care assistants to start ASAP in Cobham, Surrey. I was invited for an interview which I booked for the following day. All I wanted was to get experience and move away from the non-English speaking people as I found it very difficult to communicate with them and I also had to do more hours to earn good money.

During the years I am talking about jobs were very easy to find in the UK. None of the companies asked for references, passports or work permits during that time. The pound was very strong as well. This was before the millennium, before 9/11 and before Poland and other Eastern Europeans joined the EU. It was full of jobs you know, those kind of jobs which English people would not do. At the time of writing this book, those jobs which were easy to get are now as hard to get as *panning for gold along River Thames* - no jobs anywhere and no benefits. It's chaotic...

A lot of British people are becoming homeless. I thought; what is it that went wrong with our lovely and once very rich Great Britain? Still I am unable to get the answer. Old people in nursing homes are worried sick for their welfare, and care homes are going bust, banks going to the wall - what a life, demonstrations here, demonstrations there, riots, it's terrible!

CHAPTER SEVENTEEN

Everything is just contradictory. "Young people, if you vote for us, you will have University fees scrapped," campaign the Liberal Democrats. They managed to manipulate the young generation and got the votes. Just a few months in the Office and the 'married government' (the coalition) as a couple agreed to raise the fees! Oh my God, I thought, they want people to work and look after themselves! How is that going to be possible now, when university fees have gone up three times? I just love politicians, if you know what I mean! I love them, they make life easy for people; they make promises to people which they never deliver or even reverse... Think about it, mate! Honestly, do they or don't they?? Just like my uncle, the HONOURABLE PRESIDENT ROBERT MUGABE!! I just love him: he made every Zimbabwean a MILLIONAIRE and made many poor ZILLIONAIRES and half of the population are now refugees in other countries. How wonderful is that!

I just thought, in life it is not how you start that matters, it's how you finish. I am talking about quality control here. Are the services meeting the specific requirements? Are they dependable, are they satisfactory?? I leave you to answer that. I am just an observer! Maybe we are in the LAST DAYS!! Or maybe we are heading towards another WORLD WAR, I thought. God Almighty Help US! I prayed... *EVERYTHING ELSE SEEMS TO BE FAILLING, I cried!!*

On one occasions whilst travelling to work on a train, I

observed a young man running very fast and in-front of a fast train which appeared to travel faster than the wind - and the man died instantly. What, suicide? "Oh God Almighty, help me, why did I have to witness this?!" I cried and prayed for the dead man. The people on the train did not seem to bother about the deceased but about the time they were losing. "Now we are being delayed by this lunatic!" they murmured.

This made me wonder what exactly was happening in the Queen's country. Young men committing suicide in broad daylight? It was heart-breaking. I never dreamt or thought that people would kill themselves just like that in England. I got the shock of my life that traumatised me for some time. I just wondered why I had to witness such sad events, especially since I had expected life to be all rosy in London. I thought about myself, that I was working and earning a reasonable amount of money and feeding my entire family, even my extended family. What about people born here? I assumed life would be much, much better for Britons.

This is when I realised that life in London was not as easy as I thought it was. For me it was easy as I always converted my wages at the current exchange rate of the pound against the Zimbabwean dollar and ended up having a surplus. I did not bother about cable TV, credit cards, or store cards. Everything I earned was purely for my family and for me. The fact that I compared what I earned to that of my colleagues at home kept me going as I knew that my weekly wages were enough to pay ten headmasters and forty teachers monthly, in terms of the salaries in Zimbabwe those days.

CHAPTER EIGHTEEN

WHERE THERE IS SHIT THERE IS BRASS!

AS I LEFT the migrant-infested Chocolate and Cookie factory in Esher, Surrey, I was pleased that I now worked with people who could understand me in the care home setting. The first week I was on training and was supposed to just observe since I was on induction. I battled with the smell of raw shit as I observed Barbra cleaning Maisie Carpenter. When Barbra finished cleaning Maisie, she started going again. "Let's hoist her onto the commode, dear," said Barbs. We quickly hoisted Maisie onto this chair that had a hole in the middle. The smell was terrible and then Maisie kept on going and going.

"Did they give her something which is causing her to go like this?" I asked Barbs.

"No dear, Maisie eats and eats, non-stop. She eats a lot of puréed food including prunes and when she goes, she goes for England," joked Barbs. "This is quite normal for her," Barbs continued, "sometimes she will dig into her pad, reach

CHAPTER EIGHTEEN

for her poo and plaster the walls with it."

"Why does she do that?" I asked.

"It's due to old age, dementia, and the laxatives that she takes regularly; I think she takes two Senna tablets, Lactulose and Movicol every night and she has porridge with prunes every morning," said Barbs. "These old people get repeat prescriptions, some of which are not necessary. Once prescribed they stay on them for life, how unfair is that."

I just thought, well, the UK must be a very rich country, if they can waste resources that way. Honestly, prescribing three different types of laxatives that serve the same purpose to be administered every night for the rest of someone's life! I just wondered if Maisie really needed all that medication, but had to swallow my words.

Dementia was such a big word for me, I had never heard of it before. Care homes were there in Zimbabwe but mainly Athol Evans and Bhumhudzo which are funded by the Salvation Army; only those who did not have families were put into the nursing home. It is a taboo, in Zimbabwe, to put your parents in a care home. The whole country would talk about you, even the cheapest newspaper *Kwayedza* will make trillions in a day, with locals buying and wanting to know about a fellow Zimbabwean who has thrown his or her parents into a care home!

We then hoisted Maisie up. Barbs put a big yellow plastic pad on her. I glanced into the pot - it was half full, just as big as a head of a new-born baby, but kinda loose.

CHAPTER EIGHTEEN

"Take the pot to the sluice please, Tanaka," said Barbra.

I quickly grabbed the pot and put the lid on and headed straight for the door. I thought, that was a relief, since I was struggling to breathe in Maisie's room. I just wanted a breath of fresh air. I had my plastic apron on and my latex gloves on. I thought fine, I am well equipped for the job as I realised I was given the GAAFOFY (go away and find out for yourself).

I held the pot in my hand. GOSH, it smelled and I battled with the smell! I walked down the corridor to the sluice room. I used my foot to open the sluice machine as I was taught, and placed the pot in. There were no instructions on the sluice; all I was taught was place the pot in and press the green button to start it.

Luck was not on my side that day - I am sure it must have been Friday the 13th. I pressed the green button without realising that the sluice door or lid was not closed properly. SPLASH!!!!!!!!!! SPLASH!!!!!!!!!!!!! SPLASH!!!!!!!!! came the hot water mixed with human shit. Mate, I was covered in it, swimming in it, and I was baptised in it! I screamed for help, but it was already too late - I was covered in human shit from head to toe. As you know, I resented shit from the time I was growing up, but this time I had to mingle with it and I blended with it. The time I fell into an African public latrine was much better: then I had simply slipped and fallen into it, but now I was covered with the stuff - it went almost everywhere on me. I was marinated in it. My brain froze and I could not move; I

CHAPTER EIGHTEEN

stood there like a zombie as the sluice continued to splash out the shit. I was in a state of shock.

One of the senior carers rushed in and slammed the sluice door really hard. Still frozen, I could not even do anything to help myself. There I stood stupidly like a sewer attendant as I recalled Amish's reference to the term. Sure, where there is shit there is money: I was driven by the compelling belief that what I earned in a week was enough to pay five teachers' salaries in Zimbabwe (in the mid-90's).

"This is how you shut it; in future make sure it's really shut before turning the green light on," said Elaine. "Come with us, come on sweetheart, this must have been a shock for you," she said kindly.

"It's all my fault!" cried Barbra. "I had been told that Tanaka has never done care work before, yet I let her take the pot to the sluice." She added: "I am very sorry my love."

"No dear, it's not your fault, it's my ignorance," I replied.

The girls were really nice and kind to me. They led me to the shower. One of them went to fetch two bottles of shampoo and body wash.

"Take your clothes off, Tanaka," the girls demanded as I was in a state of shock. They helped me to undress and made me sit down on a shower chair.

Man, life is full of shit! This was just more shit than I ever thought of, real puréed shit all over me. I saw it, felt it, touched it, tasted it and scented it. *Ho-owhu, ho-owhu!* I vomited and vomited, I retched and retched and regurgitated till I vomited my stomach and lungs out. This was even worse than the time I treaded on the poo and slipped and fell: it was horrible and spooky. Why on planet earth do I keep on be being baptised in poo, I wondered!

The girls showered me and poured all the shampoo in my hair. They washed and washed me till I was clean.

"Shit, shit, real shit, fucking real shit," I swore as I kept on spitting.

My mind raced back to the time when I was growing up and the thought of the public toilet crawled into my head. I resented those toilets but now I was swimming in raw human shit! I thought people had said there is gold in London! No, I thought, there isn't any gold but loads and loads of human SHIT, bloody SHIT and BLOODY FUCKING shit and more shit! I got really paranoid and confused. Is this the kind of job that I have to do, I thought? Nah, NAH, there *must* be something better to do out there than intermingling with human waste… Perhaps Amish was being sarcastic about those sewage attendants, he must have meant carers and nurses! "Shit, fucking shit!" I swore again.

The value of the pound had made me travel many, many miles away from home. It was the life of the colonial whites that gave me and others the impression that life was easy abroad. The time I am talking about one could live like a king with only fifty grand in one's portfolio. Seeing whites

CHAPTER EIGHTEEN

affording chefs, cooks, nannies and housemaids back in Zimbabwe made me think that if I were to go to work in London for six months I would be rich like my white colleagues. It was only a dream after all.

Whilst I was in the shower, Matron had driven into town to get me a new pair of knickers and an ultimo bra (man, it was my first time to see such a beautiful bra that made my boobs look bigger!), a new pair of jeans and a jumper. Why do people waste money on boob jobs when there is such any amazing product on the market, I wondered? She bought me some perfume, deodorant and body powder. The girls towel-dried me and left me to do the last bits. I dressed myself and Matron asked me to go and have a lie down in the staff room. She came in with a hot cup of chocolate.

"Have this and drink it quickly, and cover yourself with a duvet," said Matron. "I am very sorry Tanaka," she added.

"It's not your fault," I replied.

"It is," she insisted. "Barbra was supposed to have come and shown you exactly how to use the sluice before sending you. You told me at the interview yesterday that you had never done this job before, so you were supposed to be with someone, not left on your own." Matron was such a nice lady and she did not know what to do. "Drink your hot chocolate and try to have a rest. I mean, try to close your eyes. I will come and get you at 5 p.m. and take you home."

I drank my hot chocolate quickly but I was still in a state

CHAPTER EIGHTEEN

of shock. Matron called the home owner, Mr Fathergull, and told him what had happened.

Mr Fathergull was a very rich man. He drove to the nursing home in his Ferrari. He brought me a card which said he was sorry about the accident. He offered me £5,000.00 compensation and one month's salary of £1,000.00. Matron asked me to take the weekend off and come back to work on Tuesday. I thought, what! Six grand! I could not believe it! They asked me to sign a piece of paper that I had accepted the money and was not bound to make any further claims.

Matron advised me to go and see a Doctor straight away and explain what had happened. I had some blood tests taken to check if I had picked up any infection such as Hepatitis. I was given a Hep B vaccine and asked to go back again to have my blood checked which proved negative to Hepatitis B.

For the first time since arriving in London, I managed to have a break and rested for four days. I just realised that my God had performed a miracle to compensate me for the money that Sheila had stolen from me! I had a total of about £8,000.00 on me including all the money I had worked for and some which I had brought with me. I confided in my flatmate that I did not have a bank account. He told me to take my passport and go to the bank and open a bank account.

I chose to go to Esher High Street to open my bank account, as I was scared that if I did it in London, I might be deported since Sheila had warned me that I could be deported any time. I opened my account with my visitor's visa and no questions were asked. I deposited my money and sent a thousand pounds home. The thought of the shit all over me haunted me for a while and I suffered from flashbacks. It was terrible. The desire to be like my rich friends back home when I returned home kept me going.

Honestly, there is Brass in the Healthcare Business, especially for those who have nursing homes and those who provide care to individuals in their own homes. "Where there is shit there is Brass," I thought again, but this applies mainly to the employer, not the employee... For employees it is a secure job, so they will be able to pay their bills but never do anything else; regarding the employer, it enables them to earn whilst they sleep and whilst employees are running around like headless chickens and being baptised in muck and shit! Instead of getting their hands dirty, employers keep on investing and investing, thus making their money work for them.

CHAPTER NINETEEN

THE EXPERT BUM CLEANER (AKA CARER)

AFTER MY THREE DAYS OFF, I came back to work and completed my induction programme. I became very competent in ass wiping and poo scrubbing and started working independently. My appetite had gone as I felt a huge lump in my throat all the time. Human shit is not something to mess about with; it stinks and it's sickening. I thought about it every single second. I could smell it everywhere till I got so used to the smell that it did not bother me anymore. I could come from cleaning poo and go straight to eating my food and thoroughly enjoy it. Someone has got to do the job, I thought, and it has to be done. Well, this is what I have to do for money and even trained nurses are doing it, I reassured myself and carried on. I was now a qualified sewer attendant. Seeing shit on a daily basis became just like seeing mud with the exception that mud does not smell bad like shit.

As I became very experienced in helping clients to wash and dress, feeding them and of course cleaning the bums of

CHAPTER NINETEEN

those who were incontinent, I joined an agency in Guildford, Surrey, and started working and earning real money. I earned eight pounds per hour during the weekdays, nine pounds per hour during the weeknights and eleven pounds per hour for any shift on Saturday and twelve per hour on Sundays. I started to earn about five hundred pounds per week from the agency and about eight hundred and fifty pounds for my full-time job which I only worked for three days per week. Since I had no-one in London I devoted my time to working more than having a social life. As I worked, I learnt that nurses earned about twenty pounds plus to about forty pounds and above on bank holidays per hour whilst working for an agency. My desire to become a nurse grew stronger. My only huge drawback was lack of academic qualifications.

I started making inquiries about universities and entry requirements for the nursing course. I was told there was an entry exam called the D.C test which I tried and failed. Within no time the Access to Nursing course was introduced. I decided to continue working for a few months.

I worked in and around Surrey in posh hospitals such as the Royal Nuffield and Mount Alvernia and a few NHS hospitals. I looked after some people in their own homes. This is the time that I learnt that Surrey was a very rich county. I used to look after some people who had massive houses with indoor pools. This quickly erased the thought that only those in London where rich. I started feeling a great

CHAPTER NINETEEN

desire to be like these people, especially after reflecting on my own life in Zimbabwe.

I really fancied being like the posh people who lived in Surrey and Grosvenor Park, in central London. This is the kind of life I want to lead, I thought, but how can I do it? This is the question I kept asking myself. My whole life had been driven by self-belief. I knew pretty well that anything is possible as long as I believe that I can do it, and apply myself to it.

"Keep on dreaming girl," I told myself, and, "Follow your dreams," came a little voice in my head.

I kept wondering, if there is so much demand for carers, why can't I recruit people to work for me whilst they are earning their money? I could be earning whilst I am sleeping, I thought. The thought of having several people working for me kept on going on and on and on in my head, but I did not know what to do and how to do it, since I was in a foreign country. Honestly, the recruitment industry was a niche market and a real gold mine those days. This was before the year 2000, when life was so good in Great Britain and when young people wanted to carry on with their lives and not stop working to look after elderly parents. The parents' money, locked in houses, had to look after them; for those who had it and those who couldn't afford care fees, Social Services and the NHS continuation of care paid for the care bill.

I am sure the Millennium brought all the recession and

CHAPTER NINETEEN

due to the expansion of the EU, migration from Asia and Africa, the small island of Britain is going to explode, I thought; the Gulf War and everything considered, it's just chaotic; and what about the heaps and heaps of food they throw away on a daily basis? Isn't that money they are throwing away? This is when I was starting to get used to the British life. I realised that the majority of people in England spent the day hunting for bargains, buying from charity shops, Iceland and from the car boot sales. I never dreamt that life could be that difficulty in the United Kingdom before boarding the plane. I am sure if people who are abroad start seeing how much people suffer in the United Kingdom, honestly, no-one would want to come here. I blamed it on Propaganda as people always get to be shown the nicest places and things in the developed countries, yet in Africa and Asia all people are shown are poverty-stricken areas, with people scavenging through the garbage to earn a living; they are never shown any nice places, hence all of us are flocking to London, New York and other well-known cities in the developed countries....

CHAPTER TWENTY

FEMME FATALE WITH THE AMERICAN MILLIONAIRE

MY SIX MONTHS visit turned to a year; illegally, mind you. A year turned into two years, and two years into five, and five into ten and then fifteen years. I got addicted to the UK and the smell of raw shit in care homes, and thought it was just lovely. I hardly knew my neighbours except for my housemates who worked hard like me, only seeing each other on Sundays, when we cooked food for the whole week. Eventually I began feeling exhausted and feeling sick and tired of working too hard doing eighty bloody hours a week. Let me try the dating scene, I thought - I might be lucky and meet a rich *murungu* and all this would end.

I was now thirty-something, if you know what I mean. I had reached that age where most women do not feel very comfortable talking about their age, so it's always thirty-something. I thought maybe I would strike it lucky and walk down the aisle again before hitting forty, then gradually forty-something, then half a century.

CHAPTER TWENTY

I was now more experienced in life, yet facing the battle of the mid-life crisis. I knew that life can be full of disasters which are part and parcel of the life journey; and that life will never be a straightforward journey. I was told that in London men do not approach women on the street. The dating scene was totally different from that of my Zimbabwean culture. I just had to give it a go, and start dating again whilst I was still thirty-something. I could dress up nicely when I wanted to, for no special reason other than because I knew my life itself was the special occasion - I had to make the most of it while I could.

I placed an advert in the London telephone dating ads. The telephone number in the paper was very clear and big. "To place an advert, ring the free number **0800 800 0800**." How nice, I thought, to be able to place an advert for free! "To listen to your messages call 0909 06609 6969 and calls cost one pound fifty per minute." I can't tell you how much my telephone bill was that month as I tried to listen to the messages that were left for me! I finally gave up when I realised that I was just increasing the profits of British Telecom.

I returned a call to one of my interested parties who had left his number and landline.

"Hello," came a female voice.

"Hello," I replied. "Can I speak to Ian please?" I asked.

"Ian is a married man - what do you want from him?" the voice of a white woman replied, irritated. "I know he has

CHAPTER TWENTY

placed an advert in the paper to try and get to me; we have been married for the past twenty years! We are only going through a rough patch; I hope we will get through it. I advise you to leave my husband alone, please."

"Okay, bye," I said and put down the receiver, my heart pumping with fear. It was a compensatory mechanism just in case I got harmed and bled; hence my heart pumped fast and faster to ensure an adequate supply of blood!

I had a lot of responses, but the majority of them were married man. I don't need a married man, I thought, I am a widow, single and available, so why should I date a man who is already taken? I placed my boundaries, which meant no to married men, no to very old men and no to very young men; still, I remained very surprised that married men behaved as if they we not married!

I was okay sex-wise, as I had learned the art of lovemaking from the magazines and sex videos I had smuggled from South Africa. Thanks to the South African government I did not appear as a fool and ignorant in a western country. My only problem was how to become a real woman.

My desire for full and big pants followed me from Zimbabwe to Britain. I wore my high heels - that was not a problem even if I walked like a crazy ostrich! The only problem was showing off my very hairy legs. My hairy pussy was something else (lol), but it was out of sight! It was a real animal. My armpits were not hairy at all; they were clean-

CHAPTER TWENTY

shaven. I had to learn how to become a real woman. Though I knew that I could give a bloke a good head, I still lacked confidence on account of my hairy bits. When I looked in the magazines, I saw that all women displayed smooth waxed legs. I did my research and found out that it is a very painful procedure. Shall I do it, or not, I asked myself? Finally, I gave it a go and walked into a Beauty Salon. I tried having my hairy legs waxed and screamed the whole place down! No, I am *not* doing it, I thought, for it seemed more painful than childbirth; but with childbirth I at least had the compensation of ending up with my baby. But waxing - why, what am I dying in pain for, to pull men? No, I refused and I left the Beauty Salon and headed for my bedsit. I could hear people laughing from the Beauty Salon, and I swore, "I don't bloody care, you don't know me so what!!!" I resolved that I would dismiss waxing, which was my final thought that helped me to gather myself up and leg it.

I used to have facials and manicures at home, but in England I could not afford all that luxury since I went to Western Union religiously on a weekly basis to send money to relatives and friends. I was depriving myself for a good reason.

I had to learn what it is that men wanted before risking the pain of rejection. As I struggled with my thoughts, I later realised that Nick had wanted me badly, to the extent that he even blackmailed me, stalked me and lost his life; I also had a full blown affair with Roy who had previously promised

CHAPTER TWENTY

to bring me the moon and stars had I asked for them. He had bought me a very expensive house, loved to fuck my hairy pussy and even loved the feel of my hairy legs. So I knew already that I was a *femme fatale*. He loved the hairy monster that I have, so why should I try to tame the harmless wild creature, I thought!

I decided not to do it. I threw the high heels away and went for semi-high heeled shoes, a cheap but pretty handbag and of course my usual perfume, Channel COCO, which I was now addicted to. I used black eye liner to line my eyes lightly and applied a lilac eye shadow which was blended with a touch of grey. I lined my lips with a black lip liner and wore a pretty red sleeveless dress with a hem just above my knees. With purplish lip gloss my lips looked fuller and sparkled.

I held my head high, proud to show it off with my hair enhanced with Brazilian hair extensions, and stuck out my chest as the perfect fitting red and black ultimo bra supported and enhanced my boobs; for the first time I wore this bra I felt like one of the top models who had risked their lives to go under the knife. I walked lively and confidently towards my blind date, swinging my hips like a classy lady would. My hips felt wider in this tight-fitting small red dress. The dress made a perfect S-curve as the small red dress followed my spine down my bum, which stuck up as if I had been wearing a bum support or enhancer! I felt comfortable in my own black hide. It just felt perfect to be *me*. At least I walked

CHAPTER TWENTY

comfortably in my semi-high heels, 'coz I did not want to walk like an ostrich in high heels.

My decision to join Date-loners, a dating agency that would send a list of potentials, was a good one as I had to choose the man I wanted to go out with till I found the perfect match. As I waited quietly and nervously outside Green Park tube station, my mobile phone rang. I reached for my phone and saw the name Lenny flashing as my phone continued to ring; before answering, I looked around to see if there was anyone standing nearby using a mobile phone. I did this deliberately as I wanted to check on my blind date first. If I found anything that I disapproved of, I was prepared to gallop a mile without looking back and just turn my phone off.

I stared across the road and eyed a tall, dark guy who was broad shouldered, his chest conveying the message that he was fit and a gym member. He wore a light blue shirt that had two buttons undone to reveal his chest slightly, a black belt with a pair of black trousers and a pair of neatly polished black shoes. In his right hand he carried the pink newspaper, *The Financial Times*. He had passed the bill already as shoes and belt meant much to me, as did carrying the *Financial Times* as opposed to *The Sun* - all of which struck the right note. His shirt was neatly tucked in, which was also to my approval. His hair was neatly cut, no visible tattoos or piercings or earrings. I screened him from top to bottom till I was satisfied. After my instincts had approved of my blind

CHAPTER TWENTY

date, I finally braved it and answered my phone. I must admit I am a bit old fashioned, as piercings and tattoos put me off.

"Where are you?" I asked, pretending I had not checked him out.

"I am at Green Park station, how about you?"

"Same here, I am at Green Park station."

He turned around to try and locate me.

"What are you wearing?" I queried.

"A light blue shirt and I have a pink newspaper in my right hand."

"Oh, I can see you! I am across the road, dressed in my small red dress," I said waving at him.

I took a few steps towards him to show him that I was a lady of class who allows the gentleman to take the initiative as a man. I let him make all the effort to cross the road toward me rather than me going across the street for him. I glided slowly towards him as I swung my hips to meet him halfway. I could see his smile and the look of approval that was on his face. My heart pounded and raced with excitement as I seized the opportunity to show off my lovely lady humps and the Zimbabwean class in me. "What a pull," I said to myself.

"Hey," he said, as he turned his phone off and placed it in his pocket. With an outstretched hand he reached for mine to shake hands.

"Hello," I replied.

"Can I?" he asked, leaning over to give me a kiss on the cheek.

CHAPTER TWENTY

"Of course," I replied.

"You are just what I imagined you to be," he smiled. "I am Lenny by the way, nice to meet you at last." As he spoke I noticed his neatly shaped white teeth which were as white as snow, his blue eyes, his neatly jelled hair, his well-nourished hide, his well-manicured nails; also, the smell of his mouthwash and aftershave had something to say about him.

Could he be some unknown celebrity, I thought quietly? Well, he could be just an ordinary person who has made an effort for his blind date, I thought again.

"Thank you, and nice to meet you too," I smiled in return. "I am Tanaka, as you know."

"Where can we go to find some quiet time so we could have a chat?" he asked.

"I'll let you decide," I answered, allowing Lenny to be a gentleman. I did not want to take the lead but to follow.

"Right, leave it to me. I guess a lady like you would not want to be seen in some smoky pub! I'll take you to a quiet wine bar across the road. The price of drinks only attracts beautiful ladies like you," he added.

I did not want to diminish myself in his eyes by suggesting that of course we could go to a pub, but remained firm and confident, and I replied, "Sure, these pubs are a bit too noisy and smoky."

Having lived in London for a few years I could figure out straight away that Lenny was not English but American, due to his behaviour and accent.

CHAPTER TWENTY

In the wine bar we ordered our drinks which Lenny paid for. It was a beautiful wine bar with some expensive art on the walls, nice wallpaper and very cosy and comfy chairs. We talked as we sipped our drinks. It was as though we had met before. Everything was just perfect and Lenny was a gentleman. He sipped his drink slowly as he studied me carefully. I could see his eyes dilating and his smile of approval spreading to his ears.

I tried very hard to impress Lenny, especially regarding my accent, to make it sound more British than Zimbabwean - you know, swallowing the TEEs this time.

For some reason he picked this up. "How long have you lived in London?" he asked.

"All my life," I replied.

He laughed hysterically. "No babe, you can't have lived here all your life!"

"Why?" I asked with a smile.

"It's your accent, my love. It sounds a bit like Mandela's, which means you might be from the southern part of Africa," he said with a smile.

"Yes my love, I am originally from the southern region of Africa but brought up here; it's just that at home we kept on speaking our language." I lied deliberately, as I wanted Lenny to think that all my family lived in London - just in case he was one of those men who made women disappear in London.

CHAPTER TWENTY

"I see," he chuckled and sipped his drink.

We had so much to talk about but I never gave away the information that I was on my own in London. A few minutes into our date a friend called to check if I was okay.

"So, that was one of your family members checking up on you? You are safe with me, you know," he added.

"Sure, that's my sister," I lied. (It was a flatmate I had asked to check up on me.)

"Sooner or later, I shall meet all your family," said Lenny with a broad smile.

I continued to sip my drink slowly as I examined Lenny in close detail.

I did not want the date to be an interrogative one, but to allow things to come out naturally. We sat down and continued sipping our drinks, chatting away and giggling - it was all fun. The people who were in the Wine Bar just viewed as a couple who had known each other for a while. There was never a dull moment or a quiet moment. We talked about the decorations of the Wine Bar, the paintings, the people, us and about most of the silly and stupid things that people do to get money and to grab attention.

My first date went really well and I was pleased with myself.

Lenny told me that he liked me and wanted to see me again. He was an American who was in London on a business mission but he did not mention this on our first few dates.

CHAPTER TWENTY

On our second date we went to a romantic French restaurant somewhere near the Ritz in central London. The date went well. We ended up going back to Lenny's flat somewhere around Waterloo.

As we walked into the hallway, I noticed there was a collection of high quality paintings. The walls, the tiles and the carpet - everything was remarkable. He had white antique leather sofas which were very beautiful. The floor was tiled with some high quality imported tiles. In the centre of the room was a very large white sheepskin rug which was very fluffy. He co-ordinated his living room with some red and black ornaments and lighting. It was like the kind of rooms one sees in magazines, films and show homes - it was beautiful. The flat was beautifully scented and he had these heavenly scented candles lit and placed in every corner of the flat. For a short period of time I forgot who I was and had to pinch myself to make sure I was still alive and not dead.

Lenny gave me a tour of his flat. The flat had this high quality Laura Ashley wallpaper and paint. It was decorated to a high standard. A beautiful chandelier hung from the ceiling. He showed me his photographs, his children's pictures and the lady who he called "the bitch I once loved."

"Thank God I am a free man now," he said, and went on to say, "Darling, I do not want to put you off by talking about this woman; she is the mother of my children and will always be. I loved her very much, till the day I caught her red-

CHAPTER TWENTY

handed having sex with my best friend who was also my best man at our wedding. God knows how long they had been fooling me and doing it behind my back till that day. I thought I had three children only to be told on the day I caught her in bed with my best mate that my daughter, who is now sixteen and the youngest, was not mine but hers and his. Her DNA also proved it, so, I ended it." He continued: "I don't want to talk about it, but tonight I shall call my eldest daughter to convince you that I am a free man and back on the market; and now that I have met you, I can't tell you what a relief it is to know there are no more cheaters in my life!" He chuckled, "Now, where were we?"

OOOOOuuuuccccchhhh, I cried, deep down inside, making sure that Lenny did not hear. "Not any more cheaters," I recalled. "Does he really know who I am?" I sighed quietly.

He continued to show me around. He had this massive bed; everything was high quality antique furniture, not the chipboard flat-pack kind from the local shops. "I buy most of my stuff from Italy," he said, and added, "I love Italian stuff."

As we continued round the flat we could see the workmen working on the London Eye from his window, as it was in its early stages of construction. After sipping a glassful of red wine, I never felt embarrassed showing my hairy legs and these very large pants I had on! I just thought, it's time to show *murungu* what I am really made of. Starting with

CHAPTER TWENTY

strip tease, I pulled my zip on the front of my dress down to reveal my huge melons.

"Surprise me," said Lenny. I did not want to give him a clue that I had been in this situation before and was accustomed to this sort of behaviour, but played the part of a good girl. All of a sudden the demon took hold and I jumped on Lenny's lap, forcing him to lie down on his back.

"Hands above your head," I ordered. I quickly reached for two chiffon scarves that were in my handbag. With one I gently tied his hands above his head and onto the bed, and used the other as a blindfold. I worked my way from top to toe, using my tongue accordingly, over and over again till he groaned with excitement, and shouted "I am on the highway to heaven!!" with excitement. He reached cloud nine! I untied him thinking he had had enough!

Slap went his hand on my bum! He pulled me closer to him and kissed me passionately, like some movie star in a romantic movie; finally, he threw me onto the bed so that I lay on my back facing the ceiling, and he worked on me from top to bottom returning the favour! Talk about what the French do! It was received with honour, several times I guess, till I was saturated with desire! For a few minutes I forgot who I was, and that I did not have money or papers. I was in another world yet to be discovered, the world the young ones desire to find out about. Finally, Lenny charged like an angry bulldog. "Bend over misses!" he ordered. He reached for my

CHAPTER TWENTY

laces (*matinji*, labia minora down below), and played with them, his lips glued to mine till his prick was as hard as RHINO HORN! "I like taking you from behind, but in the holy and moral hole," he said, thrusting his thingy into my holy hole. I could feel its warmth and when he did the male jive, I could feel it hitting my cervix. Like a jockey on a horse, he rode me really hard, slapping my bum as he rode. "Now lie down, I want it from the front!" Hear me out before going back to bowing down and worshiping in the good old missionary position. I reached Planet 9x9 screaming and making loud noises, till I heard him screaming too! "Fucking shit!" he groaned as he sprouted his seeds with much generosity! "This is just so fucking good!"

Within no time my demon left me, having performed its indispensable skills - miracles would be a better term! We looked at each other as we lay cuddling and gasping for breath, just like Bolt on the Olympic track after running a marathon and winning a gold medal, smiling from ear to ear to express the winners' emotions!

After our steamy session Lenny concurred that I was highly talented. He told me point blank that what I did with him was totally out of this world. I had to make all the effort in pleasing him, since he was my last resort. *WHEN EVERYTHING ELSE HAD FAILED, as I thought, this might get me out of poverty - marrying for money.* I became a real animal in bed, but deep down I didn't want a man for

CHAPTER TWENTY

financial independence; I just didn't know how to start a business in a foreign country and how to raise capital, and above all, how to become a resident instead of a visitor.

"I am sorry for my unshaven legs and a bushy pussy," I told Lenny.

"Don't be silly," he replied. "It's not about Brazilian waxing or big boobs dear, you don't have to be like River Jayden the busty model to keep me, my love," he went on.

"What is it all about then?" I asked shyly.

"It's about how you handle your man, and knowing the right places to go for and doing it properly, your body language and the way you speak when you want something - that's what counts," smiled Lenny. "Your armpits are clean-shaven, your breath smells nice and your pussy is irresistible, and you talk sensibly," he added and continued: "You know what, Tanaka, in life you can bring the world under your feet, but only if you know how to; and what to say at the right time. So in bed I found out that you know how to do it, but I need to teach you how to make money. I don't want to see you working so hard for money. You can make money just as quickly as clicking your fingers - that is, if you know how to, and I want you to be able to make money whilst you sleep."

"Oh I see," I said. I tell you, he made me blush but made me wonder again about making money whilst I slept! He was the second person I had heard saying that within a space of five years.

CHAPTER TWENTY

"I thought as a woman," I ventured, "I have to impress my man by what I wear, and by having smooth skin."

"As far as I can tell you dear, you don't have to change a thing; you are just perfect," said Lenny. "Most women spend money on expensive clothes, G-strings, having boob, nose and lip jobs, designer vaginas; yet they are really useless in bed and when we come to the act, well, it's just appalling!"

Once again, I realised that my natural thick lips and my padded VAGINA aka BUSHY PUSSY, BADLY PACKED KEBAB were very powerful assets, not liabilities that needed regular maintenance; only soap and water, deodorant, Channel Coco, mouthwash, flossing my teeth all the time, and of course my usual manicure and pedicure did it for me as well having a touch of class. I just felt free to please Lenny and to make sure that he was satisfied, which was my paramount priority, and his compliments boosted my confidence and my self- esteem. Within no time, I won Lenny's heart; he loved me to the extent that he would have brought me the moon and the stars had I asked for them.

I was not shocked to hear this from a *murungu*, since Roy had previously made nice comments about me. I became very confident and started seeing Lenny on a regular basis. My life became really good now that I had met Lenny. The only problem was that Lenny was an American businessman and as such he had to take several trips back to the States to see his children and for business purposes.

CHAPTER TWENTY

He was very caring, considerate, passionate and generous; you know what I mean - he was very, *very* generous. He was a man of high integrity and a man of substance. He made sure that if I cancelled my shift to meet up with him, he would treble my wages for that week or pay my wages for the month multiplied by four or five, and he would just say, "Here you are my gorgeous girl, go and spoil yourself; money means nothing to me, I can lose it all now and get it all back tomorrow because I know how to make it; right now while I am with you, I am making more by the minute. I do not regret any minute of it because we can stay in one of London's most expensive hotel, ask for room service for a year, tip the waitresses, and will still have more money - simply because I am making more every second and I want to teach you how to make money whilst you sleep, too!"

How nice could a guy be! Surely, he was very kind, considerate and generous. We never went Dutch on meals or drinks, for he always footed the bill. I always offered to pay my way, but he would always say, "No babe, you don't have to, that's my duty as your man, and one thing that inspires me is that you are not with me for the contents of my wallet but for who I am, and that's why I love you. I have had a few women who fell for me for the wrong reason, but with you, Tanaka, everything just feels so natural and it is has been a case of one thing leading to another." I felt loved and well looked after, as I was being spoiled. It was so easy and it didn't

CHAPTER TWENTY

take long for Lenny to win my heart and my submission, and it was not long before I heard those famous words "*Je t'aime bebe*" from an American guy.

"*Moi aussi, Je t'aime,*" I replied shyly.

"So you speak French?" queried Lenny.

"Only a little bit," I replied smiling.

"One of these days I will take you to Paris," he said. ("*Oh my God, please do not even think about going there, Lenny please,*" *I thought and prayed quietly for this Paris conversation to end. How can I go to Paris? I am living in England as an illegal immigrant, I thought quietly.*) Lenny continued: "We could spent some quality time together in Paris as we get to know each other and I will buy you dozens of your favourite Coco Channel." He pulled me closer to him to give me a wonderful long, lustful and lingering kiss. He took my hand and we crossed the road to a posh restaurant in the Green Park area. Thank God, the Paris talk did not surface again.

We stood outside one of Green Park's posh restaurants that we had chosen to have a meal, reading the menus, and I recalled that it was the place where I had done my first few shifts on my arrival in London. It looked different as we entered the restaurant using the front door entrance; I had previously used the back door entrance before being greeted by the smell of rubbish bins full of left-over food when I worked as a kitchen porter. I told Lenny that I had worked in the restaurant before as a kitchen porter. I did not expect the answer he gave me and it shocked me.

CHAPTER TWENTY

"Darling, we all started from somewhere in our lives, and the thing I like most about you, Tanaka, is that you don't lie about your past or feel ashamed; you know what, if you had hung on in there, maybe by now you might have had your own restaurant. People who succeed in life have had humble beginnings - much better than sitting by a tube station entrance asking people for change." He paused, looking at me with a smile. "Do you want to go in there tonight not as a kitchen porter but as a posh customer? I will escort you so you can greet your former boss if you like," he added.

We went in and had diner. No-one seemed to recognise me; there was a girl whose accent sounded Polish who was doing exactly what I used to do. I felt sorry for her as she washed up non-stop, crockery coming like shit.

When we had finished we walked to catch a black cab to Lenny's Penthouse. We stopped by the cash point as Lenny wanted cash to pay the cab driver. "Have a look, Tanaka," he said. He wanted me to see his bank balance. I counted the figures after the comma, and there were more than nine figures. "You are a multi-millionaire, aren't you?" I gasped.

He took out the cash, more than he needed which was almost his daily limit, and he held me tightly and whispered, "Yes, darling, I am a multi-millionaire. I have made my fortune from corporations and properties; that is why you heard me saying I will teach you how to make money while you sleep, and that your money should generate more money for you. I am glad that you fell for me as I fell for you, without knowing how much I am worth. This means you are honest and that you did not hook onto me for the contents of my wallet."

Immediately, I knew that there must be a reason why I kept on pulling millionaires and multi-millionaires. For some strange reason, if I had a relationship with someone without money, it did not seem to work; yet if I had a relationship with someone with loads of money, there was a spark of MAGIC. I knew straightaway that I was destined to be rich, not by marrying a rich man, however, but by working hard and applying what the rich taught me. I started viewing my life as a millionaire even if I did not have the money. Lenny taught me that in life it is who you socialise with that influences and makes an impact on your life. If you mingle with junkies you will end up being one of them; if you mingle with lazy people you will end up being lazy; if you mingle with the wise and intelligent, you will end up being wise and intelligent; finally, if you mingle with the rich you will end up being RICH or be perceived as one.

"Texas is where I come from, babe," he went on. "When you are ready, I would like to take you to Texas; we work hard and we play and work BIG and we buy Big - everything is big in the USA," he said with a smile on his face. "I want to teach you strategies that will change your life forever, because I love you so dearly," he added. "I want to make you a Millionaire or a Multi-Millionaire within the next five years,

CHAPTER TWENTY

not from my money but I will show you how to do it without any money to your name - that is, only if you are willing," he chuckled. I felt butterflies flying around in my tummy.

"Gosh, isn't he some fraud?" I wondered naively.

I asked Lenny to excuse me whilst I used the rest room. *Me having millions*, I giggled to myself. I jumped in the restroom with excitement and said a small prayer. I pinched myself. I looked at my face in the mirror to make sure it was still me, the African girl who had been previously baptised in poo. I went into the toilet cubicle, lowered the toilet seat and quickly climbed on it, and there I sang and danced! Two ladies who were in the restroom thought I had lost it! I continued to smile and giggle till the excitement evaporated. I viewed myself in the exact type of house I wanted to live in when I had my millions. I finally left the restroom, walking confidently towards Lenny, exactly as a rich confident woman would do.

Those people who say money does not bring happiness are bloody liars, because this changed my way of thinking! I did not know anything called stress when I dated Lenny, because he was stress-free. As you know, stress is contagious and can cause most relationships to break down, especially where money is a problem. I must admit, I was over the moon with happiness, though I missed my children dearly. The fact that kept me going was that my kids received loads of foreign currency on a weekly basis, in Zimbabwe sent via Western

CHAPTER TWENTY

Union. (The fact that my immigration status was not good stopped me from keeping money on me or in my bank account, as people always said that when one is an illegal immigrant, at the point of deportation the Home Office officials will take all the money off you as it will be considered a result of illegal working.)

I kept on seeing Lenny for a year on and off, since he had to fly to the States some of the time. The only stupid thing I did was never to ask for his American contact details, and I never brought him to my bedsit… since I felt ashamed of my lodgings. I did not want him to visit my bedsit in Tooting, which did not have any hot water or heating. I was a tenant in a shared house which was made into bedsits. There were five of us in a three-bedroomed house; the lounge and the dining room had been turned into bedrooms too. We only met in the kitchen and shared the bathroom; none of us realised that we were buying the house for someone, or had any brains to realise we were making someone rich whilst he or she slept. Lack of insight, ha! Nevertheless we were very happy as tenants aka lodgers.

I felt much more comfortable staying in Lenny's Penthouse; when it was up for rent we would go into five star hotels such as the Hilton, staying there till he purchased another flat or house. It was a life that most people would only dream about.

But unfortunately fate struck again! I lost contact with

CHAPTER TWENTY

Lenny when I lost my mobile phone whilst I was running to catch a train to work. It was a pay as you go mobile phone, one of those that were as big as a brick, the one that did not involve any monthly statements or bills being sent for the calls. I cried like the day my dad died for my mobile phone as I watched it getting crushed by electric, fast trains; going for it would mean death by crushing and electrocution! The telephone number was just too long for me to remember - it had about eleven digits. So, again, *EVERYTHING ELSE HAD FAILED* for me! *OOOooouuuchhhh!* And it was before I was taught how to make money whilst I slept, before I was Out Of Poverty!

I started working like a mad woman again, doing ninety to one hundred hours a week; sometimes doing twenty-four hour shifts, going from a long day to a nightshift - hoping to raise more money to go back home, you know; but I had not foregone Plan A - to become RICH, or Plan B - to become filthy, filthy rich before I turned fifty-five! I knew and felt that I had riches in my blood; all I needed was to implement the ideas by acting upon the strategies I had learnt from the RICH people I mingled with...

CHAPTER TWENTY-ONE

IN SEARCH OF LOVE AGAIN

I REJOINED Date-loners, hoping to meet Lenny again, but it did not happen. I ended up meeting another guy who was an Englishman. He was about fifteen years older than me. He was so far the oldest man I had dated in my life. Gosh, this man, who I shall call Sean, was not my type at all; this was surely what they mean when they say that opposites attract.

Sean came to see me using trains from the Harlow to South West London where I was now living. I did not like him at all in the beginning but he kept on phoning me, telling me how much he liked me and that love grows over a period of time.

Let me just give it a try, I thought. Tell you what, if I had seen the car that he drove those days, honestly, I would not have dated him. I had always valued my men by what they drive and the kind of shoes they wore and also if they had a belt on

CHAPTER TWENTY-ONE

their trousers. Their purse always came after all the above.

Sean and I started dating. Little did I know, Sean was in the process of re-mortgaging his three-bedroomed house so that he could downsize and buy a two-bedroomed flat and free up a few bucks as well. Therefore, Sean decided to come and camp in my one-roomed bedsit which I rented in a shared house. He was the first person who chose to come and spend some days at my place whilst the other guys I had dated previously preferred me to go to theirs, or meet up in some nice hotel. He did not have any class at all! He was just a common guy and too common for me to date. With my seventy hours per week, I earned twice his weekly wages. I really don't know why I got involved with him in the first place.

As time went by he started answering my calls, listening to my voice messages and reading my mail. I did not take it seriously or take offense over it and just carried on. He never contributed to the bills but just lived with me. Every Friday he had to go to see his son to pay maintenance to a previous partner, which was not bad at all. I never thought that I was being used and believed I was in a relationship. Within a few weeks he declared his love for me and started rejecting the use of condoms. "I want to marry you," he said all the time, but he never actually proposed.

Sean was the most boring man I had ever dated. He kept on talking about his previous girlfriends with me. He had dated another black girl from Ghana called Yana, who was

CHAPTER TWENTY-ONE

twenty years younger than him, and Liza from Harlow. Every single day I had to be told stories about Yana, Liza and Jacquie. I just wondered what I had got myself into. I was told that Yana, as an African girl, just wanted someone to use accommodation-wise so that she could live in Sean's house rent-free, and she accomplished her mission. When she bumped into people who knew her she apparently introduced Sean as her landlord, never as her boyfriend.

When Sean met me, he knew pretty well how hard I worked and how much money I earned and how much I had in my account.

After six months together I fell pregnant. This is when my life went into a complete standstill, since I suffered from morning sickness. I got no financial support from Sean even though he knew I had to pay my bills in England as well as send money home to my kids. Sean was the most unkind and selfish man I had ever dated. He thought about himself most of the time. Even in our lovemaking he wanted me to give him a good head all the time, yet he never went down on me. How selfish is he, I thought! It's time for TABBY BYE-BYE, I thought - it has to end.

One day he brought me an old pink woman's shaver and said, "One of my ex-girlfriends left this in my house - you can have it if you like." Gosh, I felt so pissed off and showed him the door! I told him point blank that with me, love, what you see is what you get, take it or leave it! I told him that if he

CHAPTER TWENTY-ONE

wanted me, he had to accept me for what and who I am, and not to try and change me.

I went on to tell him that since we met he had never done anything for me and that all he did was to talk about his ex-girlfriends, text them in the middle of the night, and so on. I just wanted to end it. Instead of supporting me financially and emotionally, he brought me an old lady's shaver! What a horrible guy he is, I thought. Even if my pussy was bushy, I always kept the area between my legs neatly shaved to enable me to wash my bits properly and to keep foul smells away.

It was tough to end the relationship since I was pregnant.

One day, when I was heavily pregnant, I received a last-minute call from the Nursing agency that there was a shift available in Guildford, Surrey. The shift was a fifteen-hour shift which was supposed to earn me £150. I accepted the shift without realising that my weekly travel card had expired on that day and I was supposed to get my weekly wages into my account on Saturday at 12 midnight. The problem was, I had to wake up early in the morning on Saturday to travel to Guildford. I took my savings card which was the only one I held at that time, for I had no credit cards or anything else. I went to the cash point, keyed in my secret pin number, without success. I tried three times and got the same message: "You have insufficient funds available to complete this transaction." I had no buffer allowance, no overdraft. The

CHAPTER TWENTY-ONE

queue was getting longer behind me but for some strange reason, I did not notice this; all I wanted was for the ATM to dispense some cash to me. I stood there like a ZOMBIE, until a man of middle-age tapped on my shoulder and said, "If you keep trying you are bound to lose your card." This is when I noticed that the queue had grown longer. I tried to call Sean from my mobile, but all I could get from him was hysterical laughter. "You must be joking, calling me this time for ten pounds! Or you are trying to check up on me?" He refused to come to my rescue and said he was watching England playing against another team to qualify for the world cup. He suggested I borrow from my housemates, but at this point they were all at work. I stood aside, still holding my card and watched everyone withdrawing their money and leaving. Once, again I stood there and thought, what should I do WHEN EVERTHING ELSE HAD FAILED? I needed the money in order to earn more money!

As, I stood there thinking hard and praying quietly, a cold wind started to blow towards me. It was a relaxing sea breeze in the middle of London. I felt something catching on my foot and looked down, and *there* was a £10 note - the very amount I needed to get me to work! At first, I could not believe this miracle. I looked around to see if there might be someone who just let the money be blown towards me. There was absolutely no one. I picked up the money and rushed to my bedsit. I found it difficult even to explain to Sean what

CHAPTER TWENTY-ONE

had happened as he kept nagging, wanting to know who gave me the £10 note. Even at the time of writing this book, I have no idea how it happened, but I believe it was sent by GOD.

On Sunday Morning I had more than £500 pounds in my account which was paid by the agency from the previous week. From that day I remembered not to send every penny home and taught myself always to have some money in my purse, which I never used unless it was for the purpose of attracting more money. This is also when I realised I should not depend on a man for money - due to Sean having failed to send me £10, which he could have transferred into my account over the phone without even having to drive to my place.

Later on during the course of our relationship, I still remember being invited to a party in Clacton-on-Sea. It was Sean's nephew's birthday party. I took a train from London to Clacton-on-Sea. We stayed the night in a Bed and Breakfast. The next day I had to return to London as I had to go to work at a nursing home in Surrey the following day.

"I will take you in my car," said Sean, "that way you could save yourself some money." I agreed as I thought it was more sensible.

I climbed into his very old car, the make of which I cannot even remember. The passenger door did not close properly. It was freezing cold and the car heater was not working. I was shivering and trembling with cold; I had never felt that cold before. Instead of Sean being sympathetic, he

CHAPTER TWENTY-ONE

laughed and giggled as he saw this as very funny. We finally reached his house which was also freezing cold, since he had turned the heating off. He had turned the heating and the hot water off whilst away to save money, or perhaps had never turned the heating on since he lived in my bedsit. He did not offer me anything in his house till I asked for a cup of tea and for some hot water so that I could soak myself. All this time Sean was laughing and I could not make any sense of it. I could not figure out if it was because of embarrassment or ignorance. Honestly, was it worth the twenty pounds I was saving by not using the train? The alternative was taking the risk of ill health or at the worst, freezing to death!

From that day I created this statement on saving: *"Why save for the future when you are putting your health a risk? How will you realise your investment in the future when in the future you are no longer there, killed by hypothermia when you could have bought a coat, a blanket or a cup of tea?"* I learned to spend my money accordingly and to let my money take care of me, rather than me taking care of it.

I finally got the cup of tea which I drank very quickly, and for two hours I felt my unborn baby moving inside me. I asked if the water was hot and he replied that it was. "Show me the bathroom please," I asked. In my life I had never ever seen a bath that was so dirty! I could not believe my eyes. I just wanted to die! Since this was my first visit to his house, and I was also pregnant with his child, I tried my best to be

CHAPTER TWENTY-ONE

polite. I tried hard to clean the bath but failed. I just realised that I didn't have to soak my body but just my feet. I soaked my feet and hands till I got myself warm.

I made myself warm by wearing outside clothes whilst indoors. It was not funny, the house was freezing cold - just like its owner. There was never anything sensible that I was told by Sean. He never had any plans or ambitions. It was all about his ex-wife and ex-girlfriends. Since I was fed up hearing about his exes, I just blurted out: "Your wife whom you always say cheated on you with your best friend was really wise! Who would settle for this!" Every minute I get told that Yana was his best friend, over and over again; when we accompanied my friend Lucy on an outing, people used to think she was my daughter, and then he would burst into laughter. I was starving, feeling very hungry and there was nothing to eat. I just told him that I had had enough of his exes and I stormed out. I found my way to the train station and back to my bedsit in London. I got myself plain boiled rice and beef in black bean sauce from a local Chinese take-away, and ate my food whilst it was still hot. Then I took a shower and made myself a milk drink and went to sleep. I just realised that some men really do not know what to talk about in a relationship. I just felt sorry for him.

Finally, when he managed to get his money from the sale of his house, he went straight to the travel agency and bought two plane tickets to Zimbabwe. For Sean, this amounted to

CHAPTER TWENTY-ONE

a large sum of money, which made him go a little bonkers. He behaved in a way that made you think he had received a life-changing amount, but in reality it was only £20,000 - which he had to use to buy a better second-hand car, and furniture, plus move to a new flat which he intended to downsize to. I could tell from his behaviour that he had never handled large sums of money, as he would wake up in the middle of the night saying he could not sleep because he needed to plan how to use the money wisely.

He was now looking for a holiday in Zimbabwe at the same time; he had not consulted me but just went and bought the plane tickets. I later told him no, "I can't go back to Zimbabwe."

"Why?" he asked.

"I am still waiting for my papers," I said.

"So you are illegally here?" he asked.

"Yes, I am," I replied.

"Oh my God," he sighed. He then went to call his sister and told her all about the failed trip. The sister jumped to conclusion and said, "I told you, Sean, that the girl wanted to use you for papers so that she could stay in Britain!"

Honestly, I swear to God Almighty that I had fallen for that guy with all my heart, as my culture had always taught me that for a woman to be complete and become whole she had to have a man in her life. I did not know about the sham marriages as I was just so naïve that time. I was scared of being in a foreign country and never wanted to break any rules, and also had I wanted to use him for papers only, I would not have fallen pregnant, for I was taught that children do not seal a relationship.

From that day onwards I suffered from an onslaught of verbal diarrhoea and physical abuse. I was pulled and pushed from the bed to the floor whilst pregnant with Shana. I was pushed out of a moving car whilst pregnant. I tell you, I saw the light since I had never thought or dreamt in my life that there could be some bad white guys like that. My view of white people had always been favourable. I learnt my lesson the hard way that day and I wished I had followed my instincts and refused to go out with Sean. A car that was following behind saw what happened and the driver offered me a lift to St George's hospital. I was rushed to the maternity department to have checks made on me and my unborn baby. I thank God because my unborn baby was safe. I sustained some minor bruises.

I was discharged the following day and referred to Social Services. Social Services told me that the Home Office could offer me accommodation but I had to go to Wolverhampton. I refused to leave London as I did not like the idea of moving up North or to the Midlands. My case was reported to the police but I later decided to say I jumped out of the moving car as I did not want to cause any trouble. However, I decided to put a stop to the relationship. The stop I had put on the

CHAPTER TWENTY-ONE

relationship did not last very long, for he came back and persuaded me to take him back.

He asked me what I wanted him to do. I asked him to invite my eldest daughter from home, which he did and I paid for the flight. At least I had someone to talk to! My daughter was as excited to see me as I was to see her. Sean then started behaving like a spoiled child, complaining that I was ignoring him. My daughter was twenty and an adult. I thought Sean was going to give us some space and go back to his place so that we could talk about what had happened at home and to me whilst in England.

GOSH!! This horrible man chose to stay in my bedsit, sleeping in my bed in the same room with my twenty-year old daughter who slept on the couch! There must be something wrong with him, I thought. In actual face he had nowhere to stay since he had sold his house, which he never told me about. He later bought a two-bedroomed flat in Clacton-on-Sea. He went to buy new furniture and a second-hand car. After moving his property to Clacton he then came back to London. Again he just wanted to sleep in the same room with me and my daughter; honestly, in my culture this is taboo. Little did I know that since this man had always gone out with younger girls and was starting to develop an interest in my daughter! I just warned my daughter about his previous relationships with girls who were young teenagers and some who were twenty or more years younger than him.

CHAPTER TWENTY-ONE

The following day, Sean asked if he could take my daughter to Clacton with him and help her to look for work. Initially I agreed. He acted very quickly and said he wanted to leave straightaway. They got ready and left. Before they had reached central London, my instincts told me to ring him and ask him to bring my daughter back. I had just realised that I had not been to his new flat, so I did not know his address or telephone number. I told him that I had just received a telephone call from home with the news that someone from our family had died. I lied deliberately, as my instinct told me to act quickly.

When he brought my daughter back, he was angry and his face had turned red. I knew pretty well that he was up to no good. Instead of asking me who had passed away, he was going on about my daughter Pat who had refused to sit in the front seat in his car and went to sit at the back. I am sure my daughter might have sensed something herself. I apologised for my daughter's behaviour and asked him to leave.

I later told my daughter why I did that and that no-one had died at home. She told me that she herself did not feel comfortable with the arrangement anyway, but could not say anything as she thought I knew what I was doing. As time went by we later visited his flat in Clacton. Since he had his plans he insisted that my daughter stayed behind whilst I returned to London with him. In actual fact, it was now easier for him to commute to work in Harlow from my place than

CHAPTER TWENTY-ONE

making daily journeys to and from Clacton to work in Harlow; little did I know, I was being used. I could spend two weeks without seeing my daughter even though I spoke to her several times a day on her mobile. I told him one Saturday that I had to go to Clacton to fetch my daughter, just in case she needed to catch a train, for then she would know how to get home.

On our way to Clacton I had to put my ear plugs in as he was going on about feeling tired, and the journey was too long for him to drive. This was a one and half hour journey that stretched to six hours. He kept on stopping and going to sleep. The truth is he was not happy with the idea that I wanted to accompany him and see my daughter. We finally reached Clacton-on-Sea and he asked me and my daughter to accompany him to his sister's. His sister lived in the cheapest area of Clacton-on-Sea, in an area called Jaywick, yet felt so proud that you would think she lived in one of the upmarket houses around Surrey. She never spoke to me or my daughter; all she did was smoke one cigarette after another in a house with a pregnant woman.

Sean's sister never liked me as she thought and had told her brother that I wanted to marry him for papers, i.e. for the sake of a SHAM MARRIAGE which I had never entertained. Both brother and sister had no idea that I had in the meantime claimed asylum and that the Home Office already knew I was in the country.

CHAPTER TWENTY-ONE

Boxing Day Invitation

Towards the end of the year I was invited to have a meal on Boxing Day by one of Sean's sisters. Yvette was a lovely lady and we got on very well. I had met her twice previously. I accepted the invite and was looking forward to meeting her and her family. My daughter and I felt very honoured to be invited. I felt quite overwhelmed as this was going to be my proper Christmas with a family, as I had always worked on Christmas and Boxing Days for all the previous years I had worked in London. On those previous occasions I chose to work on Christmas Day simply because I did not have anywhere to go and anyone to celebrate Christmas with.

As time dragged on I felt heavily pregnant and tired. I could not work anymore. I continued to work nevertheless as I did not have any choice. I wanted to save enough money for my three children in Zimbabwe and to buy clothing and all the necessities for my unborn baby. Life was really tough. It was also the first time I had to work whilst pregnant with my fifth child and in the age-group of thirty-something; you know what I mean - thirty-something and pregnant in a foreign country, with an unsupportive partner and without official immigration papers!

Since, I needed money I worked till I was eight months pregnant. In December I had a massive fallout with my childish partner Sean. This was when I was pushed out of a

CHAPTER TWENTY-ONE

moving car. It was all about his ex-girlfriend who kept on phoning and texting him nonstop. I was too naïve to see that he was leading a double life. I was told he had to do what she wanted or else he would be barred from seeing his son. When I was taken into hospital, I was told by Social Services, counsellors and nurses that I was better off without him. I decided not to talk to him or see him again.

I was told that I was not welcome in his house or in his family's house. I didn't give a damn and carried on as usual. I booked myself to work both on Christmas Day and Boxing Day. I asked Matron if I could stay at the Nursing home with my daughter over Christmas since there was no public transport and I did not drive. Matron was very understanding and kind; she arranged for someone to pick me up and drop me back home so I could rest well and look forward to resuming work the following day. She arranged for the chef to include me and my daughter for Christmas dinner. We enjoyed our Christmas and Boxing Day with the old people at the nursing home. I really enjoyed it as I provided care for people who could not do anything for themselves who nevertheless still received an income. I worked till the end of January when I was eight months pregnant. Sean did not bother to see me but kept on phoning every two days or so. I started telling myself that I would survive with or without him. I had actually predicted something like this would happen, which is why I asked Sean to help me bring my daughter over because I needed someone to talk to.

CHAPTER TWENTY-ONE

In February he started coming back, pleading with me to take him back, saying he was sorry. I found it really difficult to understand him. He offered to buy clothes for his unborn child and wanted to be part of her life. I hated him so much especially after all the abuse he had put me through. His sister rang me and asked me to accept his offer of buying clothes and all the preparation stuff for the unborn baby including a Moses basket.

He asked me to go to Mothercare with him to buy the items which I needed and have time to talk. I refused to go with him, so he suggested that my daughter Pat go with him instead. Pat walked to Mothercare and met up with Sean. She chose all the basics. When she had finished she brought the things home. Sean followed her and asked to be let in. We allowed him in. He started talking, complaining and moaning about the things my daughter had chosen. It was terrible. I thought this man must have some mental issues as nothing seemed satisfactory to him. Nothing I did for him was right, yet he declared his unconditional love for me. I was just confused. In my life I had never known anyone who behaved like that. It was just like some who have bipolar disorder. It was terrible and totally unpredictable. One minute he was laughing uncontrollably, the next he was completely agitated and became a different person. The next moment he was this very nicest of men and spoke continuously about how nice he was. Oh God help us, I thought!

CHAPTER TWENTY-ONE

"Mum, I think Uncle Sean is a sick man," said my daughter. She was just fed up with his behaviour.

"Yes, he is," I concurred. We were fed up and just wanted him to go. Once again we didn't get on and he drove back to his flat.

The following week I was surprised to find Sean knocking on my door again. One of my housemates let him in - unfortunately, for I would not have let him in! "I have brought sad news," he announced. "Your other daughter in Zimbabwe has just phoned on my landline as she thought that Pat might be there and she said your mum has passed away."

I just froze with shock! "How could she go when she knew my daughter would be born this month, in a week's time!" I cried. I just pretended to be brave but deep down my heart was bleeding. It was very painful and it hurt me to the bone. "Now, I am a complete orphan," I sobbed, "no mum and dad, two siblings gone and a husband within a period of three years." I had to endure the pain of losing a dear mum and make sure that I had done all that I was supposed to do.

I pulled myself together and made my plans. My baby was due in few days, and my case with the Home Office was still pending the decision of the adjudicator. I thanked Sean for bringing the news. I grabbed the phone, rang home and spoke to my daughter who explained what had happened. In my family they all looked to me for support. No-one at all did much to help. When dad died, I footed the funeral bill on my

CHAPTER TWENTY-ONE

own. Now mother had gone I had to see to her funeral. I went to the cash machine and withdrew some money which I sent via Western Union. I instructed my daughter on the type of casket to buy. I chose the hymns and planned everything the way I thought mum would have wanted. Everything was bought and delivered and mum was buried the following day.

Once again my so-called partner from Hell started saying bad things. I just wished he had gone back to his place after delivering the news, but he saw this development as a way of coming back. He nagged and nagged: "What did you have to send all that money home for?" I got really pissed! I had previously explained to him that our cultures were totally different. I had sent money to foot the funeral bill because no-one else could have done that, I explained. My bipolar partner lost it once more: "Why didn't your mum have any funeral insurance?" he asked. I was just surprised that he had said that, as I told him before that insurance for homes, cars, life, let alone funeral, were for the rich people. My parents were not rich; even in the UK I had seen people dying and getting assistance for the funeral expenses from the Department of Works and Pensions. To me he just proved to be very unreasonable, unkind and cruel.

"Some people do not understand, mum," said my daughter.

I didn't know what to say but just cried. Later on I tried once again to explain to him that in Zimbabwe people do not

CHAPTER TWENTY-ONE

get benefits. People pay for everything themselves and their families are meant to support each other during difficult times. I could not understand Sean, since my money was my money and his money was his money. We never talked or planned about money; he did his own thing with his money and I did what I wanted with mine. The reality is because he used to open my mail he knew exactly how much I had in my account. I had saved money enough to take me through my maternity leave. Since Sean was after money he just blurted out a heap of rubbish which made me say a little prayer for him, asking God to forgive him. The following day when I was supposed to go to Croydon for my immigration problem to let the officials know I was still in the country and had not absconded and that I would be going into hospital for an operation, Sean offered to give me a lift in a better second-hand car he had bought following the sale of the house. I was surprised that on our way to Croydon, he asked me to give him £3,000.00 so that he could marry me. That is when it came quite clear to me that the guy never loved me in the first place. I told him that I was not going to do that because I had a genuine case and that he should not bother or think about marriage for money.

On hearing this he lost it again and went into his typical funny and horrible mood. I was just fed up and did not want any more of his abuse. We finally arrived in Croydon at Lunar House, Wellesley Road. It took quite a while before my turn came. I had to have all the necessary documentation ready, including a photo for a new card which they had just introduced for asylum seekers, and had to have my fingerprints taken. I was told that I should get in touch with my solicitors as soon as I had my doctor's confirmation that I was fit from the operation, so that I could have the outcome of my case's determination as soon as possible.

Simply because I took a while inside Lunar House, Sean, who remained in his car when I went in, thought that maybe I was going to be deported; which actually surprised me when he said this on my return. Never mind, I had to go into hospital that night, since I had to be kept in a state of nil by mouth from midnight till the time of the caesarean section. I had made my decision that I didn't want Sean to be present on the day, since the very thought of his presence stressed me up and caused my blood pressure to shoot up to the ceiling. I had to have an operation to deliver my baby and did not want Sean around.

I told the midwife that I did not want Sean present during and or after the operation. However, the midwife who admitted me forgot to hand the message over to her colleagues when she went off duty.

I was sent to the ward with my brand new baby girl Shana. She looked a bit like a Chinese child with lovely brown eyes and brown hair. She looked just perfect!

The nurses gave her her first bath and dressed her up

CHAPTER TWENTY-ONE

nicely in a pink sleep suit. Within no time Sean turned up in the maternity ward and begged the nurses to let him in so that he could see Shana. They asked him who he was and he lied to the nurses that we were married and he was my husband. They let him in and showed him where I was with Shana. He brought with him some white and baby pink artificial flowers in a basket. He didn't say much and just asked if he could hold Shana. He did not even bother to ask how I was. I did not want to talk as I was tired and in pain - all I needed was a good rest. When the midwives saw that I was in pain they gave me some strong painkillers. They asked Sean to leave as they knew that I would be asleep within no time. When I was fast asleep Sean asked the nurses when I was likely to be discharged and he was given the date and time of expected discharge.

I spent the next four days in hospital. On the day of my discharge, Sean turned up early to offer me a lift home. I did not know what to do as I was not able to walk far. I had no option but to get into his car. When I got in his car he started apologising for his bad behaviour and wanted us to start afresh with our new baby. He pleaded with me to come to Clacton with him. He tried to convince me that since I had been operated on I needed help with the baby at night and during the day. I thought he was being sensible and gave in. Again I was made a fool. Sean drove us to Clacton. He persuaded me to give up my room which I was renting as he thought that I

CHAPTER TWENTY-ONE

was wasting money on it. I followed his orders and did what he asked. My daughter later joined us as she was living in a room in London. She later found a job as a healthcare assistant in one of the nursing homes in the same area.

When Sean had invited my daughter into the country the Home Office became suspicious and thought that something was amiss; after all, it seemed odd for a man of fifty to invite a girl of twenty into the country. She was allowed to stay in the country for only fourteen days. I rushed around to find a university or college that could enrol her for a course. The colleges and universities charged a lot of money, and I had no choice, but to pay the high fees so that my daughter could get a visa and continue to study and work in the UK. Sean volunteered to enter his name on my daughter's visa application form as a sponsor. The deal was that he was not in fact volunteering to sponsor her but was just assisting so that she could get her visa. It all went well, and my daughter was finally allowed to stay in the country as a student.

When I was in Sean's flat, life became difficult as the orders were just too much for us. I was not allowed to answer the door or collect letters from the letterbox. I had bought some pink cards with the wording, "She is finally here and she is a girl," in which the name and weight and date of birth are entered; I wanted to send these to my workmates and friends from the church as well as my family in Zimbabwe.

Sean did not seem impressed by the idea of me sending

CHAPTER TWENTY-ONE

cards announcing the baby had finally arrived, and just snatched the cards off me and blurted, "Who do you want to send these to? All my relatives already know that you have a baby and none of them should have those!" He ripped the cards into tatters and threw them in a bin. I just felt confused, as I could not understand this man's behaviour at all.

On the 7th of March it was my daughter's first week and she was now seven days old since she was born on the 28th of February; my workmate called Ruby had rung me to say she wanted to hear the baby crying. I told her that the baby was fast asleep; however, if she phoned in the next fifteen minutes to half an hour, she would be awake as it would be time for nappy changing and feeding.

Co-incidentally, the phone rang at around the agreed time and the baby had woken up and was crying for a feed after I had finished changing her. With much excitement, I just picked the phone up and said, "Good timing Ruby, here is your baby girl crying, listen to her!" Little did I know that it was not Ruby but Sean's ex-girlfriend Jacquie, the one who used to text him in the middle of the night and caused us to row about her. I took the milk bottle and I placed the teat in the baby's mouth so that she could start feeding as I talked to Ruby on the phone. To my surprise the line went dead and there was no one on the other end. I started wondering who had rung. I dialled 1471 to get the number of the last caller and got the message: "You were called at 13.15, unfortunately

CHAPTER TWENTY-ONE

we do not have the number to return the call as the caller withheld their number." Straightaway Jacquie rang Sean and told him that I had rung her and told her to listen to my baby who was crying and that my baby was a girl, for that matter, which I had not said at all. Within the next five minutes Ruby rang to ask if the baby was now awake. I told her yes, she was but she was now feeding. I asked Ruby if she had called a few minutes before and she said she hadn't. I explained to her what had happened and she reassured me and said not to worry as strange things like that happen when one is excited, adding, "The person will probably ring again if the call was urgent." Little did I know that I was in trouble with Sean.

When Sean finished work at two o'clock, he did not waste time and drove straight to his flat. I could sense that something was not right as he walked in with his face very red and looking very angry. He plucked the baby from my arms and threw her onto the bed. He stopped the baby from feeding as he took the bottle away and put it onto the worktop in the kitchen. "Now you have some explanation to make, young lady!" he said, pushing me onto the couch.

I fell backwards and wondered what all this was about. I asked him to explain to me what it was that went wrong instead of pushing me about. At the same time the baby started crying. I told him that I wanted to go and get the baby so that I could continue feeding her - then we could talk when the baby went back to sleep.

CHAPTER TWENTY-ONE

"No, leave her," he said, fuming with anger. "I want to know why you rang Jacquie to tell her about your baby! I never wanted her to know about your baby," he barked again.

I told him, "I swear on my baby's life, I did not ring her."

"Yes, you did," he insisted and continued shouting at me. "I did not want her to know that I have a baby with you and that you are living with me here!" he said.

"Why, what's the problem?" I asked. "You told me that you two were finished, and since you have a son with her I think you would have wanted your son to get used to the idea that he has a baby sister."

"Because that is how I want it!" he yelled. "I did not want them to know!"

I started crying, and told him that I was not an idiot and would not have done anything stupid just to upset people.

"Yes, you do silly things, you are evil!" he shouted.

"Well, as I have told you, I did not ring her!" I insisted. "Check with British Telecom and T-Mobile, they will give you a list of all calls made today from my mobile phone and your landline."

He continued shouting. I told him that I was not putting up with all this rubbish and I just wanted to go. I wanted to go into the bedroom to pick up my baby who was crying, but he stopped me. I was left with no option so I picked up the phone up and dialled 999. I knew that even if I did not say a word, ringing from the landline the police would know where the call came from. Within no time the police turned up!

CHAPTER TWENTY-ONE

He started blaming me, saying, "Look what you've done now! You've been shouting and some horrible neighbours have called the Old Bill - now look, the police are here!" He thought that possibly one of the neighbours had called - he did not realise it was me. I told him I called them. He asked me how I did it. I told him I dialled 999. "Idiot," I told him, "I am sick and tired of your abuse!" *He never thought that I would have the courage to call the police as he considered me to be illegally in the UK.*

Can you guess what he did? As soon as he saw the police, he rushed to pick up the baby who was crying and started feeding her. He opened the door and went to meet the police with a big smile on his face. He twisted the story and pretended he was the nice one and indeed very nice. He never mentioned the telephone call. Instead he told the police that he thought I was mad and suffering from post-natal depression, and was a danger to the baby and that I was also HOMELESS, hence living in his flat. This is what was said by the man who used to live in my bedsit!

He went on and told the police that I was homeless and was in the country illegally and was also having an argument with him because I wanted him to marry me so that I could stay in the country (aka marriage of convenience). The police said to him, "Fine, we just want you to stay outside whilst we talk to Tanaka." They took the baby from him and brought the baby to me.

CHAPTER TWENTY-ONE

They asked me to explain what had happened. I told them everything, including the telephone call which I had received and I how I replied to the call as I was expecting a call from my friend Ruby. The police contacted Ruby and asked her about it and she confirmed what I had said and also told the police that she could show them her phone bill when it arrived. The police told me that Sean had told them that we were arguing because I wanted him to marry me so that I could stay in the country. Without saying much I reached for my purse and pulled out the small card which was similar to a driver's licence, which was issued by the Home Office. I told the police that that was not the reason for the argument. I also told them that I never wanted him to marry me. He was the one who always talked about marriage and I also told them of the incident when he had asked me to pay him £3,000.00 so that he could marry me.

I told the police that he did not know that I was an asylum seeker and that the Home Office already knew that I was in the country. The police checked with the Home Office who confirmed that they knew of my presence in the country and were waiting for me to recover from the operation which I had just had.

The police went back to Sean and told him their findings, and they told him that they could arrest him for domestic violence. He claimed that he had not abused me and that it was me who was supposed to be shipped back to Zimbabwe, since he claimed that I was an illegal immigrant. He told the police that he and his sister would look after Shana. I told the police there was no way I was going to go without my daughter. Sean was told that since the two of us were not married, the law in the country at that time said the kids belonged to their mothers, which meant that if I had been here illegally, my daughter would be considered to be here illegally too and we would be shipped back to Zimbabwe together. The police went on to tell him that I was not in the UK illegally and that according to the Home Office, I am an asylum seeker who is still waiting for her case to be determined.

This was not good news for Sean as he had thought I was going to be shipped back to Zimbabwe, leaving him to bring up Shana with the help of his sister. He promised the police that he would not create a scene again and that all was well. As time went by he asked me on several occasions to give up Shana so that he could bring her up with his sister. I told him that there was no way I was going to do something so stupid, and never would be reduced to a mere surrogate mum.

After Sean had found out that I had applied for asylum, he wrote a letter to the Home Office to try and undermine my asylum application. He told the Home Office that I had been living in the country for a long time and was working illegally under three different names. He even wrote to them saying I should be shipped back to Zimbabwe as he had heard me previously supporting Mugabe's doings. It was just too much to bear. He even phoned Social Services to tell them that I was mad and the baby was not safe with me. I was assessed by the Community Psychiatric Nurse who confirmed in their report that they could not find any source of mental illness or any dangers that could occur to the baby.

What Sean did not know was that when people are going through a bad patch, they need a friend and a comforter, not more enemies; he just didn't know or just never thought that Shana would one day grow up to be a big girl and that my life could also change for the better.

When all the members of the multi-disciplinary team sat down together they found Sean's accusation very disturbing. They kept on having regular meetings and kept in touch with me. Well, as time went by, I had to go back to London to have a six-week check-up for the baby and myself. I also had to collect Shana's heel prick test results. Even though Sean knew that I was out of work, he asked me to pay for the fuel to and from London for every trip we made to have the baby checked, which I did, as I did not want any arguments. One day we had gone to London and on our way back he had driven via his sister's place somewhere on the far side of the seaside town. It was at night and it was getting dark and cold. I asked to remain in the car with my baby while he visited his sister as I was told that I was not welcome in his sister's house. He took his time and never bothered that I was left in the car with the baby, and this is the sister he said cared so

CHAPTER TWENTY-ONE

much about Shana! I found all this very contradictory: if she really cared about my baby, honestly, she would have put herself in my shoes, sitting outside at night in a cold car with a tiny baby who was only six weeks old whilst they had a nice cup of tea in a warm house.

The following week Sean had arranged with his sister to meet up around the area where there was a pub called The Hungry Horse. I was asked to come with him and have a cup of tea and cake at a tea-house near the pub. I was surprised as this had never happened before. When were about to leave, he went into his funny mood again, shouting at me that I took a long time to get ready.

I was told off for having taken too long and that now the sun had disappeared. As we walking down Connaught Gardens East into Marine Parade, along the road towards the sea front heading towards First, Second and Third Avenues, Sean just pushed Shana's pram and let it roll on along Marine Parade, saying now the sun had disappeared the weather had turned horrible. I did not understand this kind of behaviour as I rushed to grab my baby's pram and brought it out of the road. He later realised what he had done and apologised.

We continued walking to the tea shop. As we arrived he chose to sit by the window. We sat there and had a cup of tea and piece of cake. As we were having the tea he kept on looking at his watch, checking the time. I was told it was time to go back. On our way back we saw his sister and her

CHAPTER TWENTY-ONE

husband looking for a second-hand car. He asked if he could take Shana to them so they could see her. I then realised that all this was planned, which is why he was having tantrums that resulted in throwing my baby into the road.

Once again, I was not pleased with the way my baby was thrown into the middle of the road with the pram being allowed to run down road unattended till I ran after it. I reported the case to Social Services the following day, but I was too blind to see that it was a case of domestic violence. I was told that the most available option was to move to Wolverhampton where they had houses that were readily available for asylum seekers. I refused to go to Wolverhampton as I wanted to go back to London. I had ties in London, as well as church mates and workmates in Surrey.

My daughter continued to live with me, working at the same time. She had taken over the responsibility of sending her siblings some money on a weekly basis as my savings had gone. One evening as I was feeding baby Shana, my daughter Pat rang my mobile saying she was on her way, asking if I could let her in when the doorbell rang. Since I did not want to disturb Shana who was feeding and falling asleep, I asked Sean to do me a favour by letting Pat in.

Honestly, once again you would never guess what he did! He left the bedroom to go and let my daughter in. As he opened the door my daughter screamed very loudly, to the extent that I jumped with my baby in my arms to go and see what had happened to Pat. I walked out of the bedroom into the hallway. I was shocked, as I saw Sean standing there in front of Pat completely naked! You know what I am trying to say - *completely* naked, in his birthday suit, right in front of my twenty-year-old daughter! Pat Just exploded into tears. She appealed to me: "Mum, I am just fed up with this kind of abuse! Let's do something and get out of here."

I did not know what to do. I was not allowed to work. I was still waiting for my determination from the independent adjudicator. I was told that there was a backlog in the asylum applications, but just to be patient and wait.

Once again I reported this to Social Services who found Sean's behaviour to be very unacceptable. They asked him if he had somewhere to live until my case was finalised. He arranged everything with Social Services. He then moved out and went to live with his sister. On leaving, he took everything with him. He left the fridge empty, of course. He took all the bedding. He turned the hot water and heating off, forgetting that for the past one year he had been living in my bedsit for which I paid rent on my own, as well as paying all the bills and food. Now that I was in his flat, it was not more than one week before problems began, since the house was freezing cold and did not have any bedding.

I just thought of the Salvation Army. I called the church. The Corps Officer came straight away. He brought us some bedding and some food. He showed us where to turn the heating and water on. It was my hardest experience. I had never expected anything like this from someone whom I had a child with. Sean behaved in such a way that he clearly never considered that Shana, when she grew up, might learn about how her mother was badly treated by her dad.

When I reported all these incidents to Social Services, my daughter was placed on the child protection register. I was referred to several organisations such as the Open Road and Needle Exchange, as people thought I might have been a junkie and was causing problems because I needed gear. What an embarrassment! When I went to these organisation people sympathised with me but could not help me. I just wished and hoped for the best, as I never thought that in Britain that is what they did, sending people where they rubbed shoulders with druggies and so on. I hated myself and realised that everything was a result of my own actions - because I should never ever have agreed to go with Sean to his house after my daughter's birth.

I was emotionally and physically abused by Sean, but I was too daft to see this. I must admit that I hated the people who tried to help me thinking that they were destroying my relationship which never existed. Victoria aka Bumble and Hilary worked very hard to help me out of this relationship, but I thought no, they were destroying me. Now that I have been a victim of domestic abuse, I know exactly what those vulnerable women go through. The way that people out there see abusive relationship is different from the way the victims see it.

CHAPTER TWENTY-ONE

I went into the Women's Refuge resenting Hilary and Victoria. On reflection, I can now see that had these ladies not stood firm to help me out of that relationship, something very bad could have happened as Sean had started making false accusations that I wanted to kill my baby Shana. This was reversed when I told him that for you to have Shana, you will have to kill me first, because I will never let that happen! A Community Psychiatric Nurse who interviewed me asked me if I ever thought that I wanted to kill my baby. I told him straightaway that I have five children including Shana. My husband had cheated on me but I came to London to work with the desire to support my *four* children; if I was mad and a bad mother, I would not have remembered or bothered to send my children any money on a weekly basis and to send them to better schools. Otherwise, I could have stayed at home and waited for one of my brothers-in-law to inherit me and the children after the death of my husband; but I chose not to and came to work for my children.

Guess what, Sean was sitting on the opposite side at the child protection conference! He just jumped in and said, "What Tanaka is saying is very true and I salute her for that. Since I have known her, she sends her children money on a weekly basis without fail; and I think she is a very good mother and there is no doubt that she will be a very good mother to Shana too." The professionals just looked at each other without saying a word, but with that look that said,

CHAPTER TWENTY-ONE

"But how come we are gathered here because of your accusations that Tanaka is not a good mother?" I just wondered how someone could go from accusing someone of wanting to murder her newly born baby to changing his statement just like that. I had not suffered domestic violence before, hence the delay in recognising its signs and symptoms.

I also blame this on my upbringing and my stupidity; otherwise I might not have wasted my time on Sean or hung on for so long to endure the type of abuse that I went through. I just wondered why Sean did not want his so-called ex-girlfriends to know that he had a child with me. I expected him to be very excited since he had three sons and Shana was his only daughter, but he turned out to be the opposite - nasty and very nasty indeed; in short, the most horrible man I had ever known. Never mind, with the help of police, social workers and some other non-governmental organisations, I was finally evicted. I found myself homeless with a new-born baby. So, I was now homeless, without a roof over my head and no money in a foreign country. *I appeared to be an idiotic homeless fool abroad - something I never ever dreamt about.*

As time went by, Sean tried to make sure he knew where I lived and my whereabouts. He kept on coming to my door demanding to see Shana. He never paid any maintenance as in his mind child maintenance is paid as a way of saying "thank you for allowing me to see Shana". For several months I allowed him to see Shana without paying any maintenance, hoping that he would see sense, but he never did. Eventually he requested to see Shana fortnightly and to pay £50 weekly for maintenance. He never paid his maintenance on a weekly basis but monthly, and sometimes never. The amount he owed piled up and then he would start badmouthing me to his family during my daughter's presence, to the extent that I wanted to scrounge him off his money. My daughter would come and report everything to me - until his wise sister Yvette suggested that he brought a book where I would sign when I received maintenance money and write down the arrears for him. This was only done once, till he discovered that he owed about £2,500 in child support. I never rang him to chase him for the money, which pained him more as he expected me to beg him like his other ex-girlfriend who used to ring him or text him after midnight on Friday nights, chasing him for money. I was different and smart. When he found out that the amount he owed in child support was too much, he broke off contact with my daughter. He tried to use solicitors to persuade me to mitigate and come up with an agreement. I refused as I felt happier and my daughter felt happier without Sean in our lives.

After one year and some months without contact, I was surprised to receive a call from the National Response Team who wanted to know if Sean was in contact with Shana. I feared for the worst as the lady on the phone said Social Services would be in contact with me. I wondered what on

CHAPTER TWENTY-ONE

earth I had done wrong. The lady told me that there were no concerns about my parenting but it had come to light that Sean was being investigated by the police as he posed a risk to children. Finally, someone had braved it and reported him. On hearing this, my ten-year-old daughter just started to cry, saying, "I knew my father was a paedophile; he used to sit on the toilet and fish his willy out and say, 'Shana, say hello to Mr Willy-Wonker,' and he used to wiggle his willy singing 'Willy wonker, willy wonker' to me." I froze for a minute with anger, fear and resentment. I thought I had failed to protect my daughter from that kind of abuse.

The lady on the phone said there was nothing for me to worry about, for I had done the right thing by stopping contact and they were ringing to advise me to stop contact if it was still taking place.

Immediately, I knew that my instincts had always been right when I thought there was something wrong with Sean - since he used to receive text messages from a girl of twelve at odd times whom he had nicknamed 'Bum' because he thought she had a cute bum. At last I felt I had done the right thing, protecting my daughter from this paedophile. Money means nothing but the wellbeing of my children is paramount. Honestly, we don't know who we are dating till something bad happens. This man was very cruel, yet I forgave him several times and pretended all was well. Again, what a fool I was!

At the time of writing this book, in 2012, Sean was found to

CHAPTER TWENTY-ONE

have more than nine hundred indecent images of children on his computer as well as some extreme pornographic material; he was sentenced to thirty-six months of community service and recommended to have some treatment. He was a man of sixty who was obsessed with having sex in a school uniform. However, it is always wise to follow our instincts, as I never felt comfortable with him. Now, I am glad the truth is out, but he had tarnished my image by telling lies about me to his family. I am glad now they know who exactly he is and what he is capable of. When Shana was told by Social Services about her dad she said, "I knew there was something wrong with my dad as he seemed to fancy young girls."

CHAPTER TWENTY-TWO

LIFE IN THE WOMAN'S REFUGE: HOMELESSNESS

I NEVER THOUGHT I would ever find myself HOMELESS in my life, especially in England, the Queen's country! I was now a nobody, a stupid woman, a homeless woman, a brainless woman, a single mother with a four-months-old baby who had nothing and I really could not remember who I was. It felt like I was lost in a wilderness. I was once someone, running a business in Zimbabwe, had a massive house, had sex appeal as I was still young, but now I had reached the mid-life crisis and I was living in a foreign country. I had been thrown out of a two-bedroomed flat which was actually a one-bedroomed flat and a bit, as the second room could not accommodate a single bed, worth about £50,000.00; but my ex felt as though he was throwing me out of a huge mansion worth £450,000.00 or half a million! Honestly, life sucks when you are broke.

CHAPTER TWENTY-TWO

"She is homeless and has nowhere to go: after all, she is an illegal immigrant and I am sure she will be better off if she is shipped back to Zimbabwe!" Sean screamed loud enough to draw the attention of neighbours and passers-by. I felt small, but tall enough to be seen by everyone and to face the shame. The truth is I just wanted to die and I wished the ground would just suck me in so I could disappear from the shame. My mind raced quickly to the street beggars I had seen on my second day in London at Brixton market. Honestly, I thought to myself, is he comparing me to those homeless men? I felt cheap, like Maureen in the phone advert on the telly, that says, "Maureen is cheap - just call 118-118."

God help me to keep my mouth shut until I know what I am talking about, I prayed quietly as the police, social workers and some advocate called Victoria helped us out. I had been reduced to this plight because of the man who had camped in the bedsit I rented in London for the past nine months, the same man who wanted me out of his flat just after seven days of our baby's birth. I thought, some people are poor and will always remain so due to their mean behaviour. Never mind, I pulled myself together and thought it was my fault for getting into this mess, because I had agreed to start the relationship in the first place; consequently it was my responsibility to get myself out of the situation.

I gathered all my clothes that were thrown to me in black plastic garbage bags and into the Social Services' red car and

CHAPTER TWENTY-TWO

left for the woman's refuge. I became a homeless refugee on top of being a Zimbabwean political refugee - how marvellous! Life sucks, hey, it's like a rollercoaster, I thought; but never had I expected it to be so bad because in my life I had never seen anyone thrown out of a house like that especially with relationships where children were involved. In my country it was always done respectfully and discreetly; also, everything was done by mutual agreement, where people parted on good terms. Now, being in England, I assumed things would be done reasonably and sensibly, but it turned out to be the opposite.

Life in the Women's Refuge was not a picnic. I met some women who had suffered domestic violence, some who were depressed, anxious, tearful and emotional. It was very depressing being in such an environment... and I could not cope being in such an environment. The doors had to be kept locked and people were supposed to be in by a certain time; it was just like being in the big brother's house, with cameras everywhere. I had no friends, no-one to talk to, nothing to do. I used to spend my day in town admiring shoppers as I sat opposite a MacDonald cafe watching people eating in the hope that someone might hand over their leftover bags and French fries to me. Passers-by would look at me and my baby daughter. I did not realise that the bench I was sitting on was a bench that was frequented by drunks and drug addicts, so people naturally thought I was one of the junkies.

CHAPTER TWENTY-TWO

My daughter Shana who was well trained and used to go to bed at 8 p.m. changed her sleeping habits. She used to sleep in her own cot bed which her sister Pat had bought for her for twenty pounds, since Sean had refused to buy her a cot bed.

There was no room for the cot bed in the refuge so Shana had to sleep on the same bed as me and her sister. We stayed in the Women's Refuge for a whole month before we moved out to a rented property, which was partly being paid for by Social Services. In December of the same year I finally received the determination regarding my political asylum case in which I was granted leave to remain indefinitely in the United Kingdom as a refugee. I then tried to apply for housing benefits and income support, which was very difficult to get. On Christmas Day I had a roasted turkey from the Salvation Army.

The Member of Parliament, Mr Bob Russell, wrote to the DSS on my behalf asking them why they were withholding the support that I was entitled to. It was worse for me since the thirty-five pounds that I used to receive on a weekly basis had been stopped. I just thought life was not easy and this was the first time I wished I was dead. I had all the necessary papers, yet I could not get the support from my local council. I had used up all my savings. It was chaotic and once again life was very tough for me. "Everything Else had Failed, and deeper down into poverty I had sunk" - once again! It felt like dying a second death whilst still alive.

CHAPTER TWENTY-TWO

I pulled myself up, dusted myself and started working again as a HCA. I told no-one about my daughter Pat who had met an Englishman who was old enough to be her dad and was also married, about how she left me when I needed her most. She had left me with no money, no job, no benefits; it was a nightmare. This was after I had spent all my savings on her flight and paid for a university which she never attended in order for her to obtain a student visa and be able to work. I did not have anyone to turn to or talk to; once again life sucked.

I recalled one day when I did not have anything to eat. I only had maize meal, some greens and carrots. I boiled some carrots and mashed them; I tried to feed them to Shana but she refused and continued to cry as she was hungry. Milk alone was not sufficient for her as she had grown. There were no nappies left. I called the Member of Parliament called Bob and explained my ordeal. Within an hour I saw a lady called Teresa Higgins knocking on my door. She was a councillor and had brought with her a litre of milk and a packet of disposable nappies. She was a godsend and came to my rescue at the time I needed help most. I talked to her and explained my dilemma. She felt very sorry for me and advised me to go to the Department of Works and Pensions again and explain to them that I did not have any food to eat or to feed the baby.

The following day I went into town for my usual walk. I bumped into a black girl. I was so excited to meet someone

CHAPTER TWENTY-TWO

of my colour! Sylvia was from Zambia. Sylvia offered to babysit Shana during the night whilst I went to work. I worked at a nursing home during the night and slept partly during the day. I had to look after Sylvia's son after school and during the weekends. At this time it was even harder as the thought of going back home was just scary; all I wanted was to get my kids out of Zimbabwe safely and alive.

With help from Sylvia I managed to raise enough money for my son to fly to England. When my son Ron arrived, it was not that easy, as I had to ask him to babysit his sister whom he had never seen before all night - the same night after his arrival in the United Kingdom - while I worked to raise money to support his two sisters we had left back home and to raise enough for a ticket for Lolo.

The following month Lolo finally joined me, whom I had left when she was just six years old. She was now thirteen. I failed to bring my second daughter over since she was pregnant. When Lolo arrived I was very excited to see her after so many years of absence. I had used all my wages on her flight and was left without any money for food. I managed to buy a ticket for my son to travel to Gatwick airport to pick Lolo up. We had to watch the train guards and change coaches in order to avoid being asked for train tickets; as it was early in the morning the charge was double for peak time. Since we travelled with faith we actually made it to Gatwick without paying a penny. We bought our tickets for coming

CHAPTER TWENTY-TWO

back home as it was now off peak. It was so exciting to see Lolo after such a long time, and we finally arrived back home in Essex.

The following day I took the bottle that I used to keep my one penny coins in to see if I could afford to buy food for the kids. I went to the coin star machine but it was not working. I sat down next to Lolo and we started counting the pennies, and we made up ten pounds. We did our shopping on value foods and went back home smiling. Life could be better, I thought. I wondered if I should insult God or wish myself dead, but realised that God had a purpose with my life and that everything happens for a reason. I later realised the value of the Zimbabwean saying, *Kusina Mai Hakuyendwi* - meaning one should never go very far away from one's parents; it was true, I thought, and missed my own parents like a young girl.

Life was very different in England. In my country my neighbours would not go hungry whilst a neighbour had enough to spare. We were taught to give as a community. In my country neighbours can borrow cooking oil, sugar, salt or absolutely anything. In England it was different, where it was one man for himself; even the father of my daughter opened his mouth once to me and said if you are desperate for help, go to Social Services. I just wondered about the father of my child telling me to go to Social Services - did he mean my child was an orphan? - because in my country only orphans

CHAPTER TWENTY-TWO

can be cared for by Social Services. I could not believe it and I just could not imagine a white man saying that! The impression we have always had in Africa is that all white men are very rich and very kind as well as generous. I just had the shock of my life, hearing a father asking for his child to be looked after by Social Services - yet he was a person who had all five senses, both arms, hands and legs, a head with a brain, *and* a full-time job. Shame on him, I cursed!

I continued working hard as I received no support or maintenance from Sean. I worked hard and started training at a local college. I learned how to use a computer; then did an Access Course the following year. After the Access Course, I went to University and trained to be a nurse. I did my three years of nurse training which I thoroughly enjoyed.

It was during my nurse training that I enjoyed the Sexual Health module. I did the Sexual Health module as part of my degree and wanted to explore more on this subject. It was during my research that I encountered the Female Genital Mutilation subject. I had never heard anything about Female Genital Mutilation before. It is not something that is practised in Zimbabwe. On learning about FGM, I cried as I realised how lucky I was as a child and how much I empathised with the innocent young girls who are forced to go through this painful and barbaric act.

Whilst I was a student nurse, I encountered some colleagues who were so brainwashed as children that they

CHAPTER TWENTY-TWO

actually said that if they had baby daughters they would allow them to go through this barbaric act. I just realised that ignorance has no defence and that our childhood determines who we become as we grow up. My expectation was that when people are educated, they would in turn educate others to a more enlightened level of civilisation; but with this colleague of mine, who originated from Guinea and was a Moslem, could not appreciate how bad this barbaric practice is. While I was doing my sexual health module, I also learnt that male circumcision reduced the chances of contracting sexual transmitted diseases such as HIV and Aids, while this was not true for females; however, male circumcision does not of course guarantee 100 per cent protection from sexually transmitted diseases. As far as females are concerned, really, no-one can explain or justify the real benefits of the barbaric act called FGM.

When I completed my nurse's training it was a high achievement for me, especially for someone who had left Zimbabwe without any high school qualifications. I embarked on a business course with Cambridge University as I wanted to get started in business but did not know how. I did a business degree; during the first year of the course we learnt about *entrepreneurial* skills and how to start businesses. This gave me the foundation knowledge and incentive to set up my recruitment company whilst still a student. I kept my job working alongside my business.

CHAPTER TWENTY-TWO

However, as soon as my boss learnt that I had a business, was studying for a management degree, I was dismissed automatically and unfairly; once again someone had pulled me down, I thought. I resolved that I had to make it, I had to help myself. "I will do whatever it takes to succeed!" I promised myself. I made the resolution never to tell anyone about my plans, never to brag about money, never to change in my behaviour and attitudes, never to blame anyone for my life's failures. I had to continue with my plans, doing, failing and redoing till I got it right, and now I am in a position to say the sacking was nothing but a blessing because otherwise I might have carried on being beholden to the NHS for job security and never would have achieved financial freedom.

Whilst working for the National Health Service I was bullied by colleagues and verbally abused by patients on the ward. I recall one of my patients who called me and said, "Hey Mugabe, Mugabe, why don't you go back where you came from!" I must admit I did not find this funny at all, but intensely annoying. Due to the professional conduct I was expected to adhere to, I merely smiled. I learnt that you had to smile even if it hurts! Nevertheless, I reported the patient's outburst to my manager who had a word with the patient, and the patient apologised.

The difference between people who make it and those who don't, is that those who make it know how to recover from misfortunes and recuperate quickly; when they happen to fall, they pull themselves up and dust themselves off quickly,

CHAPTER TWENTY-TWO

and start again, learning from their mistakes; they remain focussed on their goal and set sail, persevering through storms to grasp high achievements!

But a word of advice: do not wait for someone or wish for someone to come and lift you up when you have fallen or failed! Don't be ashamed to gather yourself up and to ask for help, because everyone has failed at some point!

To summarise, I learnt the hard way from this relationship and my testimony now is based on the following biblical verse:

> For I have learnt to be content, whatever the circumstances may be. I know now how to live when things are difficult and I know how to live when things are prosperous. In general and in particular I have learned the secret of eating well or going hungry, facing either plenty or poverty. I am ready for anything through the strength of the one who lives within me. Philippians 4: verses 11-13.

And the following verse inspires me every day of my life: "And to make it your ambition to lead a quiet life; and attend to your own business, and work with your own hands, just as we commanded you." (1Thessalonians 4:11.)

It is now my ambition to mind my own business, work with own hands as commanded by God Almighty, and to lead a content life.

CHAPTER TWENTY-THREE

GOING BACK TO MY ROOTS

LIFE IS NOT FAIR at all, because we can never have everything, and it is always the opposite in life. I have spent all my life trying to figure out what exactly happens with people when they are in a relationship. Some people have loads of money, zillions, but they do not have a sense of belonging; they can't love anyone or be loved by someone. Honestly, I couldn't come up with a clear answer. Life is how one makes it, I concluded.

When all had failed for me relationship-wise, I recalled Munyaradzi. Munyaradzi was a guy I once had a fling with in the early 1990s. I met Munyaradzi on a bus called Power Coach travelling from Harare to Karoi. As I walked towards the bus Munyaradzi tried to block my way. He started chatting me up but I completely ignored him, thinking he might be one of the *tsotsis* (thieves) that operated around

CHAPTER TWENTY-THREE

Mbare musika Harare. When I bought my ticket the bus conductor told me that I was very lucky as I was the last person they were waiting for to fill the bus up as no standing passengers were allowed on the bus. I walked from the door to the end of the bus but could not find a place to sit. I went back to the bus conductor asking for a refund as I could not find a vacant seat. The conductor reassured me that there was definitely one seat left as he had counted his tickets. The bus driver started the bus as a way of calling people on board, and all the passengers who were outside smoking boarded the bus. I was surprised to find out that the only place left was the seat by the window next to Munyaradzi. Munyaradzi had left his briefcase on the seat and his jumper on the one next to his, so I thought both seats were occupied.

"Come and join me," said Munyaradzi

He stood up and let me squeeze past him and allowed me to occupy the seat next to the window.

"I knew you would come to sit next to me," smiled Munyaradzi.

"How did you know?" I asked.

"Because, I knew that there was only one place left as the conductor had told us he was just waiting for one more person," said Munyaradzi.

The bus driver started the bus and it took off for Karoi. Munyaradzi wanted to talk to me but I was just too shattered and feeling bored. This was the time I had lost everything. I

CHAPTER TWENTY-THREE

was separated from Kenzo and he had grabbed everything. I had to start from the bottom again, using public transport until I had sorted myself. Munyaradzi kept on trying to talk to me, saying he did not mean any harm, he just wanted to be a friend. Well, he came at the right time when I needed a shoulder to cry on. He was very gentle, tall and attractive. He told me that he worked for a company that offered agricultural loans to farmers. I knew the company very well as most of our friends had mentioned the company.

We talked and talked whilst on the bus and we seemed to click. I told Munyaradzi my ordeal and he felt sorry for me. I told him I was okay-ish but was just waiting to sort myself out. Munyaradzi put his arm around my shoulder and pulled me closer to him.

"I don't want you to think I am taking advantage of your situation, but just to let you know that I felt drawn and attracted to you the first time I saw you," said Munyaradzi.

"Well, I do not always get on with strangers and this is my first time on a bus in sixteen years," I told him. "I have always driven myself around," I added.

"So what have you been doing in the Capital?" Munyaradzi asked.

"I had gone to find a place to rent and to order a new car that will be delivered next week," I replied.

"So, where will you be living?" asked Munyaradzi.

"In Laughton Avenue, Mabelreign, Harare."

CHAPTER TWENTY-THREE

"Can I have your telephone number please?" he asked.

I gave him my number hesitantly. I was not very keen on starting a relationship with a black guy as I was now comparing my husband Kenzo with Roy. Nevertheless, I thought, people are different, and I gave him my contact details. The following day he rang me and we arranged to meet at Karoi Hotel for a drink. We talked and talked and drank loads and loads of wine. When it was time to go Munyaradzi asked me to walk with him to his place and then he would arrange for a taxi to take me to Chikangwe Location.

As I waited for the taxi, Munyaradzi started kissing me passionately. It felt so tender that I gave in and kissed him back. He lifted me up and carried me to his bedroom. We kissed and undressed each other. Since Munyaradzi was a black guy, I had my limitations. I remained within my boundaries. I thought if I did to him what I did or what I do with Roy he would wonder where I got these skills from. I limited my responses to match those of any other Zimbabwe girl. Unfortunately, it all happened very quickly for Munyaradzi. I just thought maybe he was too excited. I did not realise that Munyaradzi suffered from what they call premature ejaculation. I thought it was a one-off, but when we carried on seeing each other I realised that it was a condition that Munyaradzi suffered from.

Well, as you know me, Tanaka, I would not settle for that sort of guy, no matter how rich he might be. I told

CHAPTER TWENTY-THREE

Munyaradzi that there was not going to be anything serious between us and we would just be mates. I later moved to Harare then eventually to London.

When Munyaradzi came round to my house looking for me he was told that I had left for London. A few years later he persuaded his parents to buy him a ticket to London. He came to London hoping to meet me. However, London is not like some small towns in Zimbabwe, where people think if someone has left for London they will one day meet on the streets. I spent almost ten years in the United Kingdom, not knowing that Munyaradzi was also in the United Kingdom. Thanks to Facebook I came across him again. After a few weeks of chatting on Facebook, Munyaradzi wanted to come and see me. It turned out he had been in the country for the past ten years! He had not sorted out his immigration and was not working. I thought, man, how can one get oneself into such a mess! I asked him and he explained that he did not have anyone to guide him. He was living in one of the NASA houses in Manchester. He feared going back home, not due to the political violence but because of the economic situation. His asylum claim has been refused three times now, but he had nowhere to go to, no house, no job, nothing. Both his parents had by now died since the life expectancy in Zimbabwe had been cut short due to poverty, diseases such as AIDs, and hunger.

When he came to my house the environment became

CHAPTER TWENTY-THREE

completely different for him. He ate nonstop, sat in front of the television all day competing with Shana for the remote control. It was like taking another baby on board. His favourite places in the house were the kitchen and the lounge. He did not seem particularly interested in me as I proved to be much more successful than him and he just felt a failure. He always told me, "I know you are a very high achiever and don't fear anyone." This time Munyaradzi wanted us to do it properly - you know what I mean, have a relationship and then eventually get married. I thought, quietly, for a moment, is he genuine or does he just want to use me for money and obtaining papers, bearing in mind he was living off an asylum voucher of about thirty-five pounds per week? His decision kind of shocked me but I just thought, what have I got to lose - let me just check him out. Since, I thought, *EVERYTHING ELSE HAS FAILED for me relationship-wise*, I might give it a go. So we started seeing each other again. However, the same problem Munyaradzi had twenty-plus years ago was still there. "It's because your pussy feels too hot for me that I fail to hold on any longer!" he said. I told him point blank, "No dear, it won't work, as I will start cheating on you and you won't like it." Munyaradzi pleaded with me to keep him and I told him that *no* meant *no*.

He asked me to teach him ways of satisfying me but if the relationship wasn't sound I felt there was little hope he would succeed. I taught Munyaradzi what to do but it just did not feel right - you know what I mean, teaching a man who was almost half a century old what to do in bed as if I was teaching a sixteen-year-old.

Since I had Sky television, Munyaradzi got spoiled for choice; he would stay up late at night watching television, till three or four in the morning, and he was also becoming very lazy. He had left his children in Zimbabwe whom he never cared about; his sister who worked in London as a nurse took the responsibility of bringing his kids up, which is not fair on siblings. I soon lost interest in him and exclaimed to myself, "GOSH! Here is yet another useless Zimbabwean man - I've had enough!" I had thought perhaps GOING BACK TO MY ROOTS might help by dating men from my country who know my culture, but it just didn't work out.

I had to foot the bills for everything, including topping up his mobile phone with credit, since he was not working and earning. If he had to visit me from Manchester I had to pay for his return trip. At some point I was hospitalised for minor surgery, and Munyaradzi did not bother to check on me as he was upset with me that I had not sent him some money to fix his laptop that had been attacked by viruses. I rebuked him, saying, "How selfish and thoughtless of a man who says he loves me!"

He made me realise that he never cared about me but my money. He later went to ask one of his cousins for money, who later rang me up and had a good go at me, saying I should

CHAPTER TWENTY-THREE

give Munyaradzi money and support him financially since he 'services' me - meaning he makes love to me so I have to pay him for his services! That's when I lost it and told his cousin the way it was and told him to get lost. I told him how useless Munyaradzi was in bed, so he could fuck off and if he wanted to be a male escort, I told him where to go - central London! I said this with anger, adding, "They are advertising for male escorts, so you can go there babe and get yourself a tax free job... of shagging old women and start having a life!"

I told Munyaradzi point blank that all he ever wanted was the contents of my purse, not me. The guy had a frozen brain - he couldn't look after his kids in Africa and all he thought about was himself. Let me tell you one of the funniest thing he once did. One day while jogging he felt thirsty so he stopped when he spotted a supermarket. He had a five-pound note in his pocket so he went in to buy a large bottle of water for one pound. He then came to me and said, "You know dear, we have run out of bread at home - could you give me a pound to buy loaf of bread?" I replied, "The amount of money that you have used to buy a large bottle of water is equivalent to a loaf of bread! Why didn't you drink from the tap and buy a loaf of bread instead?" To tell you the truth, my kids never ate the type of bread he wanted to buy. It was for himself alone. He got angry and upset. I just said *in life people need to think about others, not see others as cash machines.* He took the huff and I did not care at all. I knew that he was a user and I simply wanted him gone.

CHAPTER TWENTY-THREE

I finally closed the chapter on that one. I then tried the latest dating strategy - online dating! I posted my picture on several sites, only to discover that the majority of the potential partners' profiles are from fake people. I posted my profile on one site which I will not name for legal reasons. I received about ten requests for money as my potential lovers invariably had relatives that had died in Africa - so my potential lovers needed help! Some people declared their love for me just having seen my picture and asking what I did for a living!

I thought, here we go again - gold diggers everywhere! I assured them they were digging in the wrong hole and left them. I just thought, what a scam! One guy who supposedly fell for me told me that he was based in America and was white. He never wanted to talk to me on the phone but online, on the chat site. He later asked me if I could send him about five thousand US dollars! I just said "FUCK OFF!" and closed the chapter on internet dating. "Fucking shit!" I swore. I had stalkers online; it was a shocking and terrifying experience. I had one particular guy who happened to be on every site I joined. I just wondered if he was genuinely seeking a partner or if he was an internet dating spy. I must tell you, he freaked me out! He seemed to know all the sites I had joined. Another guy who claimed to be from Germany declared all his wealth to me before even seeing my picture and not even having spoken to me. I just wondered if he was real. However, at this point I was not looking for money, you know; it was the time when I had reached forty-something, when a woman seeks a companion rather than an older man for pocket money.

I later met another guy who told me that all he wanted was a chat and a leg over and no strings attached, since he was married. I just wondered what was happening to the world of dating. Before putting a stop to men completely, I met another guy called Pariyah. Pariyah was from Iran, a Moslem and a student at my local university. We dated for a couple of months. Pariyah was the worst guy I had ever dated in my life. He was forty-something, he hated my food, my music, my deodorants and perfumes! He told me that a woman should smell of 'natural odours' and use no deodorants or perfumes - just water did it for him. I could not bear the smell of sweat on this guy. It was terrible! Pariyah did not know what to do with a lady and how to French kiss, let alone what to do when he went down on me.

Pfuuuuuuuuuuuuuuuuuuu, pfuuuuuuuuuuuuuuuuuu, went the air on my bits! "What the flaming heck are you doing?" I asked Pariyah.

"I am giving you a blow job," he said.

"Is that how you perform a blow job?" I queried! "Blowing my pussy like a balloon!" I puffed. "You can't give that creature mouth-to-mouth like it breathes and it is short of air! You need to learn the skill, man!"

"Okay, I am sorry, let me do it this way," he said, now kissing my bits like he would do on the proper lips!

CHAPTER TWENTY-THREE

"Stop," I ordered.

He stood there in disbelief and watched me as I puffed! With his prick with a full hard on, he pleaded, "My friend, my friend, calm down please! We can do it properly, in your way; I am willing to learn as long as you have the guts to teach me!"

"Do you see me as a training college?" I protested. "Out! I want you gone before it's too late!" I ordered.

Gosh! This guy needed to attend the Sex School! He had a long prick but he didn't know what to do with it! Honestly, it's not about the size, guys, it's about knowing how to use the thingy! "Thank you for making me wet for nothing!" shouted my demon! I asked him to stop and leave me alone for I never wanted to see him again! I just wondered, why and how on earth a mature man could display such Fifty Shades of Ignorance!

I wondered how on earth some women survive. I asked him if he was married. He said he was married and in his culture he was allowed to marry as many women as he liked, and the women should not feel jealous. He also believed that women should not enjoy lovemaking as it was unholy, pleasure in sex being the reserve of men; for the woman it should be for childbearing only.

Pariyah also told me that according to his Muslim faith oral sex was not allowed, yet he enjoyed having his cock sucked more than dipping it in the vagina - what a hypocrite!

CHAPTER TWENTY-THREE

I just told him that he was not my type and I was not going to waste my time on him.

I realised that when you are forty-something, it is very difficult to meet a nice man and one has to kiss many frogs in order to find a prince. I ended it with Pariyah as I was not prepared to be treated like a non-existent woman. He went on to tell me that the reason why the Muslims are allowed to marry many women is because if the wife does something wrong, the only way a husband can punish her is by not joining her in bed. I just thought that is so selfish, and a way of treating women as second class citizens. He went on to say in his culture a woman is not allowed to divorce her husband. It is the husband only who has the right to divorce his wife. I just found it unbearable and ended my relationship with him before it was too late.

I later tried to confess to someone who I thought was a church pastor; you know, when you get to that age of forty-something, meeting proper guys is not that easy. I told this fake pastor that if he knew of any single men within his congregation who were looking for a partner to settle down with, to pass my details to them. I was just trying to be moral, you see, to show that I remained grounded in my faith and was a devoted born-again Christian.

You will never believe it when I tell you that this particular fake church pastor viewed this as an opportunity to take advantage of me and he tried it on with me. I just told

CHAPTER TWENTY-THREE

him, "No! You are a married man! And after all, you are a pastor, so how on earth could you say that to me? I am looking for a single man, not a married man!" The pastor conceded that he was a married man, and went on to say he was tied into a loveless marriage where his fantasies were not being addressed. He said his biggest fantasy involved bondage and fetish and he wanted to do it with me! "How could you look for other men when I am right here?" the so-called pastor reasoned. "I want you to chain me to the bed, you know," he went on. "I want you to pee in my face, smack me, torture me and tease me…" These lamentations of the 'church pastor' were unbelievable!

"For goodness sake!" I exclaimed in anger, "Why do you think am the best person to do that for you? Who the hell do you think I am? And how dare you disrespect me like that! Do you think I am some hooker or something!" I confronted him like an angry SCANIA or DAF bearing down on an errant rat about to become squashed roadkill!

I just thought what a hypocrite he was: one minute he is preaching against adultery and the next minute… well, the very things he had condemned became his fantasies. He started stalking me on Facebook, Twitter, Yahoo chat, and MSN. I left his church and joined a Pentecostal Church in London. Before I left, I gave a testimony in the church to let people know the reason why I was leaving. I told them straightforwardly and openly that Pastor So-and-So had come on to me, that he had made sexual advances to me. It was so sad, since his wife was present; I just wanted her to know the kind of Casanova she was married to... He also stole my business idea but it never bothered him. He was a wolf in a sheepskin.

This taught me a lesson that when one is in business one needs to appoint a powerful solicitor and accountant. If I had some firm contract which legally bound all employees and those I did business with, my business idea would not have been *stolen* by this so-called false church pastor, who asked me to extend my business to his home so he could work for me on a commission basis. I paid for the office and all the bills and he used the opportunity to recruit his own people whilst using me as a financial resource. Up to now he has never made it; some people are just parasites and suckers. I wished him all the best of luck and closed the office down, took all my office equipment such as computers and printers, though this involved the police. I needed help from the police as the pastor had started using all my office stuff for his business. I finally stopped trusting people and especially men in general. The last thing I heard was that this fake pastor had abandoned the failed business and was doing some voluntary work in Africa.

I later moved on to my wonderful Rampant Rabbit, whom I fell in love with from the day I bought him from a shop in SOHO. Even if I have to buy several triple-xxx batteries, I do not regret having him. I tell you mate, he is

CHAPTER TWENTY-THREE

definitely much, much better than Munyaradzi, Sean and Kenzo. He has given me several orgasms, yet I have given him nothing in return. He doesn't ask for money. He doesn't leave dirty socks everywhere in the house. He does not fart under the duvet or have smelly armpits or bad breath. He is just perfect. In addition to Rampant the Rabbit I bought myself a human size teddy bear. I feel much happier now.

My only problem is when I go back to Zimbabwe, even if Rabbit doesn't need a passport or a VISA, he won't be allowed into the country. I will have to think of ways of smuggling him into Zimbabwe, otherwise my holiday there won't be good at all. My friend Roy lost one of his farms and is renting the other and I do not know whether he is in South Africa or Botswana or Zambia. I will have to check with the people who are renting my house in Mount Pleasant to see if he might have left a letter for me telling me where to find him. I miss Roy badly, you know. If he was in the United Kingdom, I might have found him through People.com or through the voter's roll. I am just waiting for the delivery of peace and human rights in Zimbabwe so that I can launch my adult shop for the sex toy business, since it is a NICHE market - not now, of course, with the crazy Robert Mugabe in power, or I will be locked up for life... and Rabbit would be seized by the Customs Officer, perhaps for their own use, or he will be burnt. Perhaps I should carry a reasonable amount of money to bribe the customs officers to let me enter the country with my partner

CHAPTER TWENTY-THREE

for life, Rampant the Rabbit, rather than risk having him seized and cremated in Zimbabwe... He is just a poor sex toy after all, and is quite harmless; but this uncivilised government will not see it that way.

Zimbabwe was once a country that fed half of Africa. Maize was exported on a daily basis into Zambia, Malawi, Tanzania and other neighbouring countries. I still remember when my late husband was a manager of the Grain Marketing Board, when he used to use the words, "Oh! This year we have a BUMBER HARVEST and farmer So-and-So has filled the whole grain silo by himself and our bonuses are going to skyrocket!" As I understand it, words to this effect have never been used again - not since 2002.

CHAPTER TWENTY-FOUR

WHAT I DID WHEN EVERYTHING ELSE HAD FAILED

WHEN EVERYTHING ELSE HAD FAILED, I thought all I needed in life was to develop survival strategies, or I would sink and drown for good.

In life if one lacks fear and has the faith, determination and inspiration, everything becomes easy. *Self-belief and the "I can do it attitude" is the major drive in human beings.* The reason why those who do not achieve anything in life is simply because they give up easily; some dare not try at all, while some believe they are hampered by bad luck. Tanaka came from humble beginnings and worked hard to follow her dreams, yet she led a very normal live. When she became a Millionaire she continued to live in cheap houses in the market and drove the cheapest car in the market.

It takes a lot of hard work to become like Tanaka. She refused to be walked over and wanted to prove that anyone can do it no matter where they come from on this earth. Tanaka watched people who turned to drugs when Everything Else Had Failed in their lives, and she always told herself, "Be true to thyself, and take care of what you introduce to thy body; love thyself and keep thyself clean."

At the time of writing I realised I would need to address the issue of sexual intercourse, honestly and frankly. The idea of a woman going down on a man and vice versa, using oral sex, all too readily elicits the incredulous response expressed by the words, "WHAT, YOU MUST BE KIDDING ME!" After I observed a lot of my male and female patients producing awful discharges from their penises and vaginas ("God help us, *yuk, and she regurgitates*!!"), I realised that there are valid reasons why some are shocked by the act of cunnigulus (oral sex or "eating a girl out", as it is often called). I am not saying don't do it but be careful who you do it with; and never trust anyone who wants to do it in the dark. Feel free to examine the bits you are going to accept into your system; just like food, we examine it with our eyes and the sense of smell. Ask yourself "Is my partner clean?" and have some tests before you think of going down that route, and always, *always* use a condom. Never ever trust someone by just taking one look at them as you never know what they are carrying in their bodily fluids.

The idea of writing my first book came when I was not

feeling well and after suffering a lot of discrimination at work where I was unfairly dismissed. I thought, "GOSH!! In this whole wide world, no one will ever get rich by working for someone else!" Perhaps losing my job was the catalyst that triggered the search for new strategies, hence going into business, investing in property and starting to write to earn a passive income in the form of royalties. On a daily basis I saw opportunities and niche markets; I developed business eyes, as they are called - though I believe this is something I have always had.

Since Tanaka kept a low profile, none of her friends knew that she was a Millionaire when she became one. Her philosophy was based on the belief that once you expose yourself, you won't be able to sleep at night fearing for your life. Her children went to school without fearing that they might be kidnapped because they led a normal life. Driving around in a black Ford KA did not attract unwanted attention; she did have a Mercedes Benz for special functions, though rumour had it that it was not hers but a hired vehicle.

Tanaka also believed that if she created many friends and activities and so on, then the load would be too heavy for her to carry. In real life it is those that are very close to us that tell people about us. It is also those that are very close to us that will end up knowing everything about us, and mind you, some end up being your enemies. Staying away from people

CHAPTER TWENTY FOUR

who do not share the same insights or goals in life is the best thing. There is a saying that says birds of the same feather flock together. Tanaka dropped all useless friends, suckers, parasites and negative friends along her journey to success, and you can do the same on your road to success. She had to do away with all Mistletoe friends as they survive by sucking the blood of those who work hard to keep their bodies well hydrated and nourished, since they prefer to take advantage of others.

Some people cannot sleep at all. Some even want paparazzi to tell the world that they have produced a green or yellow poo. These people end up feeling depressed and fearing for their lives. Everywhere they go they have bored guards with them; they don't even think that the bodyguard might turn around and ask for money, poison them or shoot them. They even invite photographers to follow them everywhere and show the world everything they do and how they live inside their houses - what a shame! Every detail of their lives is known by the public - drugs, failed relationships, boob jobs, designer vaginas, having Botox injections, plastic surgery, you name it, they have done it all. You just mention their name and even a five-year-old can tell you all about their failings.

Their aim is to make headlines in the newspapers and make more money. It is very sad how people choose to lead their lives once they have money. For Tanaka, keeping a low profile is the key to success. The majority of millionaires are living ordinary lives and they don't tell the world that they are billionaires, unless Forbes were to spy on them!

CHAPTER TWENTY-FIVE

APPLYING THE LAW OF ATTRACTION

Applying the Eleven Forgotten Laws of the Universe and how I did it!

AS I SAT DOWN cogitating, I just wondered how I could make money. I thought, shall I sell my thingy or shall I become an informer? Every possible money-making idea rushed into my brain as I wondered after being denied ESA (Employment Support Allowance). It was now five months since I had lost my job in an unfair dismissal which they referred to as ill health capability which was based on disability discrimination. Still waiting to hear from ET (Employment Tribunal) for my case of unfair dismissal and discrimination, I had nothing to EAT let alone a place to sleep. I kept my eviction letter under my pillow and found it really hard to go to sleep. I sat down and pondered; the fridge is empty, the cupboard is empty, my bank balance is overdrawn, my rent is in arrears and I am still waiting to hear the result of the housing benefit which I had applied for in January; what shall I do to earn money, I wondered? The business which I had started a few years before was slowly drowning in recession. I made myself a cup of green tea and started thinking deeply. What shall, I do? "Create new sales strategies as opposed to Cold Calling," came that small voice again. "Streetwalking will not only endanger your life but… think of sleeping with every TOM, DICK and HARRY!" After all, how many prostitutes have made it to the RICH LIST by selling their female genitalia assets? The answer is none. How many streetwalkers were killed whilst on the mission, trying to make some spondulicks or bucks? The answer is countless. So, there we go, once again streetwalking became a non-effective OPTION.

Making money needs the **DESIRE to be rich, FAITH to believe that all will be well, ACTION to help myself out of the situation, INSPIRATION to develop creative ideas, DETERMINATION to have the power to arrive at a sensible decision, MOTIVATION to have the power to work towards my goals** and the, **"I can do it spirit". I simply had to apply the LAW OF ATTRACTION to turn my world around!!**

I applied all the Eleven Forgotten Laws of the Universe (please see list under The Words of Encouragement at the beginning of the book), starting with the Law of Thinking - which was the point where I now was.

CHAPTER TWENTY FIVE

A million pounds is £1000 x £1000, I thought. Then, I can do it, I told myself. "IF OTHER FROGS CAN JUMP, THEN I CAN JUMP; IF OTHER PEOPLE CAN MAKE MONEY WHILST THEY SLEEP, THEN I CAN MAKE MONEY WHILST SLEEPING TOO!" Thus I reassured myself. Maybe selling a product or providing services for £1,000 profit and repeat that a thousand times; which could be done in two years' time if I make my employees work and earn £10,000.00 profit for the business every week; as well as writing a book and selling my real life story could just be a better way, or by investing in property and making the tenants build equity for me whilst I sleep; yes, I can do it, I reassured myself, but honestly, making a million bucks is as not easy as it looks or sounds, I thought. "No BB, stop being negative," I told myself. "You can do it! There are a number of people who made it from nothing in real life," came the small voice in my head, "You can do it." I think my God was back from his vacation and wanted to prove that the devil is indeed a liar, or he had finally heard my call for help, since it took him a while to respond. As I pondered, I just wondered how some people seem to just make it from nowhere and, having nothing, become big in terms of wealth, and then lose everything and start again, **like the famous American Donald Trump** who lost everything and started again and still made it really big. Do these guys have gold blood in their system or are they all from the Midas clan, or do they come from another planet, I wondered? Are they aliens from UFOs or the dead (ghosts or demons) living among us, I wondered?

I thought, well, Lord Jeffrey Archer was near to bankruptcy before writing, but he made it big time when he wrote his first novel; where did his idea come from, I wondered? Was it from God, or his ancestors, or from the Midas family? He went into prison for perjury, yet he came out with more ideas from his experience whilst in prison and made more Zillions. What a brilliant money-making machine he is! I would actually want to meet this man in real life, I thought, for he is my hero: let me follow in his footsteps. Faith is what I need, and motivation as well as the **DESIRE** to want to do something.

As stated by Napoleon Hill, I was on the right track. He said in one of his famous quotes: "Desire is the starting point of all achievements, not a hope, not a wish, but pulsating DESIRE to win – essential to success!"

J.K. Rowlings hatched her idea of writing about the world's most popular character Harry Potter whilst on a delayed train from Manchester to London's Kings Cross; now she is worth billions, if not zillions. I thought Jay-Z grew up in poverty and was well known for going round his friends' to eat, but GOSH, look at him now! He is now worth millions, billions, trillions and zillions. If we add his wife's fortune to his, surely the couple's fortune is worth millibillitrillizillions…

CHAPTER TWENTY FIVE

Sir Richard Branson started by selling magazines to fellow college students. According to his books, he doesn't hold any degrees in education but holds degrees and degrees of massive wealth and knowledge; and he is a world icon in marketing. Looking at his brand VIRGIN, some people might have put him down in the beginning thinking that his business was linked to sex. The brand has grown out of all proportions now and is well known and loved world-wide.

Robert and Kim Kiyosaki, as mentioned in their books, where once homeless and now they have made millions, if not billions, by investing in gold and silver, properties, offering educational seminars world-wide, and writing books. They all had the DESIRE to make it, to become successful and RICH.

I just wondered and asked myself, are these people real and not aliens like E.T living amongst us? What makes them so different? Are they angels, or are they Christians, are they Goths, are they witches that rob the banks with magic, or are they mini-gods? I just wondered how people can start from nothing and end up being very, very rich. What is it that they have in common? Or what do they have that makes them different? I asked myself J the questions:

#1: What makes me different from them?
   Answer = nothing, as we are all human beings.
#2: What did they do that I cannot do?
   Answer = these guys took enormous RISKS; so if you can take RISKS you could end up being like them.

#3: What makes these guys different from everyone else? Answer = these guys removed FEAR and developed the DESIRE to become wealthy; they hatched a Plan and ACTED upon their plans till they won or received what they wanted; and they continued to work tirelessly.

I then realized that these guys did not win the lottery; neither did they inherit their fortune, but it was all down to hard work, engaging the principles of **Faith, Determination, Action, Inspiration** and **Motivation**; and for some of them the idea of making money came to them as a joke J **- when everything else had failed** for them. They broke the chain of **FEAR** and took calculated **RISKS**.

"Well, let me have some of the faith and motivation to start doing something," I prayed and abstained from food… and started to take action; educating myself and attending seminars. "I want to be like them: THE RICH, FAMOUS and SUCCESFUL!"

I convinced myself that my friends should be the RICH and not the broke; I was determined to work hard for my money, and ensure that my money would work for me. "I SHALL CREATE MY OWN WEALTH, and I SHALL BE EXTREMELY RICH, so help me God," I prayed. As I did all this, I did not forget my Creator as I believe strongly in the afterlife and that every blessing comes from God Almighty.

CHAPTER TWENTY FIVE

I had to work hard for my soul, as well as my wealth. I started viewing myself like one of the wealthy people before I became one. I started creating my life and my future by working very hard and making my money work for me as I invested for the future...

This thinking was also backed by Peter F. Drucker who wrote, "The best way to predict your future is to create it."

I rubbed my hands together and thought and thought; I asked myself, can I sing? *(As I was trying to come up with a niche product or service!)*

"No BB you can't sing, Simon Cowell will embarrass and ridicule you in front of the whole wide world, in front of your family, in your own house on your own TV, which you paid for, so don't do it!" came the small voice in my head.

Well, shall I try dancing then, I asked myself? "No BB," came that small voice again. "You can't even swim or ride a bike, let alone dance, and again Simon Cowell will be there, and this time he will put you down!" Oh if it means being murdered by Simon Cowell on television, let me forget about this get rich quick scheme, I told myself.

Well, I asked, what about going to the States then? That's the best place for people to make it, especially New York, the place where dreams are made. Jay-Z, 50 pence, Lady Gaga, Rihanna, and the guy who sang "my hump, my hump, my lovely lady lumps" made it and of course the one who sang, "Lonely, I am so lonely, I am nobody on my own." Only a paragraph repeated several times will help me make it big, I thought. ""No BB!" came that small voice again, "don't joke with the States, man!"

Yes, I will make it, I thought. If president Obama came from Kenya in Africa and made it, then why can't I? I *will* do it! "Well, BB," came that relentless voice again, "don't you know that Simon Cowell has taken over American TV?"

"What!!" I exclaimed, "Don't scare me, man."

"He will put you down," that small voice said again.

Well then, he will go down for murder, I thought. In America it is murder for murder; he will be put on death row and be given a lethal injection. So, I can do absolutely anything without the fear of being put down, I rejoiced!

"Hey BB, when I said he will put you down, I didn't mean that he would actually kill you! I meant that he will embarrass and ridicule you in front of the whole world on the television." That little voice was so persistent.

"Oh, I see, thank you," I said.

The small voice volunteered more information: "Our lovely Sherry Lee is back home, have you not heard? She didn't make it in the US. Now she is reportedly being smuggled into her matrimonial home and spending nights with her former cheating footballer husband." The small voice advised, "Stay at home and think of something better."

Again, I prayed and prayed and fasted and fasted, hoping for miracles to happen there and then. "How can I make it?"

CHAPTER TWENTY FIVE

I cried. "Prime Minister Cameron and his coalition government - collision government would be a better term! - is cutting benefits and jobs. Jobs are now like gold that has to be mined only by the brave ones!" Since the conservatives 'collided' with the Liberal Democrats and got married, there are cuts everywhere and demonstrations and strikes everywhere. "I lost my job, I can't get benefits, so what shall I do?" I cried. "The streets of London are no longer paved with gold," I cried again, "so what shall I do to earn a living? Shall I go and patrol the streets of Ipswich as a streetwalker?"

"No BB, you will get killed like those girls who were murdered by the same man."

"Shall I go looting and grab some goodies?"

"For how long will you survive on looted goodies, and what about the business owners that you loot goods from? How will they feel," came the voice again. **Do something, never make yourself cheap by selling your body, work for a living, use your brain and hands, start ACTING and BELIEVING in YOURSELF NOW! YOU CAN DO IT AND YOU CAN DO ABUSOLUTELY ANYTHING!!"**

"POVERTY and BROKE, I shall remember you for the rest of my life!" I cried. "You two get on so well, I bet you are siblings! Please leave me alone, I reject you!"

I started, crying and got really depressed and hit Prozac, Fluoxetine, Seroxat, Mirtazapine and Citalopram - name every drug for depression, I had it. None of these medicines

CHAPTER TWENTY FIVE

cured my depression till I drank some cold water and a cup of green tea with lemon, and as I continued my quest asking more and more questions each day, ideas started to pour in. The last two solutions seemed to work better and I started getting focused and took ACTION as I BELIEVED myself that I can do it.

"Stop crying BB, your life story is a very interesting one, just chill out, and get your old typewriter out and start typing!" came the small voice again.

"Oh! That sounds even scarier," I thought. "If the **geriatric President Mugabe** catches me, he will put me on his private death row!" I had never heard about his death row but I had heard about people disappearing in Zimbabwe!!

"Noo, BB, don't be silly, and stop worrying about granddad BOB, he will be fine and he will soon realise that times are changing; he will adapt to them and these days he seems much calmer. I think Diazepam and Lorezapam are working well for him, since he has appeared asleep on TV on several occasions," came the little voice again. At least he won't put me down like Simon Cowell, I thought.

I quickly went into the shed to find my typewriter. Gosh, it was covered in dust and cobwebs. I thought, maybe Harry Potter and his friends had been using it. "No, I-I-I-I am not touching it!" I cried. My mom had taught me to follow my instincts and a 'no' means 'no' to me. Okay, that's it, I thought, I am not doing! Let me just pray and fast and praise

CHAPTER TWENTY FIVE

my Lord God, as he will see me through; I thought, whatever I am going through he will carry me.

"No BB, do something man," the voice persisted, "**God only helps those who help themselves!**" In life there is always something or someone who tries to stand in your way when you want to do something. My advice is never to disregard your calling in life. You will know what your calling is "If you can feel and see it in your mind," as Walt Disney said, and once you know what it is, go for it!

"If that's the case, then fine," I agreed. I went into the shower… Tell you what, this is just between you and me: I did not take a shower at all as I thought, it will just waste time. I just grabbed a flannel, soaked it in warm water, soaped it through and went for my smelly bits. Within no time I smelt nice and fresh. I added a spray of my nice deodorant which I had bought from the Savers for one pound, brushed my teeth with my toothbrush which I bought from the pound shop, and used the toothpaste which I bought last month, for a pound when it was on BOGOF - buy one, get one free.

Now I need to get **cracking**, I told myself. I have got thirty days to write this book, I told myself. Well, I won't stop praying as I am asking for miracles, but I need energy to be able to concentrate and keep calm as I carry on writing.

"Come on BB, you are wasting time," came that little voice again. "Benefits are now taking longer and they also have doctors who have to assess you before you can get any money - come, let's go!"

CHAPTER TWENTY FIVE

I grabbed my wallet and rushed to catch the bus into town. I went straight into the **OXFAM CHARITY SHOP** and could barely believe my luck when I saw a Computer! I did not mind at all that it was an old-fashioned one with the back like a hump of a camel. "How much is the P.C.?" I asked the lady. "Fifty pounds," she replied, "but today you can have it for twenty five." What a nice lady!

"Oh God of Abraham, Isaac and Jacob, you are wonderful, thank you Jesus, Thank you my Lord," I sang. What a good God I have, I thought. I paid for the computer and ran across the road to my favourite shop: Iceland. I bought a variety of ready microwave meals for thirty pounds to take me through my thirty days of writing. I went back home, very happy with my new second-hand PC and food for the whole month, plus 500mls x 4 of milk for four weeks. I thought, now let me begin writing my story! I will not stop praying, but will stop fasting, for a month, I told myself. Maybe I might end up joining the Midas clan and end up brushing my shoulders with these big guys. Look at Simon Cowell, before he heard her sing he was prepared to put SuBo and her bushy eyebrows down, but SuBo refused. She went on to shine in America.

"Ohhhh yesSSSSS!!!! BB, receeeeeeeiiiive your blessings," came that voice again. "I claim it, my Lord," I prayed, "thank you Jesus! Maybe I will end up being a millibillizillitrillionaire." After I said my prayer I brought

myself two litres of cold water to drink. *"I wanna be a Zillionaire so freaking bad,"* I sang as I prepared myself to write my story. Maybe if I become a millibillitrillizillionaire, I will be able to help the poor and the people from my African community, first to fight against FGM (**f**emale **g**enital **m**utilation), second to help those affected by **H**IV and **A**ids, third to build **t**oilets for those who may benefit from it! I want to help many, many people in my life, build a portfolio of properties for people to rent so that families can have a roof over their heads. How sad is it to know that some people are still relieving themselves behind the bushes in some undeveloped countries, so help me Lord, as I want to help many, many people!!! Then I started typing!

As, I was typing, I could see my past and future life coming straight into my mind, and I could visualise my future... I could visualise myself living in a massive house, with a swimming pool, tennis court, double garage - you know the kind I am talking about, A VERY LARGE COUNTRY HOUSE, and I mean one with seven or more bedrooms, with extensive land, one that's worth millions.

I have to emphasise the point that Walt Disney made on his deathbed: "If you don't see it in your mind you will never ever have it." This is the law of attraction. Everything that has happened to me, I saw it first, either in my dreams or in my imaginations, then implemented the idea.

My life is an interesting story and my book WILL BE A

CHAPTER TWENTY FIVE

BEST SELLER, I declared. It will be printed in many, many languages; and it will be sold in many, many countries and I shall fly many, many miles away to different countries, to meet my fans and for book signing events. I shall be recognized across the globe as a Best Selling author!!!

I could picture myself like a celebrity with some people just wanting to touch me and see me. It was an amazing tableau. I could see myself talking to the wonderful **OPRAH WINFREY**, pinching myself and asking myself "Is it really me?" and **OPRAH** reassuring me by saying, "Yes, that's you, you have done it!" What a dream, eh?

"To accomplish great things we must not only ACT, but also DREAM; not only plan but also BELIEVE." (Anatole France.)

Once one is honest with oneself, one will be honest with everyone else. Being me is determined by being outspoken and the extrovert I am, with nothing to hide! I will always speak my mind and wear my heart on my sleeve, because that's who I AM. Take it or leave it, I will never change my personality for a million pounds.

I confided to a close friend that I was writing a story about my life. Hey, she became very negative, saying, "In the west people are not interested in reading stories about Africans." She tried by every means to discourage me. I asked her, "Don't you think this could be a NICHE MARKET, as not many people would be prepared to expose their life story or

CHAPTER TWENTY FIVE

testimony, especially if they are not celebrities?" She disagreed.

Never mind, I reassured myself, saying, **"As much our names differentiate us, so do our thoughts, wants, needs and DESIRES, which is why some people are RICH and some BROKE and some POOR."**

I have read a lot of books about self-made millionaires and found out that most of them say that they were not motivated by money but by the **DESIRE** that they wanted to do something for themselves. This is very different for me, as I will be very honest with everyone and say plainly that **MONEY** motivated me as I rejected the idea of being **POOR** and **BROKE.**

Also, there was a part of me that wanted to prove some people wrong, like the manager of a SCNH Nursing Home in Sussex who used me as a Clinical Lead Nurse for more than forty hours at fifteen pounds per hour. I was sacked without any pay because I had discovered that they had a lot of expired tablets in their drug trolley. I looked at the manager and felt sorry for her. She had to start work before 7 a.m., and they wanted me to do the same, yet the company would only start paying people at 8 a.m. I refused to work for an hour for free just to please the boss, but this manager did this religiously every day and felt very happy to please the boss. Bless her. I later found a job in Wales as a Home Manager, with a starting salary of £35,000.00 per annum.

CHAPTER TWENTY FIVE

When I read the contract I just felt sick and the thought of working for someone made me sick. I was told the management had a twenty-four hour responsibility for their designated care home - meaning if a staff member did not turn up for duty when I was off duty, I had to go in. Moreover, the company did not allow the use of agency staff during bank holidays. I just wondered, what would happen if three or four people rang off sick on a public holiday? This meant I was supposed to go in and work to make the numbers up. The contract went on to say that there are times when the manager is expected to conduct a stop-and-search examination of staff. I just felt all this was inhuman and the company proved that they did not trust their staff. I turned the job down and said to myself, I shall earn more than £35,000.00 per annum whilst sleeping and there is no way I am going to make someone rich by working for them under such harsh conditions. I also hated being told what to do.

Some of the orders were just too harsh to implement on workers, e.g. on people who are helping you to get rich. I realised why this company had always struggled to find staff: the owner did not have a good public relationship education. What I learnt during the time I was an employee is that when employees are treated with respect, they in return will look after your business as their own; but if they are treated harshly or made to work hard whilst earning less, they will not be motivated and all they will do is complain and waste much of their working time discussing the bad things about the business. Here is something that I learned from Sir Richard Branson, from his book *Business Stripped Bare* - "good employers allow their employees to run their business on their behalf as if they were running their own companies, and always promote from within." This piece of information really helped and inspired me.

Watching and seeing my bank balance changing every day motivated me even more: the accumulating zeros made my soul bubble with joy; each time my net worth added another zero, I felt like climaxing! Therefore **money and the desire to be my own boss** motivated me; and the desire to be free when I get older, not to be thrown into some council nursing home being paid for by Social Services. No, no, no, I rejected poverty!!

I attended my first wealth-creation seminar with RICH DAD Education by Robert Kiyosaki, where I was lectured by Dr Rohan Weerasinge and others, and this changed my life and the way I think and act forever. It was the best decision I had ever made, to invest in my wealth education and to invest in property. The money I paid for the training was worth it as an investment. I did not attend the follow-up mentoring programme as I did not consider it worth the amount that was being charged - £11,295 to get a property mentor and three days of training; no, BB, do not pay, said my conscience - use that amount of money as a down payment for a flat or a house and start investing; apply theory to practise. "Ask some property gurus in your area - they will be willing to share their knowledge with you for free," said my little adviser stuck in my brain. I must say I only took on board information which I found helpful. I didn't give in when others did, especially when they were asked to transfer their credit cards to other providers and ask for 0% interest and ask to have their credit limits increased to £100,000.00. For some people it did not appear to them that they were being bullied into asking for a higher credit card limit on their cards as a way to raise the money to pay for the mentoring course. People were being asked if they had parents who had homes that did not have any mortgages, even to ask *them* to re-mortgage and release equity to provide the funds for the courses.

Unlike me, some guys were slow to see that the motive was to get them to buy the next expensive course whereas the money for the course could be used to start investing. Thank God for my openness, as I refused to be bullied into getting into deeper debt and lose £11,295.00 to pay a mentor for a three-day training course. Since I do not suffer fools gladly, I was very open and said I wanted to sleep on the idea and do some research on the Company called Tigrent Learning, then come back for mentoring if I was encouraged by the comments and reviews. After reading the comments that were posted online I made myself a cup of tea and relaxed, as I was pleased with the findings and my decision. There were loads and loads of complaints about this company, some people linking it with a previous company called Whitney from Florida. I told myself that if I needed a mentor, I would find one for free. I went to ask my previous landlords and they helped me out for no cost at all.

My advice to those who want to get into the property business is this: do NOT look for expensive mentors or courses as you will need the money to set sail on your investment journey. Make money rather than lose it. If there are any OPTIONS of finding mentorship for free, I would grab that opportunity and then invest an amount of £11,295.00 on a £50,000.00 property as a 20% deposit for a buy-to-let mortgage and the change for improving the property; or invest an amount of £5,000.00 on a £100,000.00 property as a first-time buyer or put £10,000.00 down as 20% deposit for a £100,000.00 dwelling and use the balance for decorating the property. What I realised is that the guys offering the course focussed mainly on selling the next course rather than teaching, as they were running a training educational franchise. What they were really concerned about was making sure they succeeded in netting your hard-earned cash!! So, think carefully before investing in these property mentorship courses. Other property money magnets, like some other guys who operate in the same CULT, will be making money from your hard-earned cash by calling it creative financing, passive income or cash-flow. In his book *Rich Dad Poor Dad*, Robert Kiyosaki advises, "When you make your money make sure not to lose it" - so why pay for even more expensive mentorship courses?!

Little by little, step by step, I gradually created my property portfolio from the money I generated from the business *as I had stopped being an employee*. The only thing that helped me much was the DESIRE, COURAGE and SELF-MOTIVATION that I wanted to be rich and to help others. I continued to read books written by self-made-millionaires and many inspirational people. I viewed loads and loads of properties, even some of which were worth multi-millions that was way before my property portfolio had reached a quarter of a million. I aimed very high, desired to live in country houses worth millions and millions, and desired to own my own nursing homes. I would attend property auctions just to watch how some people did it; and how they developed the houses they had purchased. I would put an offer on properties before acquiring the mortgage only to have the mortgage turned down. I learned the hard way, but it was better than losing the money that I put down as my first deposit to some smart sales people as a mentoring fee. I have to admit that I made mistakes along the way; every property investor has made some mistakes along the way. I am glad that I had the opportunity to learn from my mistakes. As time went by, I knew exactly what to do. The truth is, when there is a viable project, money will flow in and you will choose where to get money from. The financial doors will open as they will be attracted by the viability of the project.

Gradually, I developed the knowledge and skills I needed to become a professional PROPERTY INVESTOR. I made so many friends who were very helpful, friends who had been there and run the course - Contractors, Valuers, Solicitors, Plumbers. My first friend in the property professional relationship was my Financial Broker who would help me to acquire the funds I wanted before house hunting. When properties became available to an estate agent, I was the first one to be contacted and to view the property, and sure enough, the funds would be readily available. I learned to tip the person who sourced the properties for me and as a result I purchased many properties below the market value, as my friends would tell the seller that they alone had managed to get an offer. I would do the house up, re-mortgage it, release some equity and quickly rush back to purchase more. It was more of a hobby, not realising that I was actually building my wealth.

The moment I started making money, my circle of friends changed; I started to attract very wealthy people like a magnet; they all wanted to mingle with me and me with them. I attracted some very rich property gurus in the auction rooms, not for personal relationships but for financial relationships and networking. I made sure that I made friendships with a common purpose or shared interests - either worshipping together, learning together, sharing ideas, finding deals and making money.

When I watched Caroline Marsh on Channel 4's 'Secret Millionaire' programme, tears of excitement rolled down my cheeks and immediately I realised that when an African Girl can do it, so can I. The girl was in her thirties, and this motivated me even more. I just wanted to be like her.

When I had made my money I realised that I would never ever need a man for financial independence; now that I have a bit of cash, the money pulls gentlemen and real men for me; the men don't pull me as I have lost my sex appeal due to the number of birthdays I have celebrated over the years. Now the opposite is true: surely money talks and money is power. Maybe they want me for my money, in which case there are always pre-nups to consider to ensure that I keep my money. In my family the norm has always been the one with money leads and decides, and I do just that.

On reflection, I can just say my boss did well for sacking me in the first place and Sean did well, too, for kicking me out of his matchbox-sized flat and by ending the relationship, because I might otherwise have continued living unhappily in a job and relationship for financial security and would not have achieved what I have achieved now.

When I started my business and investment, I did not sit down to calculate how much it would cost me. Consider the following Bible verse and learn something from it:

CHAPTER TWENTY FIVE

"For which of you, intending to build a tower, does not sit down to count the cost, whether he may have enough to finish it, lest perhaps, after he laid the foundation and is not able to finish, all those seeing begin to mock him saying, This man began to build and was not able to finish."
Luke 14: 28-30

And again, Proverbs 24: 3-4 teaches us that "Through wisdom a house is built, and by understanding it is established; and by knowledge the rooms shall be filled with precious and pleasant riches" - thus the wisdom and knowledge I gained from the 'Rich Dad Poor Dad' seminar has given me the understanding of establishing my wealth and to fill my rooms with precious and pleasant riches, as I shall not chase men for financial freedom.

Honestly, "Destiny is not a matter of chance; it is a matter of choice", as William Jennings Bryan says.

Therefore, my destiny has always been to be RICH, WEALTHY and SUCCESSFUL!

To Sean, I can only raise a glass of champagne and wish him well whilst I sing and dance to the BIG YELLOW TAXI by JONI MITCHELL - as I wave goodbye to him forever and ride on the big yellow taxi:

CHAPTER TWENTY FIVE

They paved paradise
And put up a parking lot
With a pink hotel, a boutique
And a swinging hot spot

Don't it always seem to go
That you don't know what you've got till it's gone
They paved paradise
And put up a parking lot

Now that my life has changed tremendously Sean may well nurse his regret that he didn't know what he had until it was gone - gone and gone for good, left for better horizons! This shows that some people we cling to in our lives not only make our lives miserable but can also help to freeze our brains to the extent that we forget thinking and working for ourselves. Do not let them control our lives with their remote control device! I am not saying people should not be in relationships or stop getting married, but enter into relationships for good reasons and with the right persons, especially not for financial freedom, or they may well use and abuse you, knowing that without them you are a nobody.

Women too can mistreat men when they are the ones with money. I know of a celebrity couple in the UK that divorced due to the girl being horrible and bad-mouthing her husband on television (ITV 2) and everywhere because she

CHAPTER TWENTY FIVE

was the one who had more money than he did. It was not a nice thing to watch. So when you make your millions, please, I beg you, be kind to other species on earth.

CHAPTER TWENTY-SIX

OUT OF SODOM AND GOMORRAH

TANAKA is now out of Sodom and Gomorrah and is a born-again Christian and a very strong believer - and a member of **Forward in Faith Ministries International (FIFMI), London UK, and she worships at Stratford Assembly** in East London. Tanaka believes that when one accepts Jesus Christ as one's Saviour, nothing shall remain private - and her testimony will save others and will help her to win souls and help other people to believe that no one will go to our father who is in heaven but through Jesus Christ our Lord and Saviour who died on the cross for our sins. She believes that happiness comes from within, the inner self, in accepting yourself in the way the Lord God created you, to follow your dreams, in living by God's commands and fearing no one except God the creator of heaven and earth. Her prayers have always been based on the Bible, one of her favourite verses being Luke 18 verses 35-40:

CHAPTER TWENTY SIX

"As Jesus approached Jericho, a blind man was sitting by the roadside begging. When he heard the crowd going by, he asked what was happening. They told him that **Jesus of Nazareth is passing by**. On hearing this, he called out, 'Jesus Son of David, have mercy on me!'

Those who led the way rebuked him and told him to be quiet, but he shouted all the more. Jesus stopped and ordered the man to be brought to him. When he came nearer Jesus asked him, 'What do you want me to do for you?'

'Lord, I want to see,' he replied. And Jesus said unto him, '**Receive your sight; your faith has healed you**.' Immediately he received his sight and followed Jesus praising God. When all the people saw this, they also praised God."

Tanaka also called unto Jesus and said, "Jesus the Son of David, have mercy on me please!" Jesus asked Tanaka, "What do you want me to do for you?" "I want your forgiveness as I have been living in sin. I need your blessings; pour your miracles over me for I have repented. I need to be saved at the end like Lot and his family were saved when Sodom and Gomorrah were destroyed by the burning sulphur. I also need to be a Millionaire. May your servant find favour in your eyes, as you have shown me great kindness in sparing my life. As the Lord is my shepherd and I shall not want, may he make me lie down in greener pastures and lead me beside still waters and may my soul be restored. Guide me oh Lord in the paths of righteousness for your name's sake. Even if I walk through the valley of the shadow of death, I will fear no evil, for you are with me; your rod and your staff comfort me." (You will see that quite a few words of my prayer were based on Psalm 23.) Then Jesus replied and said, "Receive your blessing, Tanaka; may your heart be filled with joy, as your faith has saved you."

Honestly, there is power in the words we speak!

"Thank you, my Lord," said Tanaka, crying with happiness.

The power of giving has generated so much positive results in Tanaka's financial life. As the Bible says, "Give and you shall receive." Tanaka gives to charity, church and helps other people who are in need.

Surely goodness and mercy shall follow me all the days of my life as I will dwell in the house of the Lord forever and ever. This was Tanaka's promise to herself.

Tanaka's motto has always been, "If other frogs can jump, then she can jump too!" She has and will always follow her dreams, have faith, determination and try to inspire others. Her aim is to make more friends and socialise with like-minded people, especially successful people and those aspiring to be successful. "I shall wine and dine with millionaires and billionaires, since we are what we think... Success breeds success, so help me God as I want to be successful; I do not seek any fame but financial freedom."

They say "if you wanna be big, play hard, play safe, work hard and make the people who inspire you the centre of your life." If you want money, look for it, for it will never look for you! **The money is with the big guys and small guys, just know who has it and how to make it and make friends with those who have it, those who do not keep company with negative thinkers. Aim to be like them, then you will be surprised by what you will achieve. For Tanaka started visualising her life as a millionaire ten years ago. She even told her children that she had a very strong feeling that she will be very rich in life - and would become a millionaire. Her children are living witnesses to this.**

Her philosophy was based on the famous saying by Walt Disney, "If you can't see it in your mind, you will never have it!"

Tanaka's other powerful philosophy is about giving; she strongly believes that if she doesn't stretch her hand to give, she will not receive anything. She gives to those that need it most, to the church in the form of tithes or collections, and to her people.

We need money - that is the reason for working hard and creating businesses. Sitting on my backside all day long like a couch potato has and will always be a *no* for Tanaka!! If one wants to live in debt, then that's an individual's choice. *If you wanna live like a billionaire so freaking bad, then start behaving and acting like one. Hard work always pays.*

Tanaka's tip for you is this: work hard and choose your friends wisely. The Lord will open the heavens, the storehouse of his bounty, to send rain on your land in season and to bless all the work of your hands. You will lend money to many nations but will borrow from no-one. The lord chooses heads, never tails. If you pay attention to the commands of the Lord your God and acknowledge that he will give you this day and will always be at the top, never the bottom, you will succeed. ("The Lord is our protector and glorious king, blessing us with kindness and honour. He does not refuse any good thing to those who do what is right" - Psalm 84:11.) Do not turn aside from his commands that he gives you today or any other day; do not turn to the right or to the left, following other gods and serving them; instead choose the straight path that leads to the destiny that God has chosen for you, knowing that "in all things God works for good with those who love him, those whom he has called according to his purpose" (Romans 8:28).

Tanaka's God Almighty turned things around for her and blessed the work of her hands. He will turn circumstances around for you too. **(PLEASE NOTE THAT I AM NOT IMPOSING MY RELIGION OR ANY RELIGION UPON ANYONE.)**

CHAPTER TWENTY SIX

Tanaka is now a Millionaire, a businesswoman, an Investor and is aiming at featuring on 'The Secret Millionaire' programme to help others who are in need. She has already pretended to be a beggar and homeless. Her aim was to see if there was anyone out there who had a heart to help a destitute and homeless African woman, let alone offer her something to eat or drink, or just a pound to buy something.

Tanaka tried her luck in the busiest street of London, Oxford Street. She had a hard day, seeing what it was really like for the homeless and destitute, as no-one offered to help her. People were shouting at her and some spitting and calling her names. The day was hard. She later saw a lady who came to her and offered her some soup and sandwiches in her soup kitchen. The lady was very kind to Tanaka and she gave all the information she needed to try and find hostels to crash for the night. Tanaka asked for the lady's telephone number and her name and address. The lady gave Tanaka a five-pound note and said, "Buy yourself a travel card and go to the Salvation Army hostels; they will be able to help." Tanaka did not go to the Salvation Army hostels but went to Trafalgar Square. There she tried again all night and the following day without any luck. She heard people talking very loudly: "See these foreigners, they come to London hoping to make it! Look what happens to them in the end." The day ended and no-one even dared to talk to her. She later realised that if one has money, one would lead a normal life and survive pretty safely in London.

CHAPTER TWENTY SIX

The following day she had a wash and dressed up nicely, with a nice frock on and designer sunglasses. She went back to Trafalgar Square with some banners saying, "Celebrities looking for people to help." Leaflets were available with the words, "Just complete a form and leave your contact details and write your requests, whatever you want - there is no limit. This is a 'make a request to a celebrity' Lotto. Post your request in the envelope together with a one-pound coin and write the name of the celebrity you wish to get help from." The amount was charged at one pound per request for one celebrity name, and five pounds for five celebrity names and five requests or wishes.

Tanaka was amazed by the response and how soon the people joined the queue. She herself had asked her very first client what she wanted. The client's wish was that Beyoncé would help her with five thousand pounds to start a business. Tanaka used her mobile phone to call one of her agents who had the name of Beyoncé.

"Hello, is that Beyoncé?" asked Tanaka.

"Yes, this is Beyoncé," came the American accent, "how can I help you today?"

Since Tanaka had her phone on speaker she was trying to convince the audience that she was actually in touch with the celebrity. "I have a girl here who needs your help please, Beyoncé."

"Okay, pass her over," came the voice on the phone.

CHAPTER TWENTY SIX

"Hello Beyoncé," said the girl.

"Hey," said the fake Beyoncé, "How can I help?"

"All I am asking is five thousand pounds to start up a business please," said the girl.

"Is that all?" asked the fake Beyoncé.

"Yes, dear, I can't ask for more."

"It's okay dear, I am sending someone right away. Bye and good luck," concluded the fake Beyoncé.

Within no time a very posh car appeared with a huge man carrying a white envelope which he handed over to Tanaka.

Tanaka opened it and inside the envelope was a card with Beyoncé's picture and signature - and five thousand pounds in cash.

Tanaka called Sally and said. "This is for you, Sal." She extracted the money from the envelope and passed it over to the girl who could not believe her luck! She was in shock and she cried. This alone convinced the members of the public and the people continued to pour in at Trafalgar square. People started to make five to ten requests at a time, or even up to ten or twenty requests per person.

Tanaka designed the scheme in such a way that in every one to two hours a winner was chosen with requests made to the likes of Bill Gates, Roy Croc, Sir Richard Branson, Jay-Z and Beyoncé, David Beckham and his wife Victoria, Sir Elton John, Simon Cowell, Sharon Osborne, Lady GaGa, Leona

Lewis, Nicolas Cage, and Dolly Parton, to name only a few. This encouraged more and more people to make a request for help from the celebrity lottery. In only fourteen days Tanaka had collected over a million pounds, yet she gave away one hundred thousand pounds. Tanaka realised how easy people gamble to get help from the rich and famous, yet making the already rich richer. Tanaka realised that most people preferred to wish that the wealthy would give them some of their money or give it to the poor rather than ask the wealthy how they created their wealth so they could get rich like them.

She also remembered her friend who had helped her on the first day and gave her an undisclosed amount. Tanaka soon realised that when one is a beggar and homeless, one receives no attention from members of the public and few will part with their change to help the needy. Just something to think about - none of us knows how or when Jesus Christ will return to this earth. No-one knows how Jehovah chooses to come and test our faith. It's not a good thing to look down upon people when they are down in life, as no-one knows what will happen tomorrow...

Life changes, you know, and God turns life around especially when you think that **Everything Else has Failed and you say NO TO POVERTY and start doing things to help yourself out! You have to work on your life and your goals, because no-one else will do it for you.**

I shall always remain me, myself and I; and have the

CHAPTER TWENTY SIX

power to make decisions for myself. If I feel like flying to New York, I'll do just that without asking anyone for permission. I will only need to notify my creator. If I feel like running a marathon, I will do just that. No-one will stand in my way to tell me that money is the root of all evil, because I have found happiness and freedom in money. When you have money, success and wisdom, your friends choose you and you choose your friends for who they are, as your friends determine who you are.

I am an independent person and shall always be one. I hate being told what to do and always will.

CHAPTER TWENTY-SEVEN

FOOD FOR THOUGHT: THE SECRETS OF A BETTER RELATIONSHIP OR MARRIAGE

The ten secrets of a better relationship or marriage

Acceptance. It is important in a relationship to accept each other for what and who you are. If for any reason you don't like what you see, it is best to leave it rather than try to change it as it will only cause problems. Never compare your partner to your ex-partner or it will just bring conflicts and argument. In order to be in a better position, make an agreement never to talk about your ex-partners. You both left your partners so why keep talking about them? It could be perceived differently, as if you miss and wish you were with them.

Communication. Before love dies communication dies first. It is always important to communicate and to understand each other in a relationship. Complimenting each other keeps the fire burning all the time; telling each other "I love you" as many times as one can in a day also helps to convey how you feel towards your partner. Be open as much as possible with each other and do not keep any secrets. Never ever say to your partner "You see, I told you, and I knew it would happen", because it only shows what you think and that you always have preconceived ideas. Always try to choose the right words and think before opening your mouth. Be a good listener and never finish the sentence for them. Make it a habit never to go to bed angry. Avoid talking about things that make you or your partner angry.

Respecting each other. Respecting each other is also an important aspect of any relationship. Always remember to appreciate what your partner does for you and never to put them down in front of friends or family. Respect their wishes and if they need some quiet time, allow this; give them some space.

Love. Try to keep the fire of love burning by keeping the two logs together, otherwise the fire will go out. Do the things that you both enjoy more often. Go for a walk, a long drive, arrange surprise dates, cook romantic meals for each other, make friends with each other, enjoy each other's company, have quality time together. Make it a habit to kiss each other before leaving and on arrival, before going to sleep and on waking up. Never let your partner guess what you want; if you want more than just a cuddle or a peck on the lips tell your partner and go for it.

Controlling. Try not to be controlling in a relationship as this is a very bad habit that kills relationships. No man needs to be mothered and no woman needs to be fathered by their partner either. Try not to tell each other what to do and what not to do; what to wear and what not to wear; help each other by complimenting and giving an unbiased opinion. Never make your partner choose between their mother, father, sibling or child or the truth will end up hurting you if they choose their mother or father over you.

Trust and commitment. Be friends and go beyond being just friends. Treat each other as best friends. Trust each other as this helps in maintaining a meaningful and long-term relationship. Maintain commitment to make your relationship/marriage successful. Never stop holding hands and show the world that you belong to each other. Work through your differences and stick together in times of sickness and hardship. Do your best and give 50-50 together and you will get 100% happiness. Strive to stay hot and alive for each other.

Create your own family values, signs and language. Try to maintain your own family values. Create your own signs, signals and secret language that only the two of you can understand. For example, if you are at the other's family try not to upset family members by saying things that will make your partner feel bad. Creating your own language and signals will help in saying things such as "I can't eat what your mum has cooked for us", then your partner will find a better way to say it to his or her mum in a way that will not offend her as well.

Money matters. It is always good to agree on what one has to do when it comes to paying the bills. Always do your budgeting together and make it a habit to be open where money matters are concerned. Agree on what amount is to be saved and never keep debts a secret. Always plan together what you want to spend money on and where to go on holidays. Please go on holidays to help yourselves unwind and de-stress!

Kindness. Always remember to be kind to one another. Always remember **to avoid** emotional blackmail and physical abuse. All relationships bind two whole individuals; neither of you is a half of the other; you are both two whole individuals. Therefore be kind and respect each other's wishes.

Sexual fulfilment. Learn all the aspects of lovemaking that you both desire and ensure that your partner is getting the best of your lovemaking. Keep your bodies clean and holy; be as open as possible - don't make your partner guess. Remember, it is always easy to have a happy and fulfilling relationship with someone you have known for years than a stranger. Make every day of your lives the same as the day you fell in love with each other. Grow old together and experiment together; repeat all the things that make you happy as a couple over and over again. Make it a duty to keep your partner happy and sexually satisfied. Lovemaking is an art that has to be learnt; and sexual enjoyment and fulfilment takes two. Some people get it wrong by thinking that what made their ex-partner happy will make the current partner happy. People are different, therefore our needs and desires are different. As the Bible says in 1 Corinthians 7: 3-5: "The husband should fulfil his marital duty to his wife, and likewise the wife to her husband. In the same way, the husband's body does not belong to him alone but also to his wife. Do not deprive each other except by mutual consent and for a time, so that you may devote yourselves to prayer. Then come together again so that Satan will not tempt you because of your lack of self-control." (NIV)

Finally, only take what you think will help you as we are all different and have our own preferences.

CHAPTER TWENTY-EIGHT

TRUE LOVE: WHAT IT IS AND WHAT IT TAKES
MY VERY OWN DEFINITION OF TRUE LOVE

TRUE LOVE is when one constantly thinks of someone, more than a dozen times a day and this goes beyond just having a crush on someone.

It is when you start failing to sleep at night because you miss them.

It is when you start seeing that all other men or women are ugly but your partner is the only one who is beautiful.

It is when your heart pumps faster when you see the one you love.

It is when a person accepts you for what and who you are and not for your money, not your beauty, physical appearance or your celebrity status.

It is when a person says he or she will die for you and really means it.

CHAPTER TWENTY EIGHT

It is when a person donates his or her kidney for you so that you can both have a kidney.

It is when a person is there for you when you really need him or her.

It is when a person respects you and your wishes.

It is when you forget about all your millions and get married to a person regardless of his or her status or wealth.

It is always when one starts meaning what one says.

It is when the other person forgets all the bad things you have done to him or her and remembers all the good things.

It is when both of you forgive and forget.

It is when someone makes sure that you are safe.

It is when someone protects you from harm.

It is when someone shares everything with you.

It is when someone feels comfortable with you, with or without make up on.

It is when someone feels complete because you are with them.

It is when someone's actions speak louder than his or her words.

It is when your partner respects your parents as you would respect his or hers.

It is when you feel very happy that someone has kissed you

CHAPTER TWENTY EIGHT

goodnight and kissed you good morning every single day, and tells you how much he or she misses you when you are not there.

It is when someone holds your hand and gives you a big cuddle anywhere on earth, and feels proud to show you to the world.

It is when someone reassures you that all will be well.

It is when someone shares a smile and laugh with you.

It is when someone eats with you and makes sure that you are enjoying whatever you are eating together.

It is when someone says what is mine is yours.

It is when someone appreciates what you do for them.

It is when someone tells you how much he or she misses you.

It is when someone respects you, cares for you and shows you all the kindness.

It is when someone cannot spend the day without talking to you or checking on you.

It is when your problems become their problems.

It is when someone lets you have all their passwords for e-mails, internet banking, etc.

It is when someone won't have any secrets from you.

It is when someone sees through you and feels exactly what you are feeling.

CHAPTER TWENTY EIGHT

It is when someone cries with you and rejoices with you.

It is when someone saves you when you are drowning or when you are being attacked by a lion.

It is when someone includes you in all decisions he or she makes about life.

It is when someone makes you feel warm when you are cold and offers you something to eat and drink when you are hungry.

It is more about what someone does for you than when he or she says "I love you" with words.

It is when someone makes you feel special, and feels proud of you and just wants to show you off to the world.

It is when someone can put up with your bad behaviour such as snoring, passing wind and even chewing with your mouth open, your bad breath and when you leave your smelling socks around.

It is when someone can move mountains for you, by making things possible especially by keeping his or her promises.

It is when someone says "we are meant to be together" and promises to hold onto you till death separates the two of you.

It is when someone takes your hand and walks with you into the future forever.

It is when someone reminds you how lucky he or she is to

CHAPTER TWENTY EIGHT

have you and when he/she tells you that he/she loves you more than a dozen times a day.

It is when someone feels at home with you and his/her eyes dilate at the point of seeing you and when that beautiful smile lights up his/her face that says, "Here you are, my love, my everything, my joy, my world and my life!"

Some of the things that we take for granted could mean a lot and help to mend relationships, such as complimenting each other; and telling each other the simple praise-phrase "I love you" as many times as possible could make a big difference.

THE END

CONCLUDING NOTES

Dear Reader,

Thank you for buying and reading my book. Please look out for more books, as I am still writing and there will be more to follow. I have listed below some of the books that I have read personally that helped my life to change for the better as I applied the **Law of THINKING, the Law of ATTRACTION, The Law of RECEIVING and the Law of SUCCESS.**

B.B. Goldsmith

THE BOOKS THAT CHANGED MY WAY OF THINKING AND HELPED TO TURN MY LIFE AROUND!

Rich Dad Poor Dad by Robert Kiyosaki. I read this book in only two days. It is a very inspiring and educational book for those seeking financial freedom. This book taught me that saying "I can't afford it" is a way of laziness and a means of giving up from trying and finding out ways of how to afford something that one needs.

The E-Myth by Michael E. Gerber. Wow, what can I say! The book is an absolute star for whoever is thinking of going into business or thinking of bringing an old idea to life again.

Business Stripped Bare by Richard Branson is an inspirational book from a Global Entrepreneur who taught me to respect my employees and to allow them to work with the feeling and thought that they are running their own businesses, and who taught me about the importance of promoting from within.

Think and Grow Rich by Napoleon Hill. This is the book that taught me how to apply the law of attraction. It includes many inspirational quotes to learn from.

IN GOD WE TRUST!

Never in a million years shall I seek financial freedom from dating or marrying a man with money for his wealth! I am independent as I am with my own money; marrying a man with money will be an added bonus but definitely not a way to earn a living; with or without a man my life will go on and I will even be much happier. Marriage is a gift from God, so please marry for the right reasons. May God Bless You All and may he bless you richly and help you to think logically as you brainstorm for business ideas. Trust in God Almighty and all will be possible.

B.B. Goldsmith

ABOUT THE AUTHOR

I was born in Rhodesia, in a small town called Karoi, where I was raised. This beautiful country that I love so dearly is now known as Zimbabwe. I have five children: four girls and one boy - four adults and one minor. I am also blessed with four grandchildren.

Raised in a poverty stricken but hard working family, I had the benefit of God-fearing, loving parents and was part of a close-knit family. Unlucky in love, I married a serial cheat, and then had a relationship with a male chauvinist pig in England who turned out to be a convicted paedophile. After being homeless for some months, I pulled and dusted myself up, working very hard to reshape my life which was then in shambles.

My road to success was not a straightforward one as there were loads of obstacles along the way; but I finally made it - it wasn't what I wanted at first but many life lessons were learned along the way. Helpful and genuine friends were added and parasites were deleted as my life progressed. It was just part of life. Time wasters - I particularly disliked them!

Writing has now become part of my life - novels, business

books, song lyrics and poems, all these genres are receptacles of my writing.

In Colchester, Essex, Worthing Sussex and Spain, I live. A devoted Christian, I am a proud member of F.I.F.M.I. (Forward in Faith Ministries International.)

I am a business woman, mentor and an investor

When Everything Else fails, Say No to Poverty I wrote for you, as a result of my actions, so that you might have the same opportunity to change your life. I wrote the book because when everything else had failed for me I persevered in rejecting poverty. I took action to gain my Financial Freedom and there will be more books to follow. My message for anyone who wants my advice is to stop blaming others for your life failures and take action to change your life. Apply the Laws of Thinking, Compensation, Attraction, Sacrifice, Receiving and Success in your lives; draw big things to you and huge and bigger things will be drawn to you. Those who have grown up in poverty and stayed in poverty have not attempted to better themselves or tried to do something to help themselves get out of their situation.

You are welcome to ask me how I did it, through my website, or ask me in person.

B.B. Goldsmith
www.bbgoldsmith.com

LET'S GET TAGGED!!

BY BB GOLDSMITH

INTRODUCING BB GOLDSMITH'S MOST HILARIOUS
CHARACTERS EVER!

Frank Zamuppette had enough problems growing up without his biological parents and having had no formal qualifications, but nevertheless wanted a job in the bank. He married the love of his life Pontentzia, whom he thought to be a sex vixen whilst he, Frank, was as pure as virgin Joseph! They set off on their honeymoon without a romantic DVD, an operational manual as suggested by his friend Martin! *A Humorous Disaster!*

Hit by recession, the couple fled London whilst Frank was under investigation involving millions of pounds from the Bank of England. They sailed across the seas and landed on the Island of Sentinel where they met four more guys who were on the run! They were lucky to survive the huge carnivorous plant fight.

They finally met Vermogen, the sacred girl, with incredible strength who had a mission for the people of the United States of America! An hilarious flight of fiction where BB Goldsmith shares her vivid imagination and brings out this fascinating adventure which will make the reader cry and roll on the floor with laughter! A fantastic must read for all fiction lovers: you will be completely engrossed from start to finish!

Coming soon in paperback and Kindle!

FROM OVERDRAFT TO MILLIONAIRE!!

BY BB GOLDSMITH

Here is a wonderful factual book, to help those aspiring to become millionaires.

This self-help book will guide you throughout your journey in becoming a millionaire.

It teaches how to start a business without capital, and with capital, how to invest in property and all the strategies to raise capital.

It teaches you how to overcome the drawbacks that stops people from moving forward!

Within no time you will be smiling your way to the bank rather than dreading the bank manager!

BB Goldsmith will show you the way - it won't disappoint you!

Coming out soon, sometime in 2013, for you to enjoy and change your life for the better!